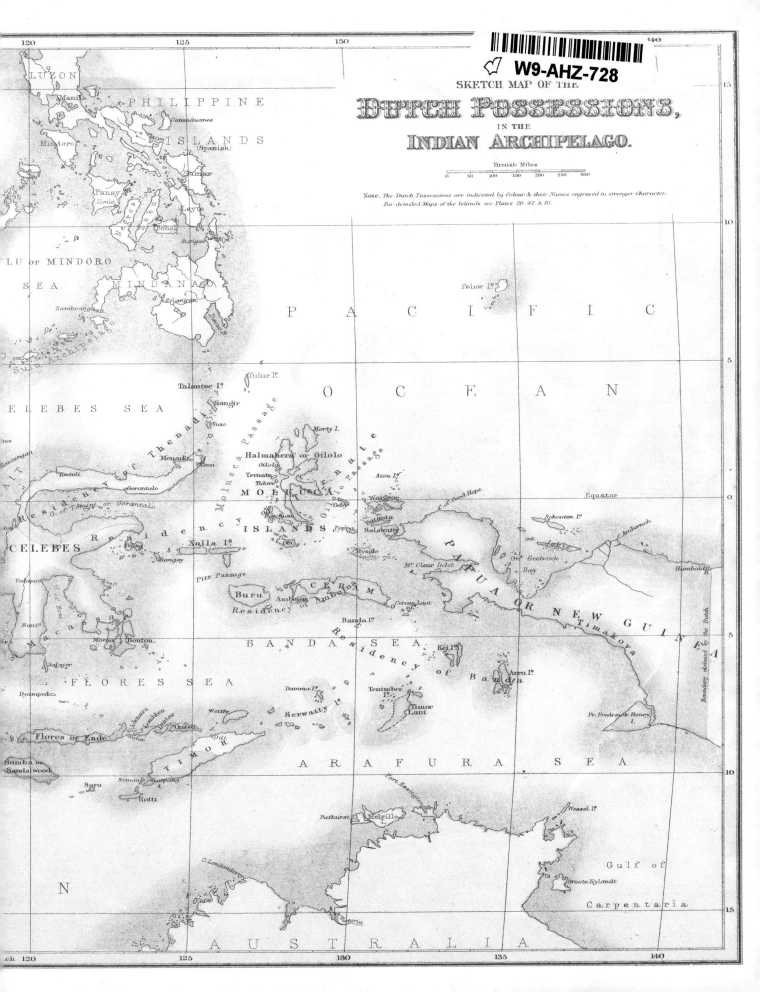

SKETCH MAP OF THE

Dutch Possessions,

IN THE

INDIAN ARCHIPELAGO.

British Miles

0   50   100   150   200   250   500

Note, The Dutch Possessions are indicated by Colour & their Names engraved in stronger Character.
For detailed Maps of the Islands see Plates 20. 42 & 70.

LUZON

Manila

PHILIPPINE

Catanduanes

ISLANDS

Mindoro

(Spanish)

Samar

Panay

Iloilo

Leyte

Bohol

Surigao

LU or MINDORO

SEA

MINDANAO

Selangon

Zamboanga

Davao B.

Sulu Archipelago

PACIFIC

Pelew Is.

CELEBES SEA

Talautse Is.

Tulur Is.

Sangir

OCEAN

Siao

Morty I.

Menado

Residency of Thenadi

Renai

Halmahera or Gilolo

Gilolo

Aiou Is.

Tontoli

Gorontalo

Ternate

Tidore

Waigeon

C. of Good Hope

Equator

G. or Tomini or Gorontalo

MOLUCCA

Geby

Schouten Is.

Otchkien

Batanta

CELEBES

Residency

ISLANDS

Popoa

Salawatty

C. Amberoob

Xulla Is.

Obi

Mysole

Geelvink

Bangay

PAPUA OR NEW GUINEA

Hanboldt

Pitt Passage

Mc Clear Inlet

Bay

Palopoo

Buru

CERAM

Amboina

Ceram Laut

Boni

Residency of Amboina

Banda Is.

Timakova

Moela

Bouton

Salyer

BANDA

SEA

Kei Is.

Arru Is.

FLORES SEA

Residency of Banda

Dyampea

Damma Is.

Tenimber Is.

Timor Laut

Pr. Frederick Henry I.

Flores or Ende

Wettir

Serwatty Is.

Lomblen

Semao

Dili

Sumba or
Sandalwood

Saru

TIMOR

ARAFURA SEA

Rotti

N

Bathurst I. Melville

Wessel Is.

C. Londonderry

Gulf of

Groote Eylandt

Carpentaria

AUSTRALIA

Victoria

This book is fondly dedicated
to those special people who are least
likely to see it, the tribal peoples
of the islands, who took us in hand,
treated us as equals, and opened
their lives to us.

RING OF FIRE

RING OF FIRE

LAWRENCE BLAIR with LORNE BLAIR

BANTAM BOOKS
TORONTO • NEW YORK • LONDON • SYDNEY • AUCKLAND

RING OF FIRE
A Bantam Book / April 1988

Library of Congress Cataloging-in-Publication Data

Blair, Lawrence.
  Ring of fire.

  Bibliography
  Includes index.
  1. Ethnology—Indonesia.   2. Indonesia—Description
and travel—1945-   .   3. Blair, Lawrence.   4. Blair,
Lorne.   I. Blair, Lorne.   II. Title.
GN635.I65B65   1988   306'.09598   87-47567
ISBN 0-553-05232-2

Published simultaneously in the United States and Canada

Bantam Books are published by Bantam Books, a division of Bantam Doubleday
Dell Publishing Group, Inc. Its trademark, consisting of the words "Bantam
Books" and the portrayal of a rooster, is Registered in U.S. Patent and Trade-
mark Office and in other countries. Marca Registrada. Bantam Books, 666 Fifth
Avenue, New York, New York 10103.

PRINTED IN WEST GERMANY BY MOHNDRUCK
GRAPHISCHE BETRIEBE GMBH, GÜTERSLOH

0   9   8   7   6   5   4   3   2   1

Contents

1

2

3

1 A Land of Waking Dreams

This is the story of a unique ten-year voyage of exploration amongst the steamy islands of the volcanic Indonesian archipelago. It begins, inappropriately enough, in the freezing winter of 1972. . . . I was struggling to complete my doctoral thesis in an icy northern England when my brother Lorne called me from London with the news that Ringo Starr had agreed to put up £2,000 and the post-production costs of our first adventure film. I had spent three years researching contemporary mysticism, and it was through John Michel, a colleague of mine who was an authority on Druid mythology and the ancient sites of Britain, that I first met Ringo. Shortly after the formation of Apple Films (a subsidiary of the Beatles' Apple Corps Ltd), Ringo and his associate Hillary Gerard had approached us to help them make a film about Arthurian legends and 'Magical Britain'. Although this project failed to come to fruition – even with Apple behind it – it was to lead us indirectly into more than a decade of adventuring in some of the most remote regions of Indonesia.

Within three weeks I had handed in my dissertation, Lorne had assembled the rudimentary equipment, and with more bravado than common sense we found ourselves on the island of Celebes in the South China Sea. From there we set sail with sixteen fierce Bugis tribesmen on a 2,500-mile voyage through the Spice Islands in search of the Greater Bird of Paradise.

For nine months of storms and doldrums we drifted amongst forgotten kingdoms of silk and gold, fire-walkers, grave-robbers, pearl-divers and pirates. Eventually we reached the Aru Islands, close to the shores of west New Guinea, where we managed to record the first ever colour footage of the golden-tailed bird in its natural habitat.

Of all the Birds of Paradise, the Greater is as rare and remarkable as it is difficult to reach. For centuries before the arrival of Westerners it

1 A contemporary Balinese painting of the joys of surfing

2 Lorne and Lawrence Blair

3 A festival mask, six feet of coloured paper to frighten away the demons

4 The Greater Bird of Paradise, which lured us to the very heart of Indonesia

had been the symbol of the soul and of eternal life; and for the Chinese, who traded with the southern islands long before the time of Christ, the bird became associated with the phoenix myth – which crept across the continents into the mind of medieval Europe, even before it was known that the world was round.

On finally seeing these creatures, mating in the high forest canopy like cataracts of spun glass, we found them to be transparent with a deeper meaning, something which lay beyond them, in the undiscovered wisdom of the islanders themselves. The birds proved to be merely the lure which was to draw us into ten years of adventure through a land of waking dreams.

Just how we got involved in this way of life is still beyond me. I'm not sure how we got here at all. Lorne, three years my junior, didn't even want to arrive. According to our mother, he was so late that she began to suspect she had the hysterical pregnancy of all time. He received his first report card when he was only four years old from a boarding school in the South of France which domestic insecurities had required our attending rather early in life. It consisted of just two words: '*folle indépendance*' – which can fairly be translated as: 'independence to the point of lunacy'.

5

Shortly afterwards we returned to English prep schools, where I quickly had my French beaten out of me in French grammar classes, and where Lorne responded by continuing to be unable to talk or, rather, to speak in any known language, for he would hold forth volubly in a tongue uniquely his own. I was frequently called out of my classes to interpret for him, and it began to be assumed that he would never talk at all. But when we emigrated to Mexico as teenagers with our mother and stepfather in the mid-fifties, he suddenly burst into articulate Spanish and English – to which he later added French and Indonesian – all of which he used to protect and further his *folle indépendance*.

It was in Mexico, during those flowering years, that we climbed the snow-capped volcanoes, dived in the Mayan wells, collected creatures and orchids and, abetted by the enlightened curiosity of our parents, delved deep into ways of being and mind unimaginably different from our own. Caught by the currents of our time, the family also became involved in Subud, a meditational method which was based in Java. Shortly after our stepfather died, our mother, Lydia, made her first leap across the Pacific to live with a Javanese guru in Jakarta, and brought back tales which inspired our first visits to Indonesia, as delegates to a Subud conference.

I was to spend a month there during the toppling of President Sukarno, while bloody revolution raged beyond the ashram walls, hoardings displayed anti-Western hate propaganda, and the British embassy was fire-bombed.

Our mentors and brothers at the Subud enclave encouraged us to focus only on the inner world, and to avoid exploring the dangerous but tempting 'illusory' world of 'Maya' outside. Lydia had barely set foot beyond the ashram in three years when Lorne turned up to kidnap her for a reconnaissance mission with him to Celebes island, eight hundred miles away to the north-east. It was to prove a magical turning point for them both.

In Makassar harbour they saw the great black-sailed trading schooners of the piratical Bugis tribe, with whom, just 120 years previously, the remarkable naturalist-explorer Alfred Russel Wallace had sailed on his historic odyssey through the Spice Islands to become the first Westerner ever to see alive the Greater Bird of Paradise. They also visited the Toraja tribe of the Celebes highlands, who believe their ancestors once descended from the Pleiades in starships. Here they discovered that their last great king had died several years previously, and still lay rotting in his widowed queen's home. He would lie here, no one knew for how long, until the tribe had painstakingly amassed the financial and ritual wherewithal necessary to launch a dead king's soul back to the stars. By going beyond the scented ashram walls of Subud, Lorne and Lydia had touched on an unsuspected world on the brink of disappearing.

6

Even after our Mexican upbringing, it was a revelation to find such things still going on, unknown to the outside world – and there were still another thirteen thousand Indonesian islands to explore, if we could only reach and film them while there was still time. We were always a family uprooted. Lydia, herself an inveterate explorer, was now aware that her three years in Java had been quite enough of an inner workout, and she returned to Europe to comb the Mediterranean for a solitary place to centre herself. She had just enough money left after selling up in Mexico to buy a small *finca* in Ibiza, where she settled in to survive on a war widow's pension and the proceeds from her annual harvest of almonds.

By our mid-twenties, Lorne and I had returned to England penniless but hopeful, with our BA degrees from Mexico in Business and Philosophy. Well – Lorne had *almost* got his Business degree, for just a week before graduating he accepted instead the position of assistant to Bob Cundy, an independent ethnographer who virtually single-handedly cranked out hair-raising adventure films, shot in all parts of the world, at a time when it was still feasible to make a living out of them. This hands-on experience helped Lorne talk his way into a production assistant's job at the BBC in London, where he was exposed to the broader spectrum of skills required to get a film on the air. But he chafed for his independence, and his brief visits to Indonesia only increased his determination to make the big jump. His nights were filled with reading abstruse research material, hatching film-plots and writing investment proposals.

7

I, too, was living a double life. My exposure to the energy and subtle abilities of my Subud brothers in Java had so ignited my optimism and sense of wonder concerning our hidden natures that I had wangled my way into Lancaster University's Department of Comparative Religion to write a doctorate on transformational consciousness, in a field which was later to be referred to as psycho-anthropology. My subsequent book was an early attempt to define the range and focus of

5 A petrol station in Celebes island – our jeep takes forty bottles

6 The great sailing ships, the prahus of the Bugis seafarers

7 The equipment we lugged all the way through Borneo

this discipline.[1] I was alternating between the academic asceticism of northern England and an enormous flat I shared with Lorne and two highly entertaining identical twin brothers in Bayswater, London. It was a vibrant time: the flowering of the sixties had lost some of its bloom, but the fruit was ripe and all around us in the protagonists of the new arts. We watched from our window as Mick Jagger gave his free concert in Hyde Park, stood on our seats at the Albert Hall for Janis Joplin's last performance, and traipsed to Avebury and Stonehenge for equinoctial celebrations. Through our tangled London flat flooded musicians and philosophers, ravers and astrologers, actors and explorers. Periodically I went back to the northern wastes again, a sort of alchemical prep school where, like Lorne, I sustained myself through the dark times with dreams of the southern islands. It was during one of the darkest that I received Lorne's excited phone call.

'We've got it!' he shouted. 'Ringo's accepted our proposal for repeating Wallace's search with the Bugis pirates for the Greater Bird of Paradise. He'd have gone for the Toraja "star funeral", too, if we only knew when it was happening. It was talk of "pirates" and "spaceships" that did it! Can you be ready to leave in three weeks?'

Of course I could. Someone had to keep an eye on him. I would be responsible for sound, second-unit camera, and most of the stills — although I'd never operated a movie-camera or tape-recorder in my life.

We departed from Heathrow with two still-cameras, two 16mm cameras with an underwater housing, a tape-recorder, a small Honda generator, a 'five-minute' Sun Gun for night filming and a pocket-sized slide-projector. At the airport we bought a sheet of tourist slides (the Changing of the Guard at Buckingham Palace, the Forth Bridge, the pearly kings and queens of London, the Apollo moon landing, etc.) to show the Indonesians something of our bizarre world.

We took a tripod, but it fell into the sea shortly after our arrival, and thereafter twisted on its axis with the serenity of a chain saw. We took a first-aid box stuffed with Lomatils, plasters, anti-malarial tablets and insect repellents — all of which proved useless to ourselves, but helpful to our reputations as 'white medicine-men'. We took a Boy Scout's compass, an aviator's map and a primitive Polaroid camera, which was to prove more valuable than our passports. We indulged ourselves with some jars of Marmite and bitter marmalade (which proved not to go well with rice) and an emergency medicinal bottle of Grand Marnier. In addition to the latest tapes by the Beatles, Joni Mitchell, Bob Dylan, Van Morrison and Neil Young, we took some reference books on shells, fishes and birds — and an 1890 edition of Wallace's classic *The Malay Archipelago*.[2] With these, but with no filming permits, since they were impossible to obtain at the time, we winged it to the steaming metropolis of Jakarta.

Whether by some trick of the Mercator Projection, or due simply to the natural chauvinism of cartographers, Indonesia seldom reveals her true proportions, or even her whereabouts. Sprawling across the equatorial seas between mainland Asia and Australia, her nearly 14,000 islands

8

8 The highland rice paddies of Bali after a warm rainfall

9 Print taken from *The Head-hunters of Borneo* by the nineteenth-century German explorer Carl Boch

10 Map of Alfred Russel Wallace's journeys through Indonesia, from his classic *The Malay Archipelago*

11 Outriggers slipping out to fish

9

10

11

include the lion's share of the world's largest and least explored. Amongst them are the last great wild gardens of the earth still harbouring uncatalogued varieties of creatures and man. In 2 million square miles of ocean, and stretching wider than the continental United States of America, Indonesia's geographical, legal and linguistic complexities have kept most of her, even today, effectively off limits to all but the most stubborn foreign travellers. Even the Dutch, who colonized the nation longer than any other Western power, were more interested in trading posts than in exploration, and vested their authority in the local chieftains who in turn vested theirs on down the line so that a great many Indonesians have still never seen a European. Since winning their independence in 1949 the government, based in Java, has sought to control its vast domain partly by making it difficult even for Indonesians to travel freely throughout their own country. The nation thus still remains largely unknown to the world, and to herself.

It was here that we sought to capture a record of the least-contacted tribal peoples while there was still time. This was both for the hell of it, as well as for the annals of the newly developing discipline of psycho-anthropology, whose aims are in part to define the global range of human ability. It was a pursuit which we could only continue, of course, so long as we managed to sell our films to commercial television simply on the strength of their entertainment value.

'Psycho-anthropology', a stepchild of anthropology and psychology, emerged as a sub-discipline at just about the same time that its purest source data – the least-contacted tribal peoples – were vanishing into extinction. Now dwelling only amongst the remotest regions of Third World nations, they represent the final fraying link in a hitherto unbroken chain of memory which stretches to the roots of the whole human tribe. Amongst them are found the last adepts of controlled altered states, out-of-the-body experience, psycho-navigation, environmental wisdom and time-honoured alternative methods of giving birth, healing, living and dying.

Reaching these peoples, of course, first required running the gauntlet of a bureaucracy which treats ethnographic film-makers with the same distrust as it does their subjects. For, having barely embarked on their first Industrial Revolution, many Third World nations tend to regard their tribal peoples with the same antagonism which caused the 'maturer' nations to extinguish theirs just a century earlier.

Further difficulties lay in raising funds in the first place. However enlightened our investors might be, they were not always convinced we would return from improbable places with improbable footage of expeditions for which no insurance company would dream of covering us. But for us the effort still far outweighed the really terrifying prospect of trying to make a living working forty-hour weeks, as our father would have said, 'like proper, responsible adults'.

Totally isolated from our own culture for long periods, we became vulnerable to forgotten times and tribes re-awakening within us. Our journeys, we found, were to take us simultaneously to some of the least-charted regions of the planet and to the least-charted regions of our own

12

12 Early maps would mark the unknown regions as 'Where Dragons and Leviathans be'

13 A blessing rite for a child in Savu, an island famed for the beauty of its ikat textiles

minds. What began for us as the effort to capture a purely objective record of what we saw gradually dissolved into a quest, an odyssey of self-discovery which actually took place amongst the last of the lands of real living kings and queens, dragons and pirates, cannibals and headhunters, mystics and magicians.

Much of our material now contains footage of peoples and events which, in the space of just ten years, have forever vanished or at least changed beyond recognition. It is odd to reflect that the firmest objective record of what we experienced now lies in the films – themselves mere illusory genii of chemicals and light, bound to 400-foot reels of processed trees and silver. Like genii, too, they must be uncorked in a dark room to dance briefly in their own time, before receding into the invisible world of memory again.

The job required the smallest possible team, for maximum mobility and minimum social impact, capable of staying for indefinite periods in unexplored territory amongst barely known peoples, while eating their food, speaking their language and sharing their lives as intimately as possible. This form of 'guerrilla ethnography' has obvious advantages over larger, better-equipped crews with more limited time in the field, but it does not include the consolations of insurance, institutional funding or any guarantees of selling the films afterwards.

Working sometimes independently of one another on separate teams, but for the most part together, we managed to capture some eighty hours of usable film spanning nine separate expeditions. This required juggling between us the hats of sleuths, writers, researchers, logisticians, cameramen, diplomats, doctors, navigators, tooth-pullers and leech-pluckers, to name but a few. Our film stock and equipment, which comprised some nine-tenths of our travelling weight, had to be husbanded first past the Pac-Man thicket of Customs and Immigration, thence through unpredictable months in the jungles, and finally out of the country again intact and undetained.

Apart from improbable luck, much of our success as a two-man team – and siblings at that – comes less from our similarities than from our differences of character. Lorne is diurnal; I am nocturnal. He can go for long periods without food; I can go for long periods without sleep. Whereas I cease to function if I can't put at least something in my mouth every day or so he, beyond a certain threshold of exhaustion, falls unavoidably asleep, bolt upright, with his eyes wide open. One of them admittedly retains a glazed, half-shut look, but the other, propped open behind his monocle, continues to observe the world with bulbous attention. This can be useful during the occasional compulsory attendance at official Indonesian functions, or when waiting in government offices for filming permits to be granted; but there have been dinner parties, at which he was the guest of honour, when he was actually thought to have died at table.

Lorne doesn't much mind what he looks like. He is not even disturbed by the fact that his beard, monocle and considerable size are not always the ideal ambassadorial countenance for delicate first encounters between East and West. Many of Indonesia's peoples, for

14

15

16

16   17

instance, who have never previously seen Europeans, grow very little body hair, and all of it straight. To come upon someone with it curling all over his face is astonishing enough to overlook at first a certain glassiness to his left eye – until, that is, he absent-mindedly lets it fall to dangle from its string. It is then that all hell has broken loose and we have found ourselves standing alone in the jungle again. Lorne excuses his monocle on the grounds that, being astigmatic in one eye and myopic in the other, he needs but one lens to neutralize the problem and that one lens is harder to break than glasses and it is easier to carry spares. Since he does 90 per cent of the filming, and is astonishingly blind, the loss or breakage of his optical eccentricities is a cause for concern. On extended expeditions there were occasions when he would break or lose even his spares, and I would find myself combing deserted beaches and jungle tracks looking for a small circle of glass on which, I was acutely aware, rested the success or failure of an entire project.

Lorne sees best when looking through his camera viewfinder – the contents of which become his whole world. It is easy now to understand why so many cameramen have filmed their own deaths. On numerous occasions I have held him by belt and legs in the rattling back of an open truck, from the edge of a storm-tossed boat, in the path of galloping Sumbanese warriors. Deaf to my shouts, he remains hypnotized by the contents of his viewfinder, which unfold before him as if on a giant cinema-screen on Oscar night, where he is an enraptured member of the audience, completely disembodied from this temporal peril.

Lorne is slow-moving, solitary, watery and, like a true Cancerian, carries his home within him wherever he goes. I am gregarious, cerebral, Geminian, and have sought, somewhat to my cost, to make the world my home. Our metabolic differences were once explained to us by a Dyak companion in Borneo as due to the fact that I belong to the tribe of gibbons, whereas Lorne belongs more to that of the orang-utan. But we are both primates, and though we have often functioned as one organism we have nevertheless brachiated through the forests of adventure at rather different levels, and have seen through different eyes. Our fears, too, are rather different. Under dangerous conditions, his chief

14 Lorne in Sumbanese headgear

15 Lawrence escaping a nine-foot-long, carnivorous Komodo Dragon

16–17 The Asmat grow no body hair, and when Lorne returned to the village a year after living with them he was aped by Entawi, a savage humourist, who greeted him sporting painted sunglasses and a home-made Cuscus-skin beard. Lorne had adopted a monocle by then – so remained marginally ahead in the game of horrid masks

concern is for the welfare of the film stock and equipment, whereas mine is more for keeping us both alive. . . .

National frontiers are the 'red zone' for guerrilla ethnographers. There were alarming stories from a French colleague who had first been made to pay an exorbitant 'import duty' for bringing his film stock into the country – and then, on his eventual departure, three times as much again for 'export duty' because, it was argued, exposed film was clearly much more valuable than virgin film. An even grimmer tale came from an Australian team which, on leaving the country after hazardous months of filming the interior, helplessly watched officials open every can of their exposed film to establish that they were not smuggling.

In those days the Customs officers were still sufficiently unfamiliar with tourists and their toys to have difficulty distinguishing between amateur and professional equipment. Everything that could be dismantled, we carried in pieces on our person. In Singapore, Lorne had begun climbing the step-ladder to the plane with the generator in his backpack, when he lost his balance and fell over backwards on to the tarmac waving his arms and legs in the air like a beetle.

In Jakarta they quickly found the generator and looked stern. We explained later it was to power a lightbulb so that we could read at night where there was no electricity. I remember Lorne saying something to the effect that it might look a bit bulky but, with their excellent petrol, in the long run it was neater than bringing hundreds of spare flashlight batteries along. The officials exchanged some old-fashioned looks, and then discovered our most incriminating object – the 16mm underwater camera housing. They already considered the ways in which foreign visitors spent their money was pretty odd. The obsession, for instance, with snapping endless portraits of complete strangers to take back home as mementoes struck them as particularly humorous. When we explained that the underwater housing was to enable us to take portraits of the fishes underwater, they dissolved into disbelieving laughter and ushered us into the country.

It was to be nine months before we finally emerged again at the other end of the archipelago – shocked, emaciated, but exalted. It was a sobering introduction to the adventurous years ahead, and the start of a most fruitful – if at times near-fratricidal – partnership which, in all conscience, one could hardly advise other would-be young explorers to emulate, unless exhaustively financed and gluttons for punishment.

For me the most dangerous aspect of the job has been not so much the very real dangers in the field as the psychological vertigo of alternating for months at a time between the utter extremes of the planet; from the film markets of California's Hollywood Hills, where I rented an A-frame, to the remotest jungles of the East. The violence of this transition became more cushioned for me in the mid-seventies, when we built our bamboo and coconut-wood home in the highlands of Bali, which for seven years now has served us as a sort of decompression chamber between the two worlds.

In Los Angeles, where I lectured for a living, I pursued my fascination for the harmonic patterns and golden-mean ratios which run so consistently through the sacred art, music and architecture of both Western and oriental mystical traditions. With the advent of the new technology of lasers and holography it was possible for the first time in history to build the ancient consciousness-raising symbols out of pure light. With the devoted assistance of several technical wizards we converted my A-frame into an alchemist's chamber of optical and electronic apparatus with which to visualize the unseen dimensions of sound and form so often described by metaphysicians.

We built holographic Kabbalistic Trees of Life, and revolving human-sized mandalas. We assembled laser sculptures of 'the subtle anatomy of man', with the acupuncture points hanging in space and the lines of 'qi' energy flowing between them in a shimmering web. There were geodesic spheres of optical plastics which appeared to explode like novas when struck with light. We also experimented with 'cymatics', the relationship between sound and form, and built meditational drums (or 'cymaflowers') whose surfaces, scattered with powders and liquids, formed perfect harmonic patterns in response to correctly chanted tones and mantras. It was an experience which revealed a whole new meaning to the mind- and body-altering sounds ritually used by the tribal peoples of the East.

From this rarefied environment of pure light and pattern, I would suddenly find myself winging across to Indonesia again, to join my brother for months of immersion in a different dimension of discovery.

For years we had studiously avoided visiting the island of Bali on the quite false assumption that its international airport and beach hotels placed it beyond our professional interest. But when curiosity got the better of us we found ourselves almost immediately drawn to a highland community where, like a long-awaiting gift, we were invited to build a house for about a thousand pounds on a verdant piece of property. Far from the tourist beaches, this idyllically simple three-storey home would serve as a sort of Base Camp One for our more ambitious sorties into the extremities of the nation. The differences between living in my Hollywood A-frame and in our Balinese house required an organism-crunching transition, which in many ways parallels the fundamental complementary opposites between East and West.

Successful living in Los Angeles requires controlling the environment, whereas in Bali it requires a total surrender. My Hollywood A-frame was hermetically sealed and thermostatically controlled. Our Balinese house has no doors, walls or windows and is protected from the occasional horizontal rain by dense surrounding vegetation, and by reed blinds which can be lowered to the floors. In Hollywood I could interact with the outside via telephones, answering machines and television. My television harangued me to buy endless varieties of insecticide and creature-killer, whereas in Bali it is taboo to move into a new home before the geckos and house-spiders have taken up residence first. These creatures are part of the Balinese pantheon of animal deities, for it is they who are the mediators in a rich and harmonious ecology of wildlife with which, to be comfortable, one must become intimate.

At night, on a dark moon, lying on my raised sleeping-platform at

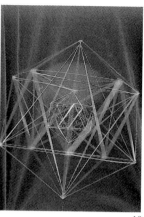

18

19

18–20 Our crystallographic and laser experiments in Los Angeles produced the same unseen vibrations of pattern and form so constantly found in Indonesian art and religion

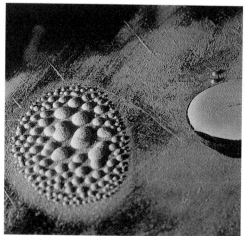

20

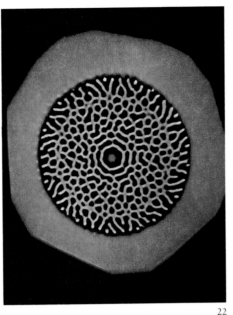

21 Nyoman Batuan, our friend and landlord at Pengosekan, painting a mandala in the village art studio

22 A mandala pattern revealed by 'video feedback', resulting from light being reflected upon itself

23 In the Ketjak, the Balinese monkey dance, the movement and chanting of the dancers create a living mandala

24 Temple offerings, the result of many days of meticulous artistry, to be consumed by the gods, dogs, and people in a matter of hours

21

22

23

coconut level, the stars are reflected in the paddies as strongly as if down was up, and half this universe dances round me as the mating fireflies move through the trees and the house. Some of them become trapped beneath the thatch, and whirl above me as diminutive galaxies of light.

Whereas in Los Angeles I manipulated costly hot and cold water in appropriate vessels throughout the house, Bali is a network of streams and rivers which, like veins and arteries, must be distinguished one from the other for their various uses. To wash our dishes, for instance, requires placing them for a few hours in a rattan basket in the swift-flowing stream deflected through the kitchen to the left of our house. The stream to our right is encouraged to pour through our bathroom, roofed with flowering creepers, in a perpetual shower. We live near-naked day and night, in close and harmless proximity with insects and snakes, in an average year-round temperature of 75°–85° Fahrenheit. Here we submit to a deep sea-change of hormonal rhythms and intestinal flora – and prepare ourselves for unknown months of deep immersion amongst the wilder regions of the archipelago.

We are also exposed to the rhythms of our village of Pengosekan, and its remarkable community of healers, farmers, mystics and artists. Nyoman Batuan, our landlord and village headman, became our friend, mentor, and in many ways our gateway to understanding the psychology of the nation. It was Batuan who explained that, although only the Gods can *own* land, they can lend it to man for his temporary use. Through his assistance our house was built in the traditional manner, and we learned that what had first seemed simply a glorified jungle treehouse actually contained remarkable hidden know-how.

The craftsmen knew, for instance, the precise critical angle beyond which an elephant-grass roof will begin absorbing rather than rejecting rainwater. The thatch is kept dry through a subtler technique. The cellular structure of a coconut tree is such that it convects moisture from its roots to its branches. Our home's eight coconut support-trunks were planted upside down so that they continue, even in death, to draw moisture from the roof thatch down into the ground, where it belongs.

It is customary to assemble the final roof in a single day. The owners provide a feast, with plenty of palm wine, to which the whole community is invited. The roof goes on in a few tumultuous hours. In this way, they tell us, there is a piece of each person in every home in the village – which helps bind the community together.

The Balinese are remarkable in that they give but half their time to the chores of food and shelter; the rest is devoted simply to the celebration of life. The festival days, the sacred plays and dance, the processions which move jangling through the villages at night quicken us to the hidden rhythms by which the island lives. Time belongs to the gods, not to the clocks of the linear West. The Hindu–Balinese calendar is annually calibrated by the astronomer-priests according to lunar and stellar relationships, so that the rites of fasting and planting, rejoicing and reaping, weeping and cremating are synchronized with the actual bio-rhythmic pulse of the island.

With Batuan and the community we have shared the all-night pilgrimages to the Mother Temple shrines on the slopes of the Gunung Agung volcano. We have felt the earth quake with them, helped when the paddies were swept away by floods. We have surrendered our fears and our dreams to them – and they have shared everything with us. In the early days, when we had some money to spare, we would contribute to the village festivals and later, when we fell on harder times, and they had become richer and more famous for their art amongst international collectors, they would support us.

Here, when I came closest to watching my own slow death from septicaemia after a motorbike accident, and Western medicines had ceased to work, I was nursed back to health by their healers. It was they who made very clear how the body is but a reflection of the life force within it. The illusory world of 'Maya' revealed its meaning – not only through the constantly shifting physical environment, but also through the all-night Wayang shadow-puppet dramas, where the shadow parade of gods and demons, creatures and people reflects the eternal dynamics between order and chaos. They recount the trials of mythological heroes on their quest for enlightenment, through the tempestuous waters of illusion. Their shadow images, like our own lives, are seen as merely the surface reflection of an unseen fabric of energy which majestically moves beyond time. Living amongst the Indonesians, where the pursuit of wisdom virtually amounts to a national pastime, the elements of Earth, Air, Fire, Water and Ether became real for me in a way they had never been in the writings of the Gnostics or the Pythagoreans. Expressed in their paintings and sculpture and stories, these elements are seen as the successive thresholds, or levels of initiation, which the warrior of consciousness must broach on his path to enlightenment.

In our ten years of wandering, we had tasted something of these trials in near-drownings, starvations, falls and fevers. We faced trials by Earth, hunting for pythons deep in caverns of human skulls; Water, too,

26

25 The still-bare ground floor of our house in Bali, shortly after we finished building

26 The colourful and intricate puppets of the shadow play of life

23

and Air, driven by storm through mountainous seas in tattered pirate-ships, or dropping vertiginously into jungle clearings in light aircraft. We ran Borneo's uncharted rapids in Dyak canoes, dived with sharks in the rip-currents of Komodo, and were sluiced off Javanese roads in monsoon flash-floods.

I thought we had also faced our trial by Fire, when in 1983 we had ignored government safety warnings and climbed the newly erupting 'Child of Krakatoa' volcano in the Sunda Straits. This was on the last day of an exhausting eleven-month shoot tracking down the healers, mystics and wise men of the islands. It was to be the opening sequence to our whole ten years of Indonesian adventure filming. Scorched and chastened, with the entire footage for our series finally in the can, Lorne returned to London to process and store the film, and I to my Hollywood A-frame to collate the slides and assemble this book. Here, over the years, I had gradually collected an Indonesian treasury of rare and beautiful things — as well as an uninsurably valuable archive of some 14,000 slides. My laser and holographic equipment lay fallow and cobwebbed. My girlfriend, after my eleven-month absence, had under-standably left me, and it was in the company of my two still-faithful black cats that I threw myself into writing. They would sit patiently either side of my word processor as I wrote into the small hours, purring appreciatively when I was pleased with myself, and opening their eyes enquiringly when I was not.

At ten o'clock one morning one of my cats leapt on my face. Until very late the previous night I had been writing about Krakatoa and trials by Fire, and was deeply asleep when the cat woke me. Suddenly I heard the guttural roar of fire from my studio above. I bounded naked upstairs to find the place merrily ablaze. I tried grabbing my slide-albums, but they were melting like a cauldron of boiling oil. I lunged for the computer which contained my first four hard-laboured chapters, and it literally burst into flames at my touch. My next thought, since saving my life's work was out of the question, was for a pair of underpants in the probable event that I would shortly find myself in public. Evidently deciding that prudery was the better part of valour, I hotfooted it down to the bedroom again in time to witness half the ceiling crashing in flames on to the bed I had been sleeping in moments before. Quickly be-knickered, I attempted the stairs to my treasures again, but they, too, were now burning. Geodesic sculptures were dropping from the ceiling and exploding around me, and my giant perspex magnifying mirrors, like contorting windows on to hell, were melting down the walls. My tapestries and books were turning into pitch-thick smoke, and the heat, from which I had hitherto been protected, it seems, by the initial surge of adrenalin through my body, now made it plain that this was the last window of opportunity for effecting a dignified, if empty-handed, exit.

I just made it out of the front door and to the end of my twenty-foot path, when the picture windows imploded inwards and the house erupted behind me through its triangular roof like Krakatoa herself. I stood there wretchedly in the street, watching the unbelievable actually happening in front of me, while my neighbours nervously hosed their

27–30 Fire-faded images of a vanishing world.

30 The black goat fated to be sacrificed in the hull of our Bugis prahu before departure

27

28

29

30

roofs against flying sparks. I had no insurance, and nothing in the bank. When the firemen finally arrived I pointed at the sacrificial pyre still burning and burbled something about my priceless slide-collection. They responded by giving the general area a few desultory squirts with their foam, but informed me the place was a total loss, and that I should be fully content with having got out of it alive. The City Fire Inspectors later concluded that the fire was caused by a 'freak focus', due to the rising sun catching and reflecting off one of my holographic magnifying mirrors. Being struck by light, the Inspectors informed me, was statistically even less probable than being struck by a bolt of lightning.

My notes and books and shells and treasures, the tools of my precarious trade, had utterly gone. The vinyl binders which had contained my slides were discovered amongst the ashes as a single, solidly welded lump. Hard and sharp as a meteorite, this carbonized giant clam finally yielded to saws and machetes, razor blades and tweezers. At its centre were several hundred perfectly preserved slides. Radiating outwards were different stages of transformation, giving an eerily beautiful look to the already exotic subject-matter. The firemen's water had contained an extinguishing agent which at specific temperatures has an exalting effect on colour emulsion. Thus my trial by Fire had shriven me of all but the Dyak tattoo I stood up in, and enough imagery to illustrate something of both the linear and the dream dimensions of an odyssey into the oceanic hemisphere of our beginnings.

32

31 At the core of the giant black
clam of burned vinyl, a few perfectly
preserved slides survive

32 Lawrence completely burned
out in Hollywood

2 Into the Ring of Fire

In the summer of 1883, from the Sunda Straits between Java and Sumatra, the volcano of Krakatoa suddenly blew eleven cubic miles of ash and rock into the stratosphere, sending a shockwave seven times around the globe. The dying ripples of its massive tidal wave lapped up the English Channel, and the volcanic debris, wreathing the planet, altered weather and harvest patterns around the world for years afterwards. Despite Kipling's dictum that 'Never the twain shall meet', the East had reached out and touched the West – with a premonition, perhaps, of the planetary holism which was to grip our minds less than a century later when we walked on the moon, looked back, and for the first time saw the whole earth rising as a single bubble of life. It was also a foretaste of the explosive energy which, within a life-span, would be ours to control or abuse.

Within a few decades, forests and animals had returned to the shattered islands which were all that remained of Krakatoa's outer rim; and from the waters between them emerged an ominous smoking mound, sometimes growing at a rate of more than three feet a month. The locals call it 'Anak Krakatao' – 'Child of Krakatoa'. It has actually raised and submerged its sulphurous head five times since its first appearance in 1925, and when Lorne and I reached it in September of 1983 it was nearly 300 feet high and so active that the government had denied us landing permits. Under these circumstances we were obliged to reach it at night, in a small open boat crewed by two very anxious and expensive local fishermen.

34

We approached the crackling silhouette through floating fields of pumice which rattled against our wooden hull, and when we stepped into the surf to haul our boat on to the beach, as black as the night around us, our bare feet sank into sand too hot for comfort. Moving like ants in a sand-trap we gasped slowly up the near-vertical rim of the secondary crater, into a storm of ash which masked the gathering dawn.

It was nearly daylight by the time we reached the summit. A few miles away, in three directions, lay the crescent islands of Verlaten, Lang Eiland and Rakata, which were all that remained of the original mother volcano's metamorphosis. Beyond them, against a curiously speckled sea, we could survey the distant coastline of Java on one side and Sumatra on the other. We could just see the hazy point where, in that August of 1883, the Dutch administrator of south Sumatra and his family had observed the tidal wave rise inexorably 150 feet right up to the veranda of his residence, pause, and withdraw again, taking some of his flowerpots, half the hillside, and the entire town with its population of some 800 people. To the south, off Java, we could detect where the mouth of the Lampong river lay, where another survivor, a fisherman, had found himself floundering in a furious inrushing sea, and had seized and ridden for miles inland what he had thought was a log, but discovered to be an equally terrified crocodile.

33 'Anak Krakatao', Child of Krakatoa, during its eruptive tantrum of 1983 – exactly a hundred years after the world-shattering performance of its mother

34 The steamer *Berouw* was carried over a mile inland from the Sumatran coast and stranded at Telok Betong (from *St Nicholas* magazine, 1900)

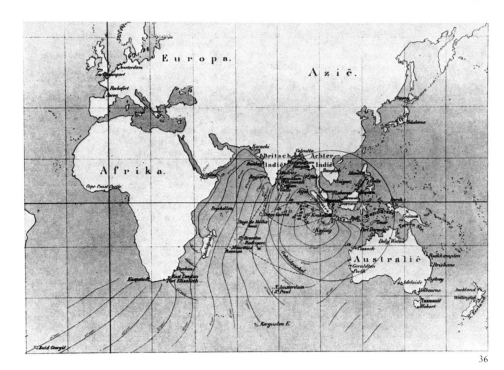

36

35

35 Exaggerated view of the corpse-filled sea around Krakatoa (from *La Fin du monde*, by Flammarion, 1894)

36 Map showing the spread of sound, ash and sea waves

37 Photographs taken at six-second intervals during an eruption in 1928

The grey ash cone on which we crouched pared away beneath us to blend with the leaden sea like an optical illusion. The only reference point to give us a sense of our height was the tiny boat on the beach beneath us, with the two fishermen, who had not only declined to follow us up the crater, but also expressed an urgent desire to avoid even setting foot on shore. Around and beneath us coiled an oily, uneasy water, flecked with floating stones. We had read in our Admiralty Pilot that the temperature of the sea round here could vary very suddenly by hundreds of degrees. Ships are advised to give the islands a wide berth, as the seabed is constantly shifting and massive magnetic anomalies cause compasses to swing wildly round the rose.

It was these haunted waters which had swallowed up nearly all the 36,000 victims who had perished in the first blast. A crewman in *Samoa*, which passed through the Sunda Straits shortly after the eruption, described seeing bodies and pumice stretching all the way to the horizon. Floating pumice fields were so thick that sailors could walk on them – and some bore bleaching human remains 4,500 miles across the Indian Ocean to deposit them along the beaches of Zanzibar.[3]

By the time we reached the volcano's outer lip it was deafeningly noisy. It was erupting rhythmically at about eight-minute intervals, which were preceded by two separate and terrifying sounds. First, as the whole island trembled like jelly, from way beneath us came what sounded like a giant rustling great sheets of brown wrapping-paper. This was followed by the bowling-alley racket of stones and boulders ricocheting off the walls of the crater as they ascended from a great depth to gush out over our heads in billowing clouds of debris and smoke. Our equipment, clothes and bodies were penetrated by the finest, hardest black dust. Every so often a football-sized boulder would thud into the ash nearby. I was reminded of the Javanese guru we had recently interviewed who claimed to teach his students how to walk through rain without getting wet!

38

39

As the sun rose, the sky became perfectly clear and blue all around us, except for directly overhead where the island was creating its own weather. It wore a personal mushroom cloud which fired sheet-lightning directly down into its crater, with thunder so head-shattering that it was hard to convince the body it had nothing to worry about. With each blast came a drizzle of hot stinging ash, which settled on our eyelashes and blistered their roots. We had difficulty in breathing, our hair stood on end, and the tape-recorder and camera electronics began initiating a synch-pulse all their own, transforming our voices into a sort of demonic rasping.

Our shooting permits, after what had been eleven months of filming, were due to expire that evening and, though shot at the very end, the sequence on Anak Krakatoa was intended to introduce the very beginning of our whole ten years of adventure films. This was indeed a place of power, shunned as studiously by modern shipping as by local fishermen, and yet it was also a chance to pay homage to the mysteries moving beneath the surface of this strange island region. Here, at the site of the most devastating explosion in human memory, we wished to demonstrate both the unity and the fragility of the earth by blowing soap bubbles across the crater. One might hardly suspect that so simple a task for so few seconds of film could prove so practically trying and, on reflection, so symbolic of our whole chain of adventures, attempting to keep aloft and alive a consecutive string of luminous mirrors against rather ridiculous odds. Considerable effort was spent first on locating the appropriate soap powder and the pharmaceutical glycerine, and then on experimenting with proportionate mixtures and blowing techniques for producing the strongest bubbles. But these glistening globes, though blown by the panting thousands, lived in that rain of ash only for frustrating fractions of a second.

Standing on Anak Krakatoa we could see and feel the fragility of the world, for we also stood at the gateway to its oceanic hemisphere. Krakatoa is merely the first of a whole chain of active volcanoes which arc down through the Indonesian islands and round the Pacific to form what geologists call the Ring of Fire. To pass beyond it is to cross the threshold into another dimension which, for all its pragmatic gifts to the West over the centuries, remains as mysteriously little-known to us now as it was for the first explorers.

It was really a scent, the aroma of spice, which first drew the West's attention to the Eastern islands. Exotic substances began arriving in medieval Venice, brought through overland trading routes and via Arab mariners across the Indian Ocean. Spices, together with tales of phoenixes and ape-people, filtered into the bloodstream of the sleeping Europeans. Nutmeg, cloves, cinnamon, and curry-powders enabled us, for the first time in history, to preserve and stockpile food across the seasons. With insurance against hunger came the ability to plan ahead, and a different structuring of time emerged. The ability to store more food than we could eat at once also meant being able to buy and sell it in real quantity – and the merchant cities arose. The resultant economics

40

38 Lawrence trying to blow bubbles on an erupting volcano

39–40 The downpour of biting black ash was the least of our problems

33

was to lead directly to the Renaissance, and thence to the Industrial Revolution. No sooner had we caught the first heady whiff of the East and altered the chemistry of our food with it than we made a quantum leap in our cultural and artistic range as well. The Age of Discovery was launched by our greedy desire to bypass the traditional trading routes and find the source of spices for ourselves. Christopher Columbus was actually looking for a quicker route to the heart of Indonesia when he stumbled on America. Spice drew us round the world, showed us it was round, and led us to confront ourselves again.

Whereas Indian, Malay, Arab and Chinese merchants had by and large traded peacefully for the exotic treasures of the islands since before the time of Christ, the marauding European buccaneers sought to own and control the real estate itself, and began four centuries of infighting. Regional spice monopolies were bitterly fought for, claimed and lost again by Portuguese, Spanish, Dutch, French and English adventurers, who spilled as much of the locals' blood as each other's in the process.

The voyage from Europe was a hazardous undertaking, with fairly poor odds on returning at all, let alone with a holdful of spice. The island aromas also came tinged with scents of the dark unconscious. To run amok, for instance, comes from *amok*, the island term for the 'killing madness', or a frenzied thirst for blood. The early spice traders also encountered the daunting 'home' team of defending mariners, the Bugis tribe, who so terrified them with their skill and ferocity that the word 'Boogie man' entered our language, and still haunts our dreams.

Marco Polo seems to have been the first European actually to have made it there and back. He was laughed to scorn for returning with tales of people who actually ate the nests of birds, which they boiled over fires of burning black stones – seven centuries before the same black stones were discovered and harnessed in Europe to fuel the Industrial Revolution. Many of the subsequent early navigators recorded a brush with the southern archipelago, long before its general shape was known. Magellan's tattered fleet, on its historic circumnavigation, lost a further ship in Indonesian waters while limping home after Magellan himself had been killed in a skirmish in the Philippines. Captain Cook

41 Latter-day pirates: the crew of a modern prahu

42 A selection of Moluccan shells

43 (over page) A war dance traditionally performed by the people of East Flores after a successful head-hunt

broached the forbidding shores of west New Guinea, and lost several men there in a fight with the Asmat cannibals, under circumstances similar to those in which he would later lose his own life in the Hawaiian Islands. More fortunate early encounters are recorded by such master mariners as Sir Francis Drake and the notorious Captain Bligh. It was after being cast adrift in a longboat by the mutinous crew of *Bounty* that Bligh managed to make his monumental open-boat voyage with a handful of faithfuls to safety, and ultimately revenge, on the Indonesian island of Timor. Drake, on the other hand, the piratical darling of Good Queen Bess, returned from a transglobal raiding adventure with a holdful of Indonesian spices, and paraded through the streets with his crew bedecked in the captured finery of the most astounding oriental silks and damasks ever to have been seen in England. Drake's most treasured Indonesian memento was a mummified 'mermaid' from Sumatra, which aroused much excitement as the proof that mythological beings were alive and well in the Eastern seas, even if their mortal remains oddly resembled the resinous union of a fish and a monkey. But we believed a lot in those days; protected by our innocence and by our conviction in our one God, under whose banner we could righteously pillage the world.

Less practical perhaps than spices, but also commanding the highest prices in the auction houses of Europe, were the precious shells which came from the Moluccas – named after 'molluscs'. Wonderfully bizarre, compared to the local species, they seemed to symbolize a sudden awakening from the drab monotones of medieval Christianity to a much richer world than had previously been imagined. Wherever we travelled amongst the islands we would collect rare and exotic shells which became for us like fragile clues in a paper-chase of changing life-forms as we moved across historical as well as zoographical boundaries.

The birth of science, and its bitterest pill, the Darwinian Theory of Evolution, was to be oddly influenced by Indonesia, and can be partly traced through the subtle relationship between Charles Darwin and Alfred Russel Wallace, which recent evidence strongly suggests produced not only one of the most revolutionary achievements in the history of science but also one of its most intriguing deceptions. For it is now quite certain that Darwin, who gives no credit to Wallace in his *Origin of Species*, would have been quite unable to write it without his essential contribution. Far more than a further unsavoury tale of professional infighting for accreditation amongst the greats, the outcome – on the principle that the discoverer leaves his imprint on his discovery – has profoundly affected the subsequent tenor of both science and the humanities.[4]

Darwin was a member of the landed aristocracy who had flirted with theology at Cambridge before becoming a highly respected naturalist. He undertook only one expedition, travelling for five years aboard *Beagle* with all the modern conveniences of the day, and spent the next forty-five years as a hypochondriacal recluse in his English country mansion, churning out voluminous erudite papers for the scientific establishment, while privately pursuing his haunting suspicion

42

that species diverged to become other species. He was fully aware of the blasphemy implicit in suggesting that human beings were not created by God as separate and distinct from nature, and of the turmoil that such a theory would release on the Victorian world. It is plain from his private correspondence that, even if he *had* discovered by himself the mechanism by which species diverge, he had no intention of publishing until after his death. But it was the arrival of the brilliant paper from the much younger, socially insignificant Alfred Russel Wallace which forced his hand – affording Darwin the full posthumous credit for Wallace's discovery, and the bequeathing to subsequent generations of a 'Darwinian bias' which is considerably less enlightened than Wallace's own interpretation. 'Survival of the strongest', for instance, and its tooth-and-claw ethic which became associated with Social Darwinism, is not at all what Wallace had meant by 'survival of the fittest', where fitness was defined by him as a far subtler and more complex weave of forces than mere pugnacious self-interest. A further major difference was in the two men's attitudes towards tribal peoples – whom Wallace recognized as fascinating equals, rather than as 'a lower order of the human race', which was Darwin's perhaps unwitting contribution to twentieth-century racism.

Wallace was a different animal, who, through a combination of circumstances and personal courage, was thrust into broader horizons. Against Darwin's five years in *Beagle*, Wallace had spent four years exploring the Amazon basin, followed by eight years, largely alone, travelling throughout the Indonesian islands expressly seeking a solution to the evolutionary divergence of species. He collected what was to amount to over 125,000 species of flora and fauna, many of which were entirely new to science. He lived cheek-by-jowl with the peoples of the region, absorbing their environment and languages. He sailed with the Bugis tribe to the haunts of the Greater Bird of Paradise, and one night, delirious with fever beneath the volcanoes of Ternate, he had a sudden vision of the entire dynamic of natural selection. Many of the explorers of the time were afflicted and often killed by malaria, or the 'ague' as it was called. 'Those who have had the advantage of experience in such matters', wrote Austen Layard, a contemporary of Wallace who had discovered the ancient city of Nineveh, 'know that one of the results of fever is a considerable excitement of the brain, consequent audacity and no small additional loquacity only limited by physical debility.'

It was in such a state of mind, suffering from malaria in the Moluccas, that Wallace had his vision. 'During one of these fits,' he later recalled,[5] 'while again considering the problem of the origin of species . . . there suddenly flashed upon me the idea of the *survival of the fittest*.'

In this ague-altered state Wallace perceived the whole symphony of evolutionary change with such immediacy that he feared it would escape him like a dream before he could write it down. Over the following days between attacks he managed to pen his brilliant fifteen-page paper called 'On the Tendency of Varieties to Depart Indefinitely from the Original Type', and mailed it to Darwin, whom he had never met, with shy requests for his comments.

44

45

The 'Ternate' paper threw Darwin into a panic. He suddenly risked losing the crowning glory of a lifetime's secret endeavour to an unknown malarial 'fly-catcher' as the humble naturalist-explorers were known. After weeks of private anguish followed by questionable closed-door lobbying of the leading minds of the Royal College of Science, Darwin found himself forced to go public on the issue of evolution for the first time, when *both* their papers were read at the Linnean Society of London on that momentous July evening of 1858. What is seldom revealed in the history books, though perfectly easy to verify, is that Darwin's contribution was less a paper than a rambling series of notes which contained nothing novel, whereas Wallace's 'Ternate' paper was the first *complete* exposition in writing of 'Descent and Divergence with modification through variation and Natural Selection' – which is the very kernel of what has become known as the 'Darwinian' theory of evolution. Although some kink in the confluence of timing and temperament may have robbed Wallace of his posthumous fame, it may also have robbed the rest of us, through this century of science, of a broader view of the hidden forces of life.

Wallace, strongly influenced by the multi-dimensional environment and circumstances under which he had perceived the Theory, had also anticipated its very limitations, which are only now being explored by Neo-Darwinists and modern theorists of evolution. To him, the 'checks and balances' of Natural Selection were only *some* of the forces operating in what he saw as the evolution of spirit or mind through matter. Recognizing amongst the life-filled Indonesian islands a way of

44 Alfred Russel Wallace as a young man before he began his adventures

45 Charles Darwin, before the *Beagle* voyage

46 Frontispiece to Wallace's *The Malay Archipelago*: 'Dyaks attack orang utan'

47 Aruese hunting the Birds of Paradise for their valuable plumes (from *The Malay Archipelago*)

48 The flying frog of Borneo parachutes on its webbed feet (from *The Malay Archipelago*)

being and mind as alien as it was complementary to Western thought, Wallace's writings were also amongst the first to gleam with an enlightened futurism. He was amongst the earliest modern scientists to confront seriously the supernatural dimensions of nature and mind, and was a pioneering author who supported, amongst other novel ideas, equal rights for women, social justice, nature conservation and land distribution.

Whereas Darwin had laboured with left-brain precision in solitary confinement with fossils and formaldehyde, Wallace had wandered, alone and open-minded, through the cauldron of the world, amongst a diversity of life unimagined by Western minds. His dream was to transform the world, as the key to the Theory of Evolution for which Darwin had striven so long. However, although his bust shares a place of honour in the apse of Westminster Abbey with that of Darwin, commemorating him as a great co-pioneer of rational science, elsewhere his memory is largely eclipsed – perhaps *because* of the premature breadth of that dream. Only in the Ring of Fire, in the Eastern islands he loved, is his name writ large – on any globe worth its salt – in *The Wallace Line*.

The Wallace Line commemorates his observation that a zoographical division slices the Indonesian archipelago in half, running down between Celebes and Borneo, Bali and Lombok, and thinly separates very old and very new life-forms. Nowhere to the west of the Wallace Line can be found the giant Cassowary, Birds of Paradise or marsupials of Australasia, and nowhere to the east of it are found the tigers, elephants, primates and early man which crossed the land-bridge once connecting Java, Sumatra and Borneo to mainland Asia. In the early days of 'Darwinism', when the race was on to find tangible evidence of the 'missing link' between apes and men, it was again from Indonesia that, from a few molars and shreds of skull, *Java Man* and *Gigantopithecus* would briefly rise to claim the title. Distressing as it was for the Victorian establishment to contemplate having descended from monkeys, it would not be long before new advances in physiology and biochemistry revealed that we virtually *are* monkeys – differing from the chimpanzee, for instance, by a single chromosome in our genetic code. And, again, the monkeys, like ourselves, are still more lizards than anything else; for, as Carl Sagan points out, by far the longest period of our air-breathing history was spent evolving through the Age of Reptiles.[6] He suggests the millions of years we spent as reptiles are what have kept the myth of the dragon alive in the art and literature of the world, and this theory also has a physiological basis. Sagan and other experts refer to our three separate brains (quite apart from our right and left lobes) each with its own biochemistry. The top, thinnest, most recently evolved *neocortex* is the rational 'thinking cap', found only in such higher animals as whales, primates and humans. Beneath it lies the *limbic system*, seat of the strong emotions and intuitive responses which we share with birds and lower mammals. Beneath that again is a bulb at the top of the spine, the *Reptilian* (or R-) *complex*, governing our deepest autonomic functions. Our biochemis-

50

49 The orang-utans, the 'people of the forest', still found in the jungles of Borneo and Sumatra

50 The distinction between animals and humans was always rather foggy to the rational Western mind until, that is, the question arose as to whether they themselves might be thinly disguised monkeys

try is part dragon: the 'R-complex', which awakens when our thinking and feeling brains are off guard, in trance, afraid or asleep, is a dragon brain. It is the root of our sense of smell and taste, fear and desire, and it still remembers the dragons we ate and were eaten by. It dreams dark dreams, but keeps the engine-room running, the peristaltic movements, the flight and fight hormones. No one quite knows what lives in that dark sea of the deep genetic unconscious.

In the early days of discovery medieval cartographers used to mark the empty, unexplored spaces on their maps as 'Where Dragons Be'. But it wasn't until 1912, from the volcanic outcrop of Komodo in Indonesia's Lesser Sundas, that the myth of the dragon became reality with the discovery of *Varanus komodoensis* – a running, swimming, tree-climbing lizard, over twelve feet long and very carnivorous. The Komodo Dragon lives off pigs, goats, deer – and man, if he can get him. He is an evolved and voracious hunter, scenting his prey with a long, pink, forked tongue which flickers over the ground like a flame. High on the Borassus Palm escarpments of Komodo stands a cross to Baron Von Reding Biberegg who died here in 1974. Although there have been several since, he is the first known Westerner to have been eaten by a Komodo Dragon.

51

The fertile biochemistry of forests constantly racked and renewed by volcanic eruption – which once prevailed throughout the cooling surface of the globe – still continues in Indonesia, and amongst her trembling islands we find time-capsules of our earliest beginnings, when dragons stalked the earth. Throughout Indonesia we found that the fears of myth are still alive today. Newspapers frequently publish macabre photographs of people who have been cut, too late, from the innards of enormous snakes, some of which reach thirty feet long. We were to meet them ourselves, when we followed the professional python-hunters into the burial caverns of Celebes island.

In the Age of Reptiles, some species sought to escape their cousins by growing smaller and climbing higher. A few sprouted wings and took to the air, without bothering to become birds first. Flying reptiles still disconcertingly glide and slither through the Indonesian sky. The eight-inch-long *Draco volans*, or 'flying dracula' lizards, swoop amongst the eaves of our Balinese house. In Borneo there are flying frogs, which parachute laterally on voluminous feet. There's even a flying snake, which flattens itself into an aerofoil and swims through the air like flying tagliatelle.

Lizards of course became birds – some as unearthly as the Greater Bird of Paradise, and others, like the Cassowary, which reversed tactics somewhere in the past and returned to the earth again. This flightless, quarter-ton relative of the Australian emu has a head like a monstrous purple turkey, runs through the undergrowth in small bands, and has been known to kick a man to death with its six enormous taloned toes. Just as the early European explorers of the North Atlantic would bring back the tusks of narwhals and pass them off as the horns of unicorns, so would the early Arabian and Indian sailors bring back the massive bones of the Cassowary as evidence of the giant 'roc' of the Sinbad sagas, or the Garuda bird of Hindu mythology, which is today the symbol of Indonesia's national airline.

Some lizards climbed higher still in that primordial forest, their claws changing into fingers with opposing thumbs. Their eyes migrated from the sides of their heads (where their cousins still keep them), to look forward with acute stereoscopic vision, and their brains began to mushroom in proportion to their body-weight. Almost identical in size and looks to this prosimian ancestor of ours is the extraordinary tarsier, a primate just six inches tall, found only in the high jungle canopy of Indonesia and the Philippines. With human-like mouth and hands, and enormous eyes in a head which can swivel 180 degrees, the Dyaks of Borneo refer to him as *hantu* – meaning 'ancestral spirit'. Like an apparition of our goblin beginnings, the tarsier still stalks the treetops at night.

Some of this goblin's progeny were later to descend to the ground again, increase in size, and stagger towards human-ness. It was from the same haunts as the tarsier that the original 'Wild Man of Borneo' – the orang-utan, or 'man of the forest' – was to reveal himself: a creature so vulnerable, so resonant with human emotion, that we could not fail to see ourselves in him.

The islanders of course do not share our Western compulsion to distinguish ourselves, the rational 'observers', from the rest of nature. Their unhesitating assumption that they contain all life as much as they are contained by it has helped them forge what to our eyes is an almost supernatural intimacy with their forests and creatures. They acknowledge that elephants and man, for instance, have a very close relationship, having climbed the evolutionary ladder side by side, losing hair together, returning to and re-emerging from the sea again, growing warm blood, emotion and long memories. They even went to war together. Like the moguls of India and Siam before them, the ninth-century island kings commanded great armies mounted on trained fighting elephants. Their wild descendants are still very much at large today, and with the gradual encroachment on their habitat there are increasing reports in the local newspapers of troupes of elephants rampaging through Sumatran villages in grand old-fashioned style. A few years ago the cousin of a Sumatran friend of ours was killed by a singularly persistent elephant. He came across it raiding his fruit garden, unwisely wounded it with buckshot, and was chased up a tree for his trouble. He remained there for what must have been an anxious day and a night while the elephant returned to and from a nearby stream with trunkfuls of water with which it was finally able to loosen the roots of the tree, push it over, then trample its victim just as his belated rescue-party arrived on the scene.

In the jungles of north Sumatra lie the long-abandoned temple ruins of Moera Takoes. Built in the eighth century by an unknown Shivite sect, they honour the elephant god Ganeesh – the Hindu patron of, amongst other things, partying, wisdom and jovial abundance. Although the people who built this temple have long since vanished, legend has it that during certain summer full moons the wild elephants arrive to roister amongst the ruins. We discovered that the temple is

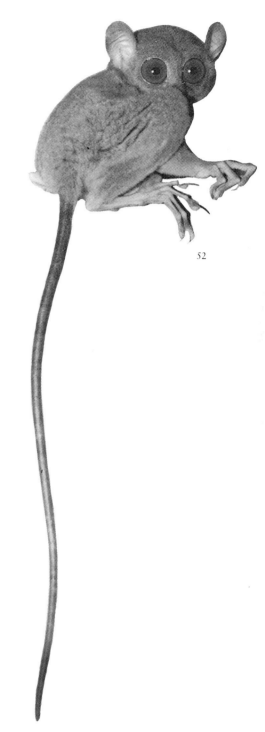

52

51 The dragons of Komodo scent their prey with flickering forked tongues

52 The Tarsier, the six-inch primate, still stalking the high canopy to remind us of our goblin beginnings

surrounded by durian trees, the fruit of which ripens and ferments through June and July. These highly alcoholic, elephant-sized olives are occasion for a drunken orgy of pachydermic proportions.

With a prickly, reptilian skin, the durian can weigh forty pounds and measure a yard across. Every year several people are killed by these preposterous objects, ripe and fermenting, plummeting on to their heads from a great height. You cannot harvest a durian, but the first person to reach a fallen fruit, even on another's land, may claim it. It smells and tastes so richly revolting that it is claimed to be the only fruit expressly forbidden in the plush Mandarin Hilton hotel in Singapore. Even in Jakarta's sixteen-storey Kartika Plaza hotel the fruit may only be consumed on three floors specially set aside for it. A durian dilettante is a breed apart: there are even special clubs which devote themselves to following the durian season round the entire archipelago – feasting and waxing lyrical on the fruit's narcotic delights.

Tigers are also particularly addicted to ripe durian. Sumatra is the only place left where tigers are on the increase, and with the human population expanding in inverse proportion to that of deer and wild pig the tigers have begun making the logical dietary transition. Shooting a known man-eater used always to be done by attracting it to fresh meat, until it was discovered that a ripe durian is a much stronger lure. There's even a joke about the 'reverse run', which can happen when several people converge at speed towards the sound of a fallen durian, to find they have been beaten to it by a possessive and alcoholic tiger.

The Sumatran tiger is more closely and deceptively striped than his larger Indian cousin, and quite a bit more intelligent. In 1956 a Dutch ship was bound for home up the Malacca Straits with a cargo of animals for the Amsterdam Zoo, when a large Sumatran tiger burst out of the forward hatch, scattering deck-hands. It sniffed the air once, went to the starboard railing, where the coastline of Malaysia was clearly visible only four miles away, and returned to bound over the port railing sixty feet into the sea, to begin swimming directly for the shores of Sumatra, a further eighty miles away and still beneath the horizon.

But more than elephants, big cats and early man moved down from continental Asia across that early land-bridge to the islands. In later years wave after wave of Confucian, Hindu, Buddhist, Christian and Islamic influences swept from the flowering civilizations of Asia and entwined with the pre-existing 'oceanic' animism of the islanders. The Wallace Line also appears to mark the division between two very different kinds of mind – the 'continental' and the 'oceanic'.

There is increasing evidence that the original island peoples did not migrate eastwards from continental Asia, but evolved independently for millennia amongst the isolated atolls of the south Pacific – resulting in a different turn of mind.[7] Little is known about early Micronesian/Melanesian culture mainly because they developed no writing, passing down their knowledge through words and music instead. But we do know that they reached a high, technology-free civilization, practised a sophisticated form of navigation, and ranged over the entire Pacific in ocean-going outriggers.

53 A Savuese girl holding intricate decorative mobiles of carefully woven pandanus and bamboo

45

Severed from the rest of the world by sea and sky, an atoll-dweller, unlike a continental people, cannot easily resolve his differences with neighbours by simply fighting or moving on if he loses. He must adapt, turn inwards, integrate with his community. Food and possessions become shared, rather than bought and sold. Decisions, too, tend to be collective, rather than autocratic. So limited are the staples, materials and real estate of an atoll-dweller that every food, object and square yard of his diminutive space becomes invested with *mana*, an invisible, inter-connecting kind of holy force, making everything individually 'alive'. Rein is given to the intuitive, or 'right brain', faculties — which perceive wholes, rather than their parts. Whereas the 'continental' mind is logical, monotheistic and autocratic, the 'oceanic' mind tends to be holistic, polytheistic and democratic. The 'earth' mind is more practical, the 'water' mind more mystical. The difference between them is further revealed by the barriers which each had to overcome in its discovery of the other. In the early days it was water, in the form of the 'endless ocean to the west', which was the first major obstacle for continental European explorers. For the oceanic explorers their obstacle was land. This is well illustrated by the oral history of the Gilbert Islanders' discovery of South America in the distant past. On sighting the desolate Andes after a voyage of *four months*, they were far from delighted, and apparently turned round and sailed back towards their atolls. They described it as Maiwa, 'the wall at the side of the world, four moons' sail to the eastward . . . a land which stretches to the north and to the south without end . . . beyond the furthest eastward island it lies – a wall of mountains up against the sun'.[8]

Indonesia is aware of being strung between the two worlds of eruptive land and tempestuous water. The nation refers to itself not as 'this sovereign land of ours', as do other countries, but to 'this, our land-and-water' – and considerable ritual effort is devoted to maintaining a balance between the two. The hereditary sultans (of which there are

54 The age-old dance of Ratu Kidul, Goddess of the South Seas, is performed by her nine hand-maidens

54

46

only two officially left) are still called 'Susunan' – the 'Life-Giving Mountain', or 'Volcano'. The Sultan of Jogjakarta annually gives the royal substances of his hair and fingernail cuttings to be deposited as placatory offerings in the crater of the great Merapi volcano. Only a few years ago, during the 'Hundred-Year Ceremony' propitiating the Gungung Agung volcano on Bali, Indonesia's President Suharto attended the sacrifice of over eighty animals, including leopards and eagles, which were cast into the smoking crater.

At the other end of the spectrum is the powerful Loro Kidul, 'Goddess of the South Seas'. We met her under various guises throughout the islands: with the Bugis pirates in the Moluccas, where we cast offerings into her whirlpool; and amongst the tribesfolk of Sumba who rely on her signal – in the form of the one night each year when Sumba's beaches briefly swarm with red sea-worm – to initiate their deadly war-sport between lance-throwing armies of mounted warriors.

We met her, too, as the patron goddess of the birds'-nest gatherers of southern Java, who pursue what must be one of the world's most hair-raising professions. Much of Java's bleak southern coast consists of 300-foot cliffs which are assaulted by breakers which have swept, uninterrupted, from Antarctica. The swiftlets which produce what the Chinese consider the most desirable edible birds' nests roost in caves beneath these cliffs. The gatherers descend the sheer cliff-face on coconut-fibre ropes to an overhang some thirty feet above the water where a rickety bamboo platform has been built. From here they must await their wave, drop into it, and be swept beneath the overhang into the cave where they grope around in total darkness filling their bags with birds' nests. They must then choose their wave again to carry them out and up with the swell so they can seize the ropes dangling from the platform. The timing must be very precise. We talked to a gatherer who had misjudged the tides and found himself unable to leave the cave for thirty-two days. In utter darkness, breathing rank air and deafened by the breakers outside, he kept himself alive by groping around for newly hatched swiftlet nestlings and the grubs which thrive in the dung on the cave floor.

It is perhaps understandable why these men, who earn their livelihood in the very embrace of the Goddess of the South Seas, should take her so seriously, but it came as more of a surprise that the Sultan of Surakarta should do the same.

Sultan Pakubuono XI of Surakarta comes from a lineage reaching back to the ninth century and, despite Indonesia's official birth into the modern age with her independence in 1949, the Sultan, like his ancestors before him, remains the uncrowned 'Pope' of pre-Islamic Javanese mysticism. For many years we sought access to him and the inner sanctum of his medieval palace, until in 1981 he finally gave us the first filmed interview ever granted by one of his line. It was then that we made the surprising discovery that the Sultan, 'the Great Mountain', is officially married to Loro Kidul. Rising from the palace courtyard is a ninety-foot phallus-shaped tower. Once a year his 'Superlativeness' is ritually cloistered in its upper chambers for a night of passionate

55

consummation with the Goddess of the South Seas. The outer walls of the palace are thronged throughout the night by crowds eagerly awaiting news of the outcome. For it is on her satisfaction with this supernatural tryst that the stability of the following year depends, and the equilibrium between Indonesia's volcanoes and oceans – her earth and water natures – can prevail.

It is hardly surprising that the Indonesians have been so profoundly affected by their kinetic environment, for theirs is the most tectonic nation on earth, boasting some 34 per cent of all the world's active volcanoes, and registering an average of three earthquakes a day measuring over 5 on the Richter scale. Of a total population of some 160 million Indonesians, about 151 million of them dwell on or near volcanoes, thriving on the rich nutrients which make their islands so fertile.

Here in Indonesia, at the most fragile geographical division between the earth's outer, congealed crust and its inner, molten magma, we also found amongst the peoples themselves the thinnest division between our more recently evolved left-brain, rational faculties, and the millennia-old storehouse of right-brain intuitive wisdom. The supernatural is constantly present, and what the West considers in the realm of the paranormal the Indonesians have raised to a fine art; the islands seethe with sorcerers, healers, sages and mystics.

Whereas the continental mind prefers a firm division between the 'observer' and the 'observed', the oceanics see no such clear distinction. The Dyaks of Borneo, for instance, have always referred to the orangutan as the 'man of the forest', treating him at least with the dignity accorded to neighbouring tribes, whereas the Europeans, on examining the first Tierra del Fuegans brought back to the West, could not decide whether to classify them as humans or animals. This approach characterizes much of the brief and rather shameful history of anthropology, where the study of Man has not been of you and me so much as of those other strange folk whose bodies, habits and beliefs were alien, but whose lands, raw materials and pagan souls were so promising.

Only now, when the tribal peoples have almost gone, has the West awakened to the fact that, rather than their lands and possessions, it is their subtle abilities and specialized environmental wisdom, forged since the beginning of time, which are of paramount importance to us all. The new psychologies of hypnotic suggestion and 'creative visualization' are increasingly aware that we are capable of infinitely more than the assumed constraints of 'physical laws' on our bodies and minds would have us believe. The Indonesians have no such constraints to overcome. From earliest childhood, through trance and possession, they practise surrendering to other than themselves. In High Javanese the word for a man means 'half a woman' and that for a woman means 'half a man'; when a couple are separated, the individuals can be possessed by the energies of their mate. Entire communities may become possessed. In the Moluccas we watched people piercing their cheeks and arms with swords, submitting to having their backs and chest beaten with boulders, eating glass, rolling in fire – and suffering no ill effects.

56

55 Balinese temple carvings

56 Trance dancers in the Watubella Islands piercing their cheeks and sewing up their lips

57 Possessed by the soul of a monkey, this man is rubbing himself with red-hot coals without burning his hands or T-shirt

57

In Ceram and Borneo, when a villager is taken by a crocodile, there are shamans who specialize in possession by the apologetic spirit of a crocodile god, who leads the community to the guilty beast. Whereas 'animal familiarization' is now only a fading memory in European folklore, it is still common in the islands, and there are shamans who claim regularly to enter the bodies of creatures to stalk the woods and fly the air at night. Like the sages of India, there are individuals with 'animal power' who can sit alone in the forest attracting wild animals to them. Conversely, people can become possessed by animal souls. In Cilicap in southern Java we have watched old men being most convincingly possessed by what they call the spirits of horses, monkeys and pigs. They began eating hay, nuts, and even raw offal in enormous quantities, until slapped out of trance by the overseers. There is also a form of transferred possession in northern Celebes in the rite of the 'dancing bamboos'. It begins with two entranced dancers fencing with short bamboos, and ends with the dancers unconscious in the arms of the community, while the bamboos continue dancing on their own as if they were slivers of paper on an electrostatically charged diaphragm.

The dramatic arts of masked dance and puppetry are also but thin excuses for shamanic possession. One of the more sinister involves the Segale-Gale puppet, which is occasionally still seen during the funeral rites of Batak chieftains in north Sumatra. Human-sized, and resting on a wheeled platform, the puppet is operated by a shaman through wires and levers extending some six feet behind it. With articulated limbs and facial expressions which even allow the effigy to weep tears and gnash its teeth, it springs fully to life before the hypnotized community, dragging the priest behind it, speaking recognizably in the voices of the recently as well as more distantly departed.

It was a form of meditational surrender and possession by a higher form of energy which first drew us to Indonesia, and the Subud ashram in Java. But this only gave us a taste of the variety of altered states we

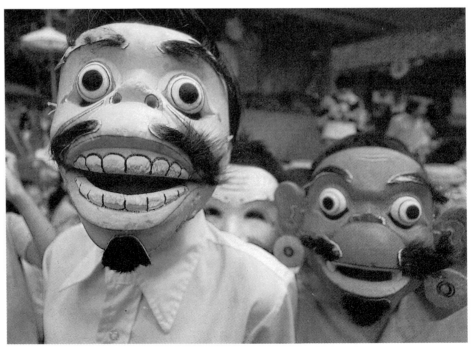

would encounter ahead. Isolated for long periods amongst little-known peoples, our sole defence lay in a sort of encounter therapy, a complete vulnerability to our hosts' ways of being and seeing. There were places where we were the first Westerners ever to have been seen, though we pre-existed in their racial memory as ugly, dominating invaders. To be a highly visible minority of two in communities which were often as expressive as they were antagonistic was an abrupt reversal of the roles we had so unthinkingly come to accept in our British prep schools. To be greeted by complete strangers with instant derision was a sobering experience, and it vividly reminded me of what it must have been like for those first black people, in the eighteenth century, walking the streets of England freely. There were coastal villages in Celebes and Borneo where the men would scowl and stride away, the women would slam their doors and window shutters in our faces, and the children would follow us down the street in howling, baiting hordes, challenging us to lose our poise. This was more a psychological war of attrition than a physical threat, but it was on just such an occasion that we used what might be called our only 'weapons' – a couple of pairs of plastic, luminous, blood-shot eyes which I had picked up in an American novelty store over Hallowe'en. An aggressive mob of youngsters had been closely dogging us for some time and, emboldened by our apparent failure to notice them or to quicken our pace, had begun throwing stones. When we stopped and slowly turned, with our bulging eyes in place, the gang scattered with such blood-curdling screams that we wondered if we hadn't overdone it, and felt sufficiently ashamed of ourselves never to use the eyes again.

In Bali, amongst the community of wise and loving farmer artists where we have our home, such a stunt would be as unbelievable as it would be unnecessary, for when it comes to the supernatural – or human trickery, for that matter – the Balinese are old hands.

The full power of trance possession first came through to me in Bali while watching the all-night shadow plays by the great dalangs, or puppet-masters, such as Madra. Though tragically killed in a recent motorbike accident, Madra was an undisputed maestro of the art, as well as an easy and informative friend whom I had known for some time, so it was a shock to witness the epic genius which came through him, and the transformation which both he and his audience underwent in that open village square the first time I saw him perform. I had to leave my place in front of the screen frequently and go behind to convince myself that each new voice was indeed coming from the same man.

The dalang is the supreme shaman of the community, and requires rigorous yogic training in breathing, fasting and energy-conservation techniques, as well as in languages and mythology. Above all he becomes a technician of controlled trance, to which he then surrenders totally – perhaps rather unknowingly as do our greatest actors and musicians. The dalang may perform for up to ten hours without a break, while singing and speaking in different voices for each of as many as 125 different shadow-puppet characters. Alternating between four different languages, ranging from the archaic Pali of medieval India,

59

58 Balinese children wearing hideous demonic masks

59 Children on the 'light side' of the screen, with the puppet master and the shadow puppets

60 (over page) The 'barong' demon, with its mirrored leather back, cavorts at festival times to frighten the evil spirits

through Javanese and Balinese, to the coarsest of contemporary 'market' Indonesian, he will simultaneously conduct a full gamelan orchestra with his feet. Through his voice and hands will pour all the archetypes of the great Hindu epics of existence, their battles and heroes, gods and demons. The national news, local gossip, your neighbour, too, all come alive and take their place to strut briefly with the immortals on the shadow screen. The dalang is the apotheosis of the wizard priest, the shamanic bard who conducts the Eternal into the presence of the community, confronting them with their deepest values and beliefs. The Balinese talk of the great dalangs who, when 'possessed by light' beyond the shadow screen, are occasionally seen to glow with a flickering nimbus, as they speak in voices not their own.

The shadow-screen becomes the battle-ground for the eternal conflict — at least in this illusory world of Maya — between the primordial opposites of Light and Darkness, Chaos and Order. Neither the demonic nor the angelic is suppressed. In the dramatic arts, which children are taught as soon as they can walk, each participant has a chance to become personally possessed by the soul of the character he is playing. One of the most fascinating of these rituals is the rarely seen 'Sangyang Dedari', in which exquisite eleven-year-old girls, dressed in the silk and gold of the Star Maidens, stand unsupported, with eyes closed, perfectly upright on the whirling shoulders of adult dancers.

I recently returned to Bali for the first time since my Los Angeles house burned down. I feared to find that it had changed, as many had told me, beyond recognition. But this was not so. There are more roads, there's even a Kentucky Fried Chicken and a small supermarket by the beach. Our house in the hills is now closer to the beaten track: Batuan's painting community has grown much larger, and more sophisticated, but its exuberant creativity is if anything richer still.

The Balinese are aware that their deities are only symbols for forces, and not the real forces themselves. They pick and choose the best of the West and incorporate it into their living mysticism. The carved demons on temple walls have begun to acquire helmets and machine guns. During the special day of Saraswati — goddess of wisdom and the arts — offerings are now made to her not only on our neighbour's canvases and paint brushes, but also on our typewriters, cameras, and tape-recorders. In the rice paddy opposite our house is a temple shrine whose highest points sport electric lightbulbs. They are not wired, but they serve as symbols for the Light of the Upper World.

Of all the islanders, the Balinese have traditionally had the most uneasy relationship with the sea. Indeed, the waters there seethe with rip currents and are turbid with virulently healthy micro-organisms. It is the only seawater I have ever swum in which infects rather than heals an open wound. We used to treat our coral cuts with iodine, unaware that the coral polyps which had entered the wounds normally thrived on iodine which they extracted from seawater — and were now extracting from our blood. Treatment with pure iodine promoted, in effect, the burgeoning growth of a coral reef in the festering wounds, and its crackling could be clearly heard if they were pressed. For the Balinese

61

61 Modern images: a hold-up, from a Balinese temple relief

62 Arjuna, the semi-divine romantic hero, from a Balinese temple relief

63 Modern Balinese painting of the myth of the Seven Sisters from the Stars arriving to bathe in the waters of the world

the ocean has always been the underworld, and source of their demons; except for a few intrepid fishermen, they used to approach it only to scatter the cremated ashes of their dead. But recent years have witnessed a remarkable example of their ability to adapt to change. With the arrival of Australian surfers in the late 1960s, the Balinese took to the water like the true temple dancers they are.

Disciplined in ritual dance from an early age, there are now several young Balinese who rank amongst the world's top competitive surfers. Our close friend Bobby Radiasa, whom we trained as a soundman and took around the islands on our last expedition, was amongst the first intrepid handful of Bali's surfers. 'It's just a matter of remaining possessed by Arjuna, who belongs to the Upper World,' he told us. 'That gets me past the fear of what lies beneath.' Arjuna is the noble shadow-puppet hero who appears to walk on air. Another young champion, Ketut Widjaya, who had been famous as a child dancer, remarked that he applies what his instructor had taught him. A Balinese, like a tree, he told us, must remember that he is strung between two worlds, balanced between the pull of gravity and the pull of heaven.

62

Both the very young and the very old are seen as being particularly close to the Upper World. A Balinese child does not touch the ground for the first three months of life. He is cradled and cosseted above the earth and introduced to gravity very gently. When he is 105 days old a 'foot-touching-the-ground' ceremony is held, when the child is ritually 'planted' in matter, and first sets foot on the earth. Until then he has merely been an angel, hovering at the frontiers of the heavenly world. He is even weighed down with bracelets and anklets, to discourage him from floating up again too soon.

Everywhere in Bali the atmosphere is leavened by the experience of being only half of this world. It is expressed in their myth of the first human child, or 'adam'. They say that before the first human was born the seven celestial sisters – the Nymphs of the Pleiades – using their sarongs as wings, used to descend to a sacred pool in Bali to bathe naked in the waters of the world. The prince, Raja Pala, lost on a hunting expedition, came across the pool and spied on the star nymphs. Obsessed with Siti, the youngest, he stole her sarong from the bank so that she couldn't fly back to the stars with her startled sisters. Despite her pleas Raja Pala insisted he would only return her wings if she first bore him a child, whose eyes might always remind him of the world she came from. This child was the first human, strung between two worlds – born of a prince and a sky goddess. But before Siti returned to the stars she told Raja Pala. 'You may have this child for his brief life on earth, but after that, remember, he returns to me.' Even today, when a child cries at night, he is taken outside and shown the stars. 'There is your mother,' they say, 'the place we all come from and where we all return, and there is no need to weep.'

63

But to start our adventure story at the beginning . . . long before we visited Bali, we escaped the ashram walls of Subud in Java, raised some money to make our first film, and found ourselves amongst a tribe who literally believe their ancestors descended from the stars in skyships.

64   Sunset in the Moluccas

65   A Toraja child in painted cloth

66   A Bugis seaman of the tribe
which once terrified the European
spice-traders

3 The Last of the Star Children

Midway between Borneo and New Guinea sprawls the great four-limbed landmass of Celebes, which has variously been compared to an orchid, or a spider, depending on your perspective. Her long shore-lines are lapped by the Java, the Flores, the Banda, the Moluccas and the Celebes Seas.

The island presented such a complex profile to the early European navigators that they assumed her to be separate islands – and her pluralized name remained all the way up to Indonesia's independence when an orgy of name-changing occurred and Celebes was renamed Sulawesi, and her capital, Makassar, became Ujung Pandang.

The sapphire waters of the coast have long been the domain of fierce sea-going tribes who were such a formidable barrier to the early European spice traders that the mountainous backbone of the island remained unexplored until the turn of this century. It wasn't until then that the Toraja tribe – meaning 'the people from above' – revealed themselves. Being ethnically dissimilar to any of their neighbours, their origin gives rise to conflicting anthropological theories, but when the Toraja themselves are asked where they came from they reply: 'Before the dawn of human memory our ancestors descended from the Pleiades in skyships.'

They still build their houses in the arc-like forms, they say, of the ships which once brought them, and their funeral rites, which for their nobility are unequalled for extravagance, are intended to launch the souls of the dead back to the stars of their origins.

When Lorne and our mother, Lydia, visited the Toraja in 1971 they found that the last great king, Lasso Rinding Puang Sangalla, had been dead for three years, and was still lying in state awaiting his final star-launch. Although this event would signify the end not merely of another king in the nation, but of a dynasty which had so far extended unbroken into prehistory, no one had any idea just when it would take place. A year later, when Lorne and I reached Celebes to make our first film, the star-gazing Toraja priests were no more certain as to when, or even if, this climactic *coup-de-grâce* to their culture would occur.

We had arrived in Indonesia speaking very little of the language, with 20,000 feet of film stock and what was left of Ringo's £2,000, intending to film our search for the Bird of Paradise with the Bugis pirates aboard the schooners which Alfred Wallace himself had sailed in 125 years before us. We had talked our way past the immigration officials in Jakarta, flown to Makassar, and checked into the rotting, former colonial splendour of the only hotel on the waterfront. We were not much concerned at discovering that we shared our beds with

lice, or that the hotel also doubled as a brothel for the town's leading gentry, because for us it had the finest view in the world. From our balcony we could see the great Bugis sailing prahus scything past us into the harbour. To watch them, the largest working sailing ships left in the world, shaped like the galleons of dreams, straining softly into port under thousands of feet of black canvas, made us long to put to sea in them.

At night we were visited by entrepreneurs in sarongs and Muslim black felt 'peci' hats, who knocked so quietly that for a long time we thought they were merely underpowered geckos. When we opened the door, they looked furtively around them and hurried inside with grimy bundles of sacking and newspaper from which they proceeded to unpack superb Chinese porcelain. These fellows fenced, it turned out, for a small syndicate of grave-robbers. We later managed to track down their elusive boss, Halim, a fragile, sharp-eyed father of twelve, in the back of his porcelain shop on the waterfront. It took weeks of winning his trust before he finally let us film his operation. We took a rickety public bus with him twenty miles out of town and then struck out on foot for several hours into the wilderness. We saw not another soul, even when we finally reached the clearing where a number of circular dustbin-sized holes had been neatly excavated in the red mud. Only when Halim whistled astonishingly loudly through his blackened front teeth, did a small platoon of grubby, half-naked men sheepishly emerge from their hiding places in the bush and recommence excavating the holes with trowels made from flattened tin cans, and thin probes of concrete-reinforcement steel.

'This my army,' Halim announced proudly and, with a sweeping gesture, 'this our private Ming mine! We have many more, further off, but this is a new one.'

We were keenly aware that the local and national authorities, to say nothing of the international archaeological community, would have been horrified by such a spectacle. And this was just one of a number of sites, known only to Halim and his team, where the early Chinese mariners had buried their dead together, as was their custom, with porcelain some of which had been fired in the imperial kilns of the Sung and Ming dynasties and dated back as far as the eleventh century. We watched one fellow as he probed the soft mud with a steel rod and then shouted excitedly. He pulled out a blue Ming vase which, after a preliminary dousing with water, appeared as good as new after its four centuries of burial.

'Fine! Fine!' Halim encouraged them. 'Many more must be here; that common bowl always means more.' He turned to us. 'See!' he said proudly. 'Why government try to stop us? This bowl mean these men and me already make more money today than three months of growing rice. My children eat that very quickly.' He grinned.

As the money man of the team, Lorne is also strongly drawn to both bargaining and gambling. I was appalled to find him investing a portion of our diminutive budget in some sixty bowls. Less than twenty of them finally made it back to England, alas – but their sale at Sotheby's made this one of the most profitable ventures we've ever engaged in, and did much to offset our subsequent post-production costs!

Makassar, still barely visited at that time by foreigners, was an eye-opener. Her chief contribution to the English language appeared to be in the areas of grease and poison. Makassar Poison, which was smeared on dagger blades to make them instantly fatal, exerted a certain fascination over Europeans. The seventeenth-century diarist Samuel Pepys, in one of his less endearing passages, describes witnessing the chilling effects of this toxin being given experimentally to a hapless dog in a London gentleman's club. Makassar Oil (a particularly noxious distillation from coconuts) was a popular hair cosmetic for Victorian men, and perhaps the greasiest of 'greasy kids' stuff' ever to have caught on. It gave rise to its defence, the 'Anti-Makassar' – the strip of linen still occasionally found protecting the headrests of seats in the older first-class carriages of British Rail. Our only other cultural memories of Makassar came from Wallace and the tales of Joseph Conrad, his contemporary, who had written:

> At that time Makassar was teeming with life and commerce. It was the point in the island where tended all those bold spirits who, fitting out schooners on the Australian coast, invaded the Malay Archipelago in search of money and adventure. Bold, reckless, keen in business, not disinclined for a brush with the pirates that were to be found on many a coast as yet, making money fast, they used to have a general 'rendezvous' in the bay for the purposes of trade and dissipation.[9]

We found the Makassarese remembered us, the Europeans, mainly as pillagers and colonial invaders. As recently as 1949 a Dutch officer had committed some appalling massacres here in a misguided attempt to regain control of the colonies for Holland. 'Belanda', the derisory equivalent of 'gringo', was screamed at us wherever we went. Hordes of hostile bicycle-rickshaw drivers would jeer at us – and it became quite hard just to walk through the streets.

The town appeared very much as Wallace himself must have witnessed it. The markets were humming with things we had never seen and would require considerable practice to begin eating. There were two types of cicada: one of them fried, for consumption; and the other alive, for fighting. For this was the season when at every doorway and table the locals were noisily betting on the lilliputian battles of fighting cicadas. They were sold in tiny cages by little boys who poked them so that they chirruped for potential customers, for the feistiness of a cicada is judged by the pitch and quality of its song.

The harbour was crammed with the great prahus which we had come so far for, but our attempts to communicate with the captains and crewmen were discouraging. Their initial abuse would give way to laughter when they understood we were looking for a prahu which would carry us eastwards. More distressingly, we discovered that the Aru islands and the Greater Bird of Paradise were no longer on their

67

68

67–8 Robbing early Chinese graves for Ming and Tang Dynasty porcelain

69 (over page) Bugis helmsmen at the steering oars of their giant prahus

trading routes and that for the last twenty years they had been pursuing the shorter and more profitable triangular passage between Celebes, Java and Borneo. We might well have to wait for six months before we found a prahu which was heading in the right direction.

We anxiously resigned ourselves to a long wait, and as the weeks passed we gradually got to know the handful of long-term foreign residents in the town, all of them eccentric survivors from days of former glory. Hans Weber, a frail, piercingly blue-eyed Swiss, had been a sea-captain here in the early 1900s specializing in smuggling Bird of Paradise feathers back to Europe when they were all the rage for ladies' hats. There was the redoubtable Mary O'Keefe — daughter of the famous sea-captain who became known as King O'Keefe of the South Seas. We also found Karl Bundt, born of an incestuous union of titled aristocrats who had fled the opprobrium of European society for the Moluccas before the First World War. This bespectacled bear of a man had been born and lived here all his life, and was now Makassar's sole expert and international exporter of the rare shells and orchids for which the archipelago had once been so famous. We were to spend many long hours exploring his meticulously catalogued treasury, practising the identification of species from our slim reference books on flora and malacology.

But it was the German Dr Werner Meyer who was to become our closest confidant and endlessly generous source of both nonsense and invaluable information. We first found him sitting bolt upright, dressed immaculately in a white safari-suit, eating gado-gado — a delicious local vegetable dish with a spicy peanut sauce — at one of the tiny mobile eateries near the market. He had a flowing white mane, and an expression of vaguely inscrutable self-possession, giving him somewhat the air of a Nordic Chinese Mandarin.

'Is this the place to eat, then?' I asked.

'Where *I* eat,' he replied. 'Good. But, for me, also free.' He nodded towards the couple who were solicitously cooking his food for him, mouthful by mouthful. 'Five years ago now, Hasim here came sick to my hospital, with no money. I make him better. Still he want to feed me for ever. So I come here sometimes,' he chuckled, 'so he stay healthy.'

When Werner heard of our filming plans he took us back to his bungalow, where he proved to have a superb cook of his own, a staggering collection of ethnographic art, and an intimate knowledge of the islands. He seldom spoke above a whisper, as if to disguise his theatrically thick German accent, and punctuated his sometimes outrageous stories with deep gurgling chuckles.

It transpired that during the war he had been a medical officer in the German Wehrmacht fighting on the Eastern Front. He was captured by the Russians, and spent two years doing hard labour in a Siberian coal mine. After his release and recovery he joined a United Nations medical programme for Third World nations, and reached Celebes in the early 1950s as part of a team of sixteen other doctors and nurses. This was shortly after Indonesia's independence, when chaos racked the nation and Celebes was terrorized by the 'Darul Islam' rebels, an Islamic fundamentalist group who succeeded in capturing the entire medical team and holding them hostage for eighteen months. Conditions were so harrowing that only two of them survived. One of them immediately returned home, never to set foot in the tropics again – while the other, Werner Meyer, the only white doctor left on the island, stayed on to become the director of Makassar's hospital. It was a position which helped him survive many subsequent close calls, particularly during the wave of anti-foreign sentiment engendered under the later years of President Sukarno's regime.

'The Bugis you cannot trust a lot,' he whispered to us. 'They like easy trading routes now and they have forgotten old navigation ways. Often they do not go where they're saying. And many sink now every year. The government is very angry with them.'

He told us unsettling stories of Chinese merchants who had insisted on travelling aboard the prahus to keep an eye on their cargo, and had somehow been lost overboard while their merchandise appeared for sale in harbours far from their intended destination. There had also been recent newspaper reports of Bugis prahus putting into the atolls east of Celebes, burning the villages to the ground, and making off with the whole year's harvest of copra – the oil-bearing coconut husks – which was the inhabitants' sole source of income.

'This Bugis journey, on sailing prahu, may be very difficult, very dangerous, now,' he warned us. 'Two people you must know. First, the General, so he can protect you, if he likes you filming; and, second, Chinese trader friend, Tan Hans Yong, who has family in the Aru islands where Bugis used to go. But much better you try film funeral of Puang Sangalla of Toraja people. I just hear it begins, maybe one month now.'

If anyone knew when this unique event might actually happen, it was Werner, for it was he who had dramatically cured the late king of

71

70 The prahus must be towed into dock with the help of paddled canoes

71 Prahus in Makassar harbour

tuberculosis in the 1950s, thereby becoming a much loved honorary member of the tribe, and the recipient of all the latest news and gossip from Torajans visiting the lowlands. This was tremendously exciting news for us, but it also confronted us with the dilemma of attempting to make two films with a budget and film stock barely sufficient for one. This would mean spending very little on food, saying goodbye to our 'emergency contingency fund', and shooting a usable-film ratio of six to one, as opposed to the more realistically recommended twelve or even fifteen to one.

Werner's 'General' turned out to be the commander of the armed forces in southern Celebes – a figure whom we would normally have done our utmost to avoid, given his political power and our absence of filming permits, but he turned out to be an exuberantly friendly man who never asked for them. He spoke numerous languages, had travelled widely abroad, and was delighted by the prospect of our filming either the Toraja or the Bugis, though he expressed some misgivings about sailing any distance with the latter. He then astonished us by lending us a jeep, with its driver, Abu, for as long as we needed it.

'First go and find out what's happening with those crazy priests up in Torajaland,' he told us. 'Then you had better start exploring the coast for the villages which still build, own and crew these prahus. Be careful of them, though; they're not used to foreigners,' he finished ominously, as Abu, a villainous-looking Makassarese Ali Baba, was ushered in to meet us. He entered the room with the pop-eyed, lock-jawed expression of one who was expecting to hear a death-sentence from his commanding officer, but he cracked into smiles of various kinds when he heard we were to be his protégés.

The General rose from behind his enormous mahogany desk, without visibly gaining in stature, and came out on to the veranda to see us off. 'Just remember,' he shouted at us, 'let me know what's happening in Torajaland; don't let Abu too close to those Toraja ladies; and bring back my jeep!'

'Tanah Toraja', or 'Torajaland', could only be reached via a hazardous fourteen-hour jeep-ride, a journey which was not enhanced by the sensibilities of our zealous Abu. Never before had we experienced a road code which considered any living things trespassing on the tarmac to be absolutely fair game. Even before we had left the outskirts of Makassar, Abu grinned into my face and asked, 'In your country, chickens fly?'

'No, they don't,' I replied, puzzled by the question.

'Well, Indonesia chickens fly – look!' he said, accelerating towards a group of hens pecking at some minor accident on the road ahead. Those that weren't instantly flattened proved to be the first genuinely air-worthy chickens I had ever seen. One of them even took off to perch indignantly on a rooftop a good sixty yards away. Despite our strong protestations, this was to be the pattern of 'flight or slaughter' for the whole journey. Human pedestrians faced the same treatment, but knowing the rules they were quicker off the mark.

72 Approaching the highlands of the Toraja tribe

64

It was even more frightening when we reached the cooler highlands, where at night people would huddle on the road for warmth, barely visible and apparently asleep, yet able to leap dexterously out of our path at the last moment. Narrow and deeply potholed, the road coiled without any protective barriers next to vertiginous drops to the valleys below. Happily there was little other traffic – and most of that appeared to be oxidizing in heaps at the bottom of the chasms either side of us. Occasionally we encountered a bus or truck hurtling down towards us, slamming on the brakes at the last minute to edge past us with inches to spare. We were never passed from behind. Abu was an army man in an army jeep, to which he was wedded as intimately as an Indian *mahout* is wedded to his elephant.

As a Makassarese, Abu, along with the other lowland seafaring tribes such as the Bajos and the Bugis, was one of the first drivers on the island. In less than a generation the pirate peoples who were notorious for forging themselves and their sailing craft through impossible conditions had acquired the ability to command undreamed-of tonnage and horsepower with their big toes. They also brought to the road some eccentric sealore of their own. It is their custom, even on their largest ships, to show no lights at night – on the principle that it is better to see than to be seen, and that it is easier to see in the dark without the distraction of lights. When night fell we were appalled to find that the same principle had been carried over to the highway. During a bright moon, headlights were kept off – otherwise they remained on only when driving on the road alone. When another vehicle approached to within fifty yards, both would turn their lights off, and pass each other in total darkness.

Six hours into the journey, and several thousand feet higher, we stopped at a small village to quench our thirst and refuel the jeep from rusty milk-cans. I was afflicted with diarrhoea – and directed to the communal latrine, which consisted of eight holes in the ground surrounded by a large enclosure of bamboo walls. About eighty villagers followed me inside, and waited expectantly . . . so I struck out for the hinterlands. About a quarter of a mile later they were still with me, and it became clear that choosing between dignity and entertaining the village was no longer an option. They made no effort to withdraw, or temper their gaze or remarks, and I struggled to maintain the sort of meditational dispassion which I'd observed in my cat on its box.

When we took off again we found ourselves climbing ever more steeply through jungled mountains. The road became narrower, the drops either side more precipitous – and we sought to engage Abu in conversation, more to dilute his fanatical sense of destination than to practise our halting Indonesian. He responded with exuberant gestures – which in no way reduced our speed and which left his hands free of the wheel for long intervals. His pantomime became most articulate when we at last reached the two vast geological features which mark the gateway to Torajaland. They are known in the Toraja language as 'Most Holy Penis' and 'Most Sacred Vagina' – though they would more accurately translate into a lighter vernacular. Half a mile away on our left towered a rounded granite outcrop, about 1,000 feet high; against the opposite mountain, to our right, lay an exfoliating fissure, fringed with forest, about three football fields long. Both features resembled their names to a baffling degree but, despite this, Abu was moved to expound upon them with such fervent body language that we nearly plunged into the ravine and terminated our lives at the very lip of the sacred symbol of where we had begun it.

It was here that the Toraja believed their first ancestors had descended from the Pleiades in starships to populate the verdant valleys into which we now descended. This was indeed another world from the coast. Misty green valleys, shot through with rushing vodka-clear rivers; emerald rice-paddies fringed with golden stands of bamboo, and primary forest towered over by soaring escarpments of granite. Through the greens and gold rose the curved and painted outlines of Toraja architecture. Houses and rice-barns, on elephant-leg pilings, rose with vivid panelled eaves to a high taper either end. They were built with neither nails nor pegs, but merely slotted and lashed together with great precision. With their narrow base, and expanding gables and roofs, they combined apparently ludicrous instability with extreme tensile strength.

The people looked different, too – more akin to the Cambodians or Siamese than to the Malays of the coast. Some anthropologists argue that they came from China, or in boats from Burma, or even from the Himalayas. None of them seemed to set much store by where the Toraja themselves say they came from. Certainly no one set any store by *when* they said they would conduct their final funeral rites. For these had to coincide, we discovered, not only with the metaphysical and astronomical indices, as interpreted by the Toraja priests, but also with the more secular calendar of the government, which had demanded the presence of several high-ranking Javanese officials for the final events.

We bore a letter of introduction from Werner Meyer to Puang Ranteallo, son of the late king – whom we at last tracked down in an

73–5 The Toraja people of the Celebes highlands

73

74

75

astonishing arena. The road, such as it was, had come to an end and the
last twelve miles to our destination were strictly four-wheel drive
through yard-deep mud, and over streams alarmingly bridged with
thick bamboo trunks simply laid next to each other, so that they
separated between our wheels if we took them at anything less than a
rush. Abu piloted us with all the aplomb of a sailor surging through
dangerous surf, and finally brought us to an entire circular village of
some sixty three-storey houses, all shaped like space-arcs.

This village had been built solely for the duration of the festival, for
the thousands of funeral guests who were expected to arrive on foot
from the far corners of the kingdom. The festival village encircled the
Rante, or 'sacred place' – which was a smaller circle of some forty
ancient stone megaliths, many of them still upright and very much
resembling a Druidical circle of Celtic Europe.

We tracked down Ranteallo in the most elegant of these structures,
which he was sharing with some thirty family members, guests, and
slaves. We were warmly invited to stay with them for the duration of the
festival, and were conducted to the top floor for a rather formal
preliminary audience with Ranteallo and his elders. We had been

warned by Meyer that he was a man under pressure. Recently converted to Christianity, bearer of the burden of funeral arrangements, father of nine, Ranteallo was the recipient of the rawest deal of his perhaps 800-year lineage. It had fallen to him to inherit not a heaven-born dynasty in an earthly paradise, but the staggering debt of correctly bringing it to an end.

We found him sitting regally cross-legged on the floor, surrounded by elders chewing tobacco, their mouths rouged and swollen with betel-nut juice. We were still fairly new to the local etiquette, so we sat in silence for a long while. For the first time I really felt myself become part of a tribal circle, accepted as an elder simply by being a foreigner. Yet as time wore on and still no one spoke I itched to ask questions.

At last I ventured, 'Can you please tell us what's going on?'

The hush grew deeper. Perhaps they hadn't understood. Lorne asked again. The prince at last leaned forward on the verge, we assumed, of uttering some revelation – but instead blocked his right nostril with his index finger and noisily expelled from his left an impressive length of mucus which plummeted precisely through a small hole in the floor.

It was but the first of a host of cultural discoveries. To the Indonesians, we found out later, one of the quainter of our many vulgarities is our predilection for depositing the contents of our noses in embroidered cloth and carrying it around in our pockets with us. These water-based peoples find our use of lavatory paper pretty funny, too. 'Cutting down forests to wipe your behinds with,' they call it. '*Our* forests, too!' the more politically minded would point out.

We were billeted on the top floor, together with the royal family and about twenty retainers. An open balcony and a low sago-thatch balustrade ran right the way round the single room and at night, when the resilient bamboo-strip flooring became everybody's mattress, the family groups, in a transparent gesture towards privacy, divided themselves from one another with colourful cotton sarongs suspended on a fragile network of strings. People would roll over in their sleep and finish up 'next door', and our own diminutive cubicle was the nightly thrashing-ground of disembodied limbs belonging to our snoring neighbours. The whole arrangement was on too small a scale for our size, and on one occasion, while making a nocturnal visit to the bushes, Lorne stumbled through the main string, snapped it and brought the curtain up (or rather down) on the whole assembled company.

But in the daytime our top balcony gave us a grandstand view of the arena in which the final events would take place. Everything below, we were sure, was exactly as it would have appeared in centuries past — apart from one major anachronism, a bright yellow construction crane, which was attempting to plant the last monolith in the stone circle.

Ranteallo explained that a stone had been raised at the death of every Toraja king, and indeed queen — though no one remembered their names beyond a few generations. His grandfather had been sent to the stars in 1912, when they still knew how to raise megaliths 'the old-fashioned way', which Ranteallo ruefully confessed to us was damn well more than he could do for his father now. For months they had been trying with divets and tackle to hoist the appropriate two-ton stone upright and into its hole.

78

'Never mind,' Ranteallo said, brightening. 'What's the point of living in a new, Christian age, if we don't use its technology? We borrowed the crane from the local department of road construction.' It certainly looked more suited to planting telephone poles than megaliths — despite the fact that the closest phone was in Makassar — and throughout the ensuing month its groans and screams would punctuate the festivities.

Slightly inset from the circle of houses was the 'death-house' itself, where the king's body, with the queen and her two attendants would be brought to observe the rites from their residence half a mile away.

We had read that the Toraja hunted heads until as recently as the 1920s, but they were feared by their neighbours less for their ferocity than for their magic, part of which was their unnerving reputation for being able to cause the dead to walk. Toraja warriors had to die in their own 'Rante', or village circle, if their souls were successfully to return to the stars. Should they die beyond the Rante, then their shamans, the stories went, could quicken their corpses long enough for them to walk home under their own steam, even without their heads. Various anthropologists had remarked on this zombie tradition – but in Makassar Werner had given us a supplementary twist to the story.

The occupying Japanese forces had apparently been so terrified by the Toraja that after a few peremptory massacres they had left them to themselves. On several occasions, according to Werner's informants, groups of Toraja resistance fighters had been taken into the forest by the Japanese, machine-gunned, and left there as a warning to others. Later in the evening their horrified executioners had reported encountering them again, in serious disrepair, shambling in single file back through the forest towards their Rante.

Werner had delivered this anecdote with the same wry chuckles that accompanied his more orthodox information. He had gone on to remark that the Toraja combined various features which were rarely found together: they had hunted heads, believed in a celestial origin, practised a primeval megalithism, built sophisticated architecture – and produced a unique written (or, rather, carved-and-painted) language, which very few scholars can read. The houses all displayed these picture-glyphs, resembling the whorls and yantras of Tantrism, which, reading from the ground up, told the entire history of the tribe, the clan and the individual household.

79

Some of the finest of these were on the walls of Puang Sangalla's house, where Ranteallo took us the following morning to meet his dead father, and barely alive eighty-seven-year-old mother. It was a formal introduction. We had been warned first to make our obeisances to the dead king before we even acknowledged his long-suffering queen.

The interior measured about eight feet by twelve, and was occupied by two 'lesser widows', a fat and contented black cat, the corpse and the queen. Five feet from her sleeping mat the dead king lay on a low trestle, swaddled in red velvet decorated with very old beaded embroidery. Beneath him a bamboo pipe extended towards a bowl of Ming porcelain into which his body fluids drained. Though by now he had largely desiccated, the odour of death was still unmistakable. Next to the bowl were his bottle and plate which visitors refreshed with palm wine, betel nut or chewing tobacco to keep his soul from feeling neglected. For the last four years the widow had been forbidden to leave her husband's side, and her legs had so deteriorated that (it being considered lèse-majesté to crawl) she had had herself carried about her diminutive space by her 'slaves', the 'lesser widows'.

80

Tradition required not only that she rot in constricted shade with the disintegrating corpse of her husband, but that she also eat a special diet for the entire period, which excluded any rice at all. She accepted our brief presence with disinterested dignity – as if she herself were now as symbolically dead as her husband was still symbolically alive.

The 'lesser widows' had an easier time of it. Slavery still existed here, but not at all in the form we were accustomed to in our Western history books. Theirs is not an unhappy lot – even though they must contend with the customary appellation of 'chicken dropping'. The

78 The yellow crane which failed to raise the last monolith

79 Our host, Ranteallo, would-be successor to the late king, Puang Sangalla

80 For four years the royal widow has had to share her living-room with her dead husband, whose body lies in a richly decorated sarcophagus

81 Complex glyphs depicting the
unique Toraja language

82 A Toraja princess watches the
rites from her richly carved house

Toraja acquire them through inheritance, but they are still 'free souls', and often become richer than their masters — since they are not so rigorously required to re-distribute their wealth. A nobleman's son will have a 'slave' of his own age assigned to him from birth, who will later attend school with him in Makassar, and sometimes even university in distant Jakarta.

In the 1960s the government sought to reduce the animist religious confusion in the nation — and centralize its own authority — by abolishing the practice of all but five officially sanctioned religions. These were Islam, Hinduism, Buddhism, Christianity and, since Bali was already so internationally attractive precisely for its rich blend of animism, the quickly invented category of 'Hindu–Balinese' religion. This would have effectively made Toraja religion illegal had it not been for a young Toraja 'slave' who had studied law while attending to the needs of his lord at university. He had brilliantly and successfully argued that the Toraja religion was one and the same with whatever 'Hindu–Balinese animism' might be — and thus Toraja religion was permitted to survive.

In many respects Toraja women are the equal of men. Sex is encouraged from an early age, and holds no shame for them. Much experimentation has usually taken place before marriage — which then tends to be very long-lived, though it, too, may be dissolved when either party wishes it. The Toraja children refer to all men as 'Father' and all women as 'Mother' — and their blood parents are not necessarily their favourites. All children appeared to be treated by all the adults with equal and, by our standards, highly indulgent affection. Thus to be a 'bastard', or the child of what we would call a 'broken home', means simply to have many parents and to be part of a larger, stronger family.

Girls are given names like 'Slippery Eel' or 'Downy Bird's Nest', and boys get names such as 'Tall Bamboo' or 'Twelve Times'. We were taken aback to learn that the late king's additional name of Lasso Rinding means 'Granite Penis' — a title he apparently did nothing to dishonour. When we asked Ranteallo how many times his father had been married, he replied rather confusingly: 'Marriages, only five. But wives! Ah! Very many!'

81

Apparently he was a man of both great passion and civility, but he was also famed for his ability to project energy. His anger, when fully aroused, was voiced very quietly, but could forcefully throw people in his presence to the ground.

When the king had died peacefully in bed in 1968 he had been left exactly as he was for the first six months to make sure he wasn't simply astral-travelling. This was also the period beyond which the Tominah priests could allegedly no longer cause the dead to walk. Only then was his black cat (a participant in many of the rites) ceremonially informed of his death, and his body reorientated towards the south-west – the 'land of souls' – initiating a whole symphony of rituals which only now were coming to a head.

'All being well,' Ranteallo informed us, 'within a week now we can transport the household and the king's Tau-Tau to their death-house in the Rante for the culminating rites.' Tau-Taus, together with textiles and carved panels, are amongst the Toraja's artistic products most coveted by ethnographic collectors. At the death of a noble, a Tau-Tau is carved in his likeness by a specialized shaman and dressed in his clothes. It will become home for his earthly shade, and will join those of his predecessors which line the balconies hewn in the death-cliffs.

The Toraja believe we have many layers of spirits, or astral bodies, which at death must detach themselves like the skins of an onion so each may find its proper place. Some of these will remain to watch over the living; others enter the bodies of white birds, such as the sulphur-crested cockatoos or white egrets which hover over the Toraja rice-paddies. Another will inhabit his Tau-Tau, while the essential soul is freed to make its journey across space to its source.

Ranteallo was a distracted host. His recent conversion to Christianity, his gruelling exposure to the banking system in his attempt to raise money for the rites, and his position as arbitrator between the old Tominah priests and representatives of the Jakarta government were getting him down. He could no longer explain to us what was going to happen next, but he gave us complete *carte blanche* to explore and question as we pleased, and suggested that we begin by taking a look at the burial-cliffs, about a mile away from the Rante, where the king's body would be interred.

Even with Ranteallo's permission to explore the death-cliffs unaccompanied we felt, on reaching them, that we were trespassing on very haunted ground. The carved balconies, some over a hundred feet high, were lined with disintegrating Tau-Taus which gave the very sinister impression of watchful armies of waking dead. The cliffs all around were honeycombed with caverns, which Lorne and I cautiously entered, brushing aside curtains of cobwebs and creepers with our torches. We gasped to find chambers of dripping stalactites piled to the ceiling with skulls and bones, ancient Tau-Tau heads and crumbling sarcophagi superbly carved with the rippled waves of the 'waters of space' which the dead must navigate on their way home.

'OK, that's it. Enough. Time to leave!' I was feeling extremely jittery.

'Hold *on*, just a *minute*!' Lorne replied. 'It's exactly like those fairy-tale books they terrified us with. Remember the Ogre's cave and the mountain of his victims' skulls?'

'Yes, quite . . . you've got the picture – time to go!'

'Look at this *carving*,' he rhapsodized. 'Do you realize how priceless this stuff is, and just lying around?' Now he was fiddling with a heap of human jawbones. 'Gold teeth!' he announced eagerly. 'Plenty of them. They must have been at that game for ages – and no anaesthetics, either. I wonder why Ranteallo didn't think of financing the funeral with them!'

We finally emerged into the sunshine again to find we were no longer alone in this forbidding place. A few Toraja children had arrived to tend to those remains of their forebears which were not in darkness. They neatly stacked the skulls and re-arranged the femurs with a pottering reverence. We had heard from Werner Meyer that the Toraja custom of burying their dead in high vaults began only a few hundred years ago when Bugis raiding parties from the lowlands began pillaging their burial sites for the booty interred with the corpses, and as recently as 1964 an army general stationed on the island had led his army on similar raids. We found and filmed superbly carved treasures lying about unprotected which, within a decade, were to be stolen, and subsequently appear in private and museum collections abroad.

We had now been in the village for nearly five weeks, and the atmosphere was heating up considerably. In every house in the Rante, as well as at every animist site throughout the valley, numerous puzzling little rituals were taking place – all of which had to be successfully completed, apparently, before the final 'star-launching' could proceed. Tominahs and small family groups could be seen squatting beneath trees or next to streams, intoning over sacrificial chickens and burning incense and symbolic offerings woven from jungle fibres. One of the strangest of these rituals we were to witness only by chance.

83 Even the children tenderly clean and arrange their ancestors' skulls

84 The Tau-Taus, almost life-size, are carved in the likeness of the dead, dressed in their clothes and placed on the balconies of the Toraja death-cliffs

85 (over page) Surrounded by the balconies of Tau-Taus, the bodies of the dead lie in rectangular vaults hollowed out of the rock

83

84

Werner Meyer had told us of a pool about five miles from the Rante, known only to the Toraja, where 'sacred eels' were occasionally 'called forth' by the Tominahs to accept blessed offerings of rice. One morning, suffering from the cumulative effects of the noise and confusion, we left our cameras behind and took only our snorkeling equipment in search of this waterhole. We found it nestling in a golden-green stand of giant bamboos, beneath a soaring cliff. Its opalescent waters seemed to be everything a Star Maiden from the Pleiades could wish to bathe in. Several of them, by the looks of it, in the form of three almond-eyed, half-naked Toraja girls, together with their young brothers, were already doing so. Far from being taken back, they were delighted by our sudden arrival, and unhesitatingly encouraged us to join them in the water. We splashed and laughed and played together for a long time, sharing their delight at looking underwater through a diving mask for the first time. They spoke no Indonesian, even less than ourselves, but talked warmly and directly to us in their tribal language, as we did to them in gentle English. It was perfectly understood that no outer differences between us, however great, had the slightest bearing on this shared moment of enchantment together, at play in the sunlit waters.

Things abruptly changed with the solemn arrival of about a dozen ceremonially dressed adults, led by a tall, bony Tominah jangling with necklaces of crocodile teeth. Our playmates swam quietly to the edge of the pool, while Lorne and I began to climb out until signalled that we could remain in the water if we wished. Sure enough, against all the odds, and with our cameras back at the Rante, we were about to watch the 'calling of the eels', a rite barely referred to in the literature on the Toraja, and which even Werner had never seen.

While his retainers squatted noiselessly behind him, the Tominah advanced to the edge of a rock overlooking the pool by about six feet, closed his eyes and opened his betel-nut-rouged mouth. Even the surrounding sounds of birds and cicadas were hushed as his throbbing ululations resounded off the cliffs above us and through the bamboo forest. After what seemed like a good twenty minutes of this he took a handful of rice from a gourd at his belt and scattered it over the waters.

We floated there, hardly breathing through our snorkels, watching small schools of transparent, leaf-like fish – which we assumed no ichthyologist had previously seen or named – but there was no sign of an eel. I wondered whether they really meant 'water snakes' – a word identical to 'eels' in their language – and I focused more closely on the lengths of bamboo which littered the bottom. The chanting continued, slightly changing in pitch, then from separate deep corners of the pool undulated six velvet-black eels, each slightly longer than ourselves, and as thick as our thighs. They converged beneath the priests barely ten feet from us and settled on the bottom in a relaxed Stygian knot. When the first handful of rice hit the water they didn't dart to the surface, but calmly waited for it to sink down to them. They ate a few grains, ignored the rest, and cruised back into their hiding places again.

The offerings had been received, the funeral could proceed.

We were shocked to discover how important this secretive and ill-attended rite was, and realized that our aquatic curiosity might well have offended these creatures on whose appearance, or otherwise, rested the continuation of the entire festival. On several later occasions we returned to the pool, and tried ourselves to attract the eels with rice from both above and beneath the water. We were observed only by an old man and two buffalo boys, who eventually informed us that the eels don't eat rice, only live food. 'They only come to the Tominah's singing,' they said. Lorne tried chanting a few limericks over and over, but we never saw the eels again, though we dived there often.

By now, the nights at the Rante were getting noisier. Hundreds of funeral guests were beginning to filter in on foot from the outlying corners of the kingdom, bringing sacrificial fighting cocks, pigs and magnificently decked-out water-buffalo. Amongst them were the rare white, or pink, variety unique to the Toraja, with china-blue eyes like a Siamese cat, and each worth twenty times more than an ordinary buffalo. The pigs were never pink – but prickly, black, red-eyed close cousins of the wild hog. Some were so bulky that they were borne into the Rante sitting upright like pugnacious lords in specially constructed litters, carried by as many as eight straining porters. They were much less gentle than the water-buffalo, which spend most of their lives doing nothing, wallowing up to their ears in mudpools, while pampered and scrubbed by the little boys who are assigned to look after them from birth. Occasionally they are led through the freshly flooded rice-paddies to turn and fertilize the soil; otherwise their duties extend only to being sacrificed at noble funerals such as these, and leaving their magnificent horns attached in layers to the Toraja houses whose residents had so generously supplied them.

We lived on chunks of fighting cock, pork and water-buffalo boiled in bamboo tubes until I thought I never wanted to eat meat again. Our grandstand view proved to have its drawbacks as day and night literally hundreds of animals were ritually slaughtered in front of us, and the Rante reeked with blood. The fighting cocks lived in the house with us, sleeping under their owners' sarongs, and periodically exploded, at all hours, with stentorian 'cock-a-doodle-doos' – or, rather, their Indonesian equivalent, for here, of course, the animals speak differently. A cock shouts 'ruka-ruka-row', a dog barks 'duff-duff' – and a cat simply says 'meng'!

During our stay we were awakened not only by the cocks, but on several occasions by piercing screams coming from the rice-paddies behind us, which would continue for some time before abruptly stopping. They were ignored by our host and fellow guests alike. Ranteallo simply looked sheepish when we first asked for an explanation the following morning, and it was left to Werner Meyer to give us an explanation, when he finally arrived to join us. He had often experienced it, he assured us, but had thought it had died out with the Christian missionary influence of recent years.

It is customary for a Toraja girl who feels amorous to walk alone into the rice-paddies shortly before dawn or after sunset and begin screaming. Any swain within earshot who approves of her scream, and feels similarly inclined, is at liberty to rush to her aid and stop her, which is the sign for other suitors to halt their pursuit and file back to bed again. Some girls apparently continue screaming despite the fact that a number of fellows have already reached her and are trying to wrestle her to the ground. She, it appears, is awaiting a particular suitor who is just not as fast on his feet as the others.

The girls were very beautiful, and flirtatious, but as royal guests there was no question of us, much as we entertained the thought, lumbering off with our torches in the direction of pitiful screams.

Now that we had been here for nearly seven weeks, we were beginning to wonder if the final climax would ever take place at all. However, one evening an imposing delegation of Tominahs arrived unannounced in our royal upstairs boudoir to inform Ranteallo that the spiritual path was finally clear to transfer Puang Sangalla's remains from its abode of four years, a quarter of a mile away, to the death-house in the Rante for the culminating month of final rites.

The king's body was borne on a litter in a sarcophagus resembling a brightly decorated, miniaturized starship. A smaller litter carried his freshly painted Tau-Tau, and a third, draped in black, transported his widows. It was a far less sedate procession than we had imagined. Foaming bamboos of rice wine were being copiously consumed by every level of society, and the two litters were furiously bounced up and down along their journey. This was to assist the layers of the king's soul to break free and find their proper places, so as not to encumber his final space-flight. Some of these layers are believed occasionally to attach themselves to the living, which can cause madness and even death. Thus the 'widowed queens' on one side and the 'dead kings' on the other raced each other violently through the rice-paddies, bouncing their burdens for all they were worth, while screaming obscene abuse and exhortations to each other. The unfortunate queen, unable to take sunlight after her lengthy seclusion, was entirely swaddled in black cloth – in which she was undergoing an exercise so rigorous that we wondered if she would emerge from it alive. But she ultimately reached the Rante and was lifted up the death-house steps looking little the worse for wear and, if anything, pinker with health.

The days and nights that followed this procession became filled with the ghostly rhythms of the Ma'badong dance – a cumulative mantric tone intended to induce altered states, which most successfully, we found, interfered with our capacity to keep a grip on the job of filming. It begins with a human circle, linked by the little fingers, swaying and chanting themselves into deep trance with the eyes closed. The circle expands, ruptures and spawns new circles – which eventually fill the entire Rante with wheeling vortexes of hypnotic sound. In the Ma'badong, we were told, they could feel all the past and future generations of their tribe resonating through them as one – they could touch their Whole People, outside time, in the here and now. There was no doubt that this unceasing hypnotizing rhythm was, as it was doubtless designed to do, dulling our left-brain 'edge', and weakening our concentration and our will. Rushing about the Rante, attached like Siamese twins by a synch-pulse cable, tripping over and swearing at each other, burying our heads for mysterious minutes in black film-changing bags, endlessly sticking our noses into other people's business was a cause for considerable levity amongst the participants.

Added to the Ma'badong there were now also spontaneous explosions of Pa'gellu dancers, young girls dressed in green and gold and the most fashionable jewellery of the time – hollow Taiwanese watches, without their works, which some enterprising pirate had no doubt made a killing on. They, too, chanted a trance-inducing song – and their swaying arm movements sought to still the 'invisible waters of space' which a dead king must cross.

The finest of the remaining buffalo, one by one, were brought into the circle, and dispatched with a single blow to the jugular from a machete. From a high bamboo platform the priests, some with battery-powered megaphones, supervised the distribution of every morsel of the sacrificial victims. The buffalos' souls, we were assured, would join the king's Celestial Herd in the afterlife. Funeral giving is a vital ingredient in the Toraja economy, which is primarily concerned with the redistribution of wealth; gifts are determined by the previous history of generosity between clans and families at their funerals.

86

87

86 The king's body is carried in a miniaturized 'arc'

87 The ghostly chants of the Ma'badong echo through the village

81

88 A practice session before the
serious ritual of cockfighting begins

Then the rains arrived, in a stifling, continuous downpour, accompanied by shattering thunder, and the Rante was transformed into a red quagmire. Rather than dampen the festivities, the storm initiated a whole new cycle of tumult with ensuing days and nights of ritual cockfighting which took place beneath a hastily assembled palm-thatched enclosure in the centre of the Rante, observable by the throng from the protection of the slanting gables of the surrounding houses. They were bold gamblers, and noisily made bets which left some people in debt literally for years to come.

The cocks symbolize the upper world of fiery courage. They are pampered and hand-fed from hatchlings and their hidden ferocity is nurtured with affection. A Toraja boy desires his own fighting cock just as longingly as a youngster might desire his first motorbike in the West.

They are armed for battle, with a single five-inch steel spur bound to their right heel with magic knots and whispered incantations. In Bali, where cockfighting is also a controlled ritual, the cocks have two spurs with honed edges, rather than a single spur with a sharpened point, so the battles differ in style and technique, according to the aficionados, rather as swordsmanship differs depending on whether a cutlass or a rapier is used.

Experience is the name of the game, and surviving the first fight is the hard part. It is more a battle of style and speed than of brawn or luck. They are quick learners, and some cocks go on to vanquish more than a hundred opponents before they themselves miscalculate and die. Losers instantly have their spur leg amputated with a machete, and we were shocked to find that a cock which even for a moment turns and runs has instantly lost. Losers are also eaten. Victors, on the other hand, are wined and dined around the community, given the place of honour at the eating circles, and generally behave themselves insufferably. Occasionally, a cock is *such* a winner that despite being a potential goldmine for its owner it is reprieved from further battle and enters the mythology of the tribe as a sort of Spartacus Chicken.

With the continual stench of blood, the din of animals, Ma'badong chants, the roaring crowds and general confusion, the days and nights began to melt into a sort of homogenous limbo, but as the ceremonies moved towards their height we noticed that Ranteallo's twenty-four-year-old niece, Rala, had begun behaving oddly. She would periodically become possessed with rage, strip off much of her ceremonial clothing, and tear about the Rante beating anyone who would stand still long enough with a knobbly bamboo cane. The children baited her into further wrath until, just as suddenly, she would snap out of it again and return to her former, demure self. The Tominahs and even her uncle seemed to think this behaviour was quite to be expected on an occasion such as this, with so much soul energy flying around.

Ranteallo himself was looking increasingly unhinged; and, now I come to think of it, so was my brother. We were all being swept into a maelstrom of energy which was beyond anyone's ability to control or even explain. With so much happening, and no central authority, Lorne and I were constantly harried by the attempt to film only the crucial events, which appeared to erupt spontaneously at any time of the day or night, while conserving the precious little film stock we had put aside for the intended Bugis film. This sense of responsibility was now being seriously eroded by the continuous Ma'badong chants, and by our increasing desire to surrender to, rather than to observe objectively, the wave of history into which we now felt ourselves being helplessly, anxiously, gathered.

On the final tumultuous day, foreign visitors began arriving: two English girls, daughters of country parsons, who had hitch-hiked round the world and about ten Japanese tourists who moved cautiously in a close-packed pod bristling with lenses. There were also two French anthropologists, a raggedly effete group of Dutch and American missionaries, from opposing Christian denominations politely vying for the Toraja's attentions, and the splendid Werner Meyer, looking like the Cheshire Cat in safari costume. There was also the party of representatives from the Indonesian President Suharto in Java. The delirious atmosphere hushed slightly as their column of official jeeps snaked its way down into the Rante. The dignitaries were led to a VIP balcony from where they inscrutably observed the goings-on from behind their mirrored sunglasses. It was they who would decide whether such rites should be prohibited as too economically wasteful, or else encouraged as a possible attraction to the future tourist industry.

Ranteallo had already confessed to us that much of the problem of fixing a date for the rites had also been the laborious process of raising money from the banks in Makassar. 'Forty times I made that ride there and back – in the *bus*, not the jeep like you two,' he told us. 'But I finally borrowed the money against four future years' harvests of rice!

'Maybe it has been wasteful,' he continued. 'Maybe it's now time to be wise virgins, and save.'

'How wasteful?' I asked.

'Well, when my grandfather went, more than a thousand buffalo were sacrificed, and the death-village, which was twice as big as this, was completely burned down. But the Dutch stopped us from doing that at later funerals. They said it was economically stupid and they would only allow us to burn down the death-house after a noble's funeral. Then the Indonesian government wouldn't even let us do that.'

Panoramic visions of the whole village circle going up in flames while our cameras captured the moment danced before our eyes.

'Well, could it be, sir,' I broached, leafing furiously through my dictionary, 'that since this is the last Big One it might be, er, acceptable to send these sixty houses to the stars with – his Highness, your dad?'

The Javanese dignitaries, who would have disapproved of the suggestion, were already stirring to depart in their jeeps for Makassar to catch their plane home. They seemed more than content to skip the final episode – the half-mile procession on foot to inter the king's body in the death-cliffs. This left just three hours before darkness in which to follow and film the culminating procession to the burial-cliffs, and to return to the Rante to cover whatever pyromanic tendencies we might have managed to rekindle there.

'Not a hope,' said Ranteallo, but there was uncertainty in his voice. 'Perhaps,' he continued, 'perhaps something should burn. . . .'

'The death-house, then?' Lorne queried, referring to the least ambitious of all the structures in the Rante.

'Each one of these big houses costs the equivalent of about two blue-eyed buffalo,' Ranteallo explained. 'We can take most of them apart and use the materials again – which is what the government wants us to do.'

'But you've already sacrificed hundreds of buffalo,' I said. 'Isn't that the chief waste?'

'Ah, no, although they do represent food and, well, family prestige, all these sacrifices are essentially offerings to the gods. How could such an offering ever be wasteful?'

'How much is the death-house worth, then?' Lorne persisted. Considerable discussion, interlaced with esoteric mathematics, resulted in the general agreement that it was worth about the equivalent of one very fat sacrificial boar.

'It is like this,' Ranteallo conceded. 'If you provide the boar – your sacrificial gift to the funeral – then we will match the gift by burning the death-house anyway, as we used to.'

We realized this would be an appallingly large slice out of our budget, and certainly a piggish way to treat a boar. It was also, we knew, a slight manipulation of events: in our first test of choosing between the interests of purely 'documentary' objectivity, and those of cinematic drama, we came up wanting. Yet we consoled ourselves with what we took to be a furtive glint of triumph in Ranteallo's eyes as he accepted our pig money, and swore to us that he would not burn the house down before we could make it back from filming the king's burial in the death-cliffs.

The boar's squeals lacerated our conscience. Briefly. And as the dignitaries stiffly walked towards their jeeps and their ride home we prepared again for battle: to film, photograph, and record sound, while keeping up with the uproarious final procession to the cliffs. Keeping up, and close to the sarcophagus, was no easy task, since it travelled along a narrow raised causeway between deep wet rice-paddies.

At the death-cliffs the Tau-Taus lining the balconies were looking appropriately terrible, staring down with their freshly painted eyes.

Puang Sangalla's Tau-Tau now carried his ceremonial keris and his cane. Its arms clutched these objects as they were individually passed up the ladder to its niche: followed by its disembodied head, with a physiognomy very close to that of the photographs of the deceased. At the top they were re-assembled again into the macabre manikin which would house his earth-bound spirit. Much higher up, an eighty-foot bamboo ladder precariously met the small square opening to the chiselled vault. We were to discover that it was just large enough to hold a corpse and two breathlessly claustrophobic busy-bodies.

'Come on,' said Lorne, as I hesitated at the foot of the cliff. 'Ranteallo said it's OK, and the ladder is perfectly safe.'

'Yes, but he isn't going *up* it,' I replied sourly.

89

89 Ranteallo, sitting beneath the totem effigy of his late father

Ranteallo was standing nearby at the front of the crowd, urging us on. 'Yes! Yes! Film for history,' he was saying. 'Quite safe. Be careful!'

The ladder was undulating like a sea serpent as the king's coffin, already thirty feet off the ground, was arduously borne upwards suspended on shoulder-straps between three men. The bamboo rungs, though wide and strong, were loosely lashed with unreliable cordage, and Lorne's and my first simultaneous step onto the lowest rung resulted in it slipping its knots and depositing us both heavily in the mud – myself for the second time in less than twenty minutes. Everyone went wild with laughter again, except for the three men above us, who received such a jolt that they nearly released their macabre cargo onto our heads.

Connected by our infernal sound cable, and distributing our weight over as broad an area as possible, we crawled upwards again, like bears pretending to be spiders. By the time we caught up with the three men at the top of the ladder, they were attempting to heave the coffin into its grotto with a series of hefty swings which caused a wave-motion to be generated in the ladder, very nearly sending us all to the ground sixty feet below. For breathless, white-knuckled moments the five of us clung there while the rhythm abated, then three of us laughed loudly, one of us scowled, and the other nearly lost his liquids. The king's body, together with a number of priceless gold and bejewelled kerises attached to the scarlet wrappings, was handed into the grotto, but just as the carved wooden cover was about to be hammered into place behind it, Lorne announced that it was imperative to film the door being closed from the inside.

The shrill creak of the hinges as we were closed into the suffocating darkness of that cliff-top grave was a terrifying sound. It had something of the squeals of the boar beneath our house a few hours earlier, whose execution we had paid for, but declined to witness. To me, it also rang of the distinct possibility that it would not creak open again – and that the next sound would be that of quickly hammered nails!

These things always take a bit of time – angles, speed of door closing, creak and so on – but this seemed an eternity. When we finally did make it back to the ground, palpitating and soaked with sweat, there was no sign of Ranteallo, and much of the crowd had already dispersed on its way back to the Rante. The English girls, as I recall, were still faithfully standing by the camera we had set up for long shots, having been asked to press the button at appropriate moments when we were not in frame.

Anxious to film the final 'fire' scene, we desperately tried to overtake the tail of the throng making its way back along the narrow causeway, but our legs were betraying us.

By now we were amongst a group of riotous children, and I asked one of them if the festival were now over.

'Yes, all finished,' he chirped. 'Just burn down death-house.'

He scampered nimbly ahead through the crowd with his friends – leaving us trapped behind a leisurely army of elderly women.

'He did promise, didn't he?' Lorne mumbled.

90 The Tau-Tau of the last king of the Toraja Star Children is carried to the highest of the vaults, from where his soul can make its long journey across space back to the stars of his origins

'Well, *pasti* means something like "for sure",' I answered.

We rounded the final clump of bamboos in a sprint – until my knees gave way completely. Lorne stood rooted to the spot, squinting furiously through his monocle. In front of us was ruin. The death-house had been transformed into a smoking carpet of a few scattered embers. It had been torched quickly, gleefully, unconstrained by any outsider's opinions of just how or when it should be done. It had been so quick and thorough that only a few people now remained around it, staring glassy-eyed, and the Rante itself already seemed oddly quiet and deserted. In fact many people had turned in and were asleep, before dark, as if in trance; others had already started for home, and would be walking all night.

Abu was absent, and would not reappear for a further thirty-six hours, so we had time to watch the painful disintegration of the space-arc village and the departure of lines of subdued barefoot guests, laden with meat and buffalo horns.

We squatted together next to the ashes of the death-house, surveying the dissolution of the Rante and ruminating on what would have been a uniquely dramatic ending to our sequence. Close by squatted a very young Tominah whom we had often seen behind the older priests but had never talked to. He addressed us now for the first time, in far more lucid Indonesian than we had ever heard from his elders.

'Do you know why Toraja houses are built with those curved roofs?' he asked.

'Yes,' Lorne said wearily, 'we do. Your ancestors descended from the stars in them.'

'Ah, perhaps,' he responded. 'What about the shape of our buffalo horns?' He gestured at the dog-eaten hoofs and roots of buffalo horn which stretched before us. 'We're a buffalo culture, aren't we?'

'According to our anthropologists,' I replied, even more wearily.

He rounded on us with spirit. 'Your anthropologists laugh at us for saying we came from the stars. They do not think we may mean the "inner stars". The old Tominahs say that this crescent-moon shape means the bottom arc of a great vertical circle of our lives – the section at which we are all most deeply plunged into matter. It's to remind us that we sweep down from the upper world, slide round the bottom of the circle, and sweep up again, no trouble, if we have any sense.'

Our young Tominah friend had disappeared by sunset, and it was well after dark by the time Abu returned, together with Ranteallo, jerking about in the front seat like a clownish version of his own Tau-Tau. They were all grins and seemed to be on top of the world. A stack of empty bamboo Tuak tubes rattled around in the back.

'Presents for my wife!' Abu gesticulated wildly. Then, revealing his terrible teeth in his grin-cracked pirate's face, he went on unconvincingly: 'Sorry so late. We got lost.'

'Sorry about death-house,' Ranteallo joined in, flapping a hand and exhaling a miasma of fermented rice. 'I lose all control when people know it will burn. Nearly burn down some other houses as well.'

'We rest for a week now,' he went on. 'We sleep and dream. And then we dismantle the Rante and sell or use the materials – I don't know quite how or what for yet but, first, sleep and dream.'

We returned to spend our last night on the top floor of the now-abandoned community house, in what was now the distinctly eerie Rante. Abu, as was his unshakeable wont, slept rotundly upright, like a benevolent corpse, behind the wheel of his jeep.

Early the following morning we loaded our equipment aboard, and left that ghostly cluster of space arcs embracing the reddened circle of standing stones. The most persistent image is of the forgotten yellow crane. Weeks earlier, around the advent of the Ma'badong dancers, it had been abandoned by its relay of inexpert operators, and had ceased to scream. It now stood motionless, upright, next to the stone which it had still failed to raise, and which lay forlornly dangling over its hole.

That monolith to Lasso Rinding Puang Sangalla, the last great king of the Star Children, was still lying in the same position when I next visited the Rante – eleven years later.

After eight miles of rough driving, we reached the local highland town of Makale, and the only petrol-pump for a hundred miles. We had filled our tank, and were eating at the open food-stall, or 'warong', just across the street when a dilapidated petrol-truck pulled in to top up the filling-station's reservoir. Its Toraja driver had left the job to the attendants, and had sat down at our warong for a meal, when I witnessed a carelessly tossed cigarette-butt from a passing cyclist ignite the concrete floor surrounding the pump and the petrol-truck with flickering blue flames, like those on a Christmas pudding. The various attendants and hangers-on departed at great speed, and Abu, Lorne and I rose abruptly and began backing away into the warong. The truck-driver, on the other hand, tore across the street, through the rising blue flames, and leapt into his cab. After a few heart-stopping moments the old engine coughed into life, and he managed to accelerate the loaded vehicle through the flames out to safety. The blue flames were quickly quenched with buckets of earth by the attendants, who crept back sheepishly, and the driver was soon calmly eating his soup with us again. It looked like a Hollywood film stunt – until we realized with chilling certainty that none of us anywhere near the petrol-pump would have survived if the truck had gone up.

So, at the very last moment of our very first film, we nearly got the fire we *didn't* want, and we began to feel more sanguine about the pyromania we had tried to incite the night before. We may not have watched the Toraja dynasty ascend through a flaming village circle, but we had witnessed one of its sons, very close, leap through a flaming hoop and land on his feet.

It was with a certain sense of foreboding – as if we had seen an omen – that we descended from this mountain fastness to the domain of the Bugis, where we knew we had just two months left to find a prahu to carry us eastwards before the monsoon set in . . . .

91

92

4 Spice Island Saga

93

The Bugis were amongst the great seafaring tribes of South-East Asia. Mentioned by Melville and Conrad, they were the scourge of the East Indiamen seeking the treasures of the Moluccas archipelago. They were the bejewelled and silken-turbaned villains who coloured the pirate archetype of our Western imaginations, wielding their blades and their sea-skills like demons, and bequeathing us their name for our night-mares. Yet, long before we clashed, the Bugis had possessed a highly complex written language, in which every letter looks rather like the cross-section of a different but closely related spiral seashell. They also had tales which recounted the trials and explorations of their Sea Prince heroes who, through numerous incarnations, led their tribal fleets through unknown waters and kingdoms of dragons and witches, whirlpools and man-eating birds, and forests of half-beasts and half-men. In length and breadth these sagas belittle our Iliads and Odysseys, yet few scholars understand them and few have ever been translated.

For a millennium or so the Bugis have followed the monsoon trading cycle – surging east on the west monsoon all the way to Aru, at the forbidding lip of New Guinea's swamps, and west again on the east monsoon beyond Borneo all the way to Sumatra.

They have fallen much from their early splendour, and are today really just roving gypsies of the Eastern seas, though they ply their various trades in the only true 'tall ships' still sailing for a living – for even the giant dhows of the Arabian Gulf are now powered by Perkins, Mitsubishi and Rolls-Royce engines. The Bugis' prahus are a magni-ficent hybrid between the original island boats and the seventeenth-century Portuguese spice-trading galleons. When Wallace embarked in one of these in his search for the Greater Bird of Paradise, he described it as far preferable to travelling in a first-class steamer of the time:

. . . how comparatively sweet was everything on board . . . no paint,

91 Macawali, one of our friendly Bugis shipmates

92 Makassarese children

93 Makassar harbour with a small 'lombok' boat in the foreground and a Bugis prahu passing the bamboo fishing platforms behind

94 In Makassar, rattan cane from Borneo is processed for export

95 Market boy selling fighting cicadas in bamboo cages

94

95

96 A lavish 'society' Bugis wedding in Makassar

97 A group of Bisus, a rare sect of androgynous priests

no tar, no new rope (vilest of smells to the squeamish), no grease or oil or varnish; but instead of these, bamboo and rattan and choir rope and palm thatch: pure vegetable fibres, which smell pleasantly, if they smell at all, and recall quiet scenes in the green and shady forest.[10]

It was in these and these alone that we were determined to reach our goal, for not only was our finance conditional on such a journey, but also it might be the last opportunity for anyone to make this historic voyage before the Bugis' prahus were gone for ever.

We returned to Makassar from the Toraja highlands with dangerously diminished funds, realizing that we had been in Celebes for two months and that the chances of finding a prahu which could carry us the nearly two thousand miles to the Aru Islands were remote. We had failed to locate a single prahu master, or 'nakoda', who had been anywhere near them, or had the slightest interest in doing so, and it was now so late in the west monsoon that there only remained another six weeks before we would no longer be able to depart without risking the winds dying and starting to reverse themselves before we had reached our destination.

From our base in our waterfront digs, we spent many harrowing weeks combing Makassar's harbour, interrogating the scowling seamen of every arriving prahu, and exploring the coastal villages with Abu. Here we saw our first knife-fight – which was clearly to the death – and Abu hustled us away from the milling throng which surrounded the two furious young combatants who rolled around like snakes in the dust attempting to stab each other with their 'badiks', the seaman's dagger which few of the locals went without.

It was during these anxious weeks of searching that Halim, our grave-robbing friend, took us to another of his Ming-porcelain burial-grounds, located several hours from Makassar and about half an hour's march from the nearest hamlet. On our way back to the main road, at the end of the day we persuaded the reluctant Halim to investigate with us the loud festivities issuing from an isolated group of stilt houses. It was to be our first encounter with the 'Bisus', a bizarre peripatetic sect of transvestite and largely hermaphrodite Bugis priests who, it later transpired, were performing the traditional trance rite to accompany rice-planting. Immediately we could sense a rough and rather unpleasant atmosphere, but we allowed ourselves to be swept up the steps of the first house into a howling throng of excitable spectators. In their midst about eight Bisus, ranging from fourteen to sixty years old, were 'performing'. They were drenched in cheap perfume, and draped with gaudy women's clothing and costume jewellery mixed with talismans and ritual power objects.

'Let's get out of here,' Halim hissed at us. 'This can get nasty.'

I was prepared to second that, but Lorne was overcome with delight at finding a sect which had long since officially died out.

Though shoved and pinched and taunted unmercifully by the spectators, the Bisus quietly drummed themselves into a glassy-eyed state, drew their kerises from their sarongs, and proceeded to whirl

92

furiously about the room while trying to twist the blades into their own throats and stomachs. There were certain crescendos when a particularly macho spectator would sweep a Bisu off his feet and kiss him furiously before roughly throwing him back into the circle again. It was an alarming and not very attractive event in which the Bisus were treated more like circus whores than like priests, yet retained a touchingly self-possessed dignity, despite the ragging they received from their 'flock' and the abuse to which they subjected themselves with their own blades. We questioned the elder of the group – a soft-faced grandmother of a man, with wise and watery eyes – who explained:

'These people, our people, don't know who we are any more. They treat us worse than their women. Our job has always been to stand just between heaven and earth – to be neither pain nor joy, man nor woman, but to stand beyond the dualities which rule this world. We can remain sensitive to the voices of spirits, and can dream of events to come – though few people listen to us now.'

The adolescent Bisus were coming out of trance, and now sat bruised and perspiring together, simpering and repairing each other's damaged make-up.

'How do you become a Bisu?' I asked. 'I thought it was illegal now.'

96

97

93

'Illegal? Ha! You don't *become* a Bisu,' the elder said. 'You're *born* one, and you usually realize it very soon. You dream and feel things like a girl as well as like a boy, and you desire to dress and behave like both. It is then that you find and join the Bisus to learn the old ways of magic. Sometimes you make a mistake, and you are not a Bisu at all, but simply what they' – he gestured resignedly at the howling spectators – 'call us all anyway, just "lady boys"!'

He looked away, embarrassed. 'At least,' he finished quietly, 'if you simply have a woman's soul, but are not potentially a priest, you can still find a place of peace and acceptance amongst us, away from the community.'

Peace was hardly the reigning atmosphere when Halim and I managed to haul Lorne and his equipment out of there. Chaos was prevailing, in which part of the ritual was to douse everyone who emerged from the Bisus' hut with buckets of water. We were particularly tempting targets and, bombarded with jeers and gallons of water, we finally fled the hamlet clutching our sopping equipment to our bosoms like hysterical mothers – little comforted by the thought that these were the spiritual mediators of the people we intended to sail with over the months ahead. . . .

During our daily rounds at the harbour front contacting the nakodas, we had met a young, strongly built Chinese man supervising the loading of cargo for Java. Next to Werner, Tan Hans Yong was to become one of our greatest friends and benefactors. He shared with us a singular fascination for tropical waters and everything in them, and had acquired the franchise for scuba equipment for the whole of the Moluccas.

In his spotless home, amongst his large and benevolent family, we were fed enormous meals, shown their exotic collection of shells and sponges, and pumped for all we knew about the outside world. The Tans were international traders, in partnership with family members based in Dobu in the Aru Islands, of mother-of-pearl shell and 'tripang' – the highly priced sea-slugs which are such a delicacy for the Chinese. Yong and his father were the first people we had met who had actually been to Aru. Getting there by the orthodox method of a succession of highly unreliable inter-island launches was a sufficiently bad experience, they claimed, let alone making the journey with the Bugis.

'Tell you what,' said Yong in his excellent eager English. 'If you can't find a prahu in the next few weeks, we'll tell you how to set about getting there the "modern" way via the inter-island ferry launches. It may not take you via many of the islands which Wallace visited, but at least you'll *arrive*. And we'll have lots of letters and little presents for you to take our family if you do decide to go!'

It was a week later, and feeling increasingly more desperate, that at the suggestion of Werner Meyer we visited the isolated hamlets of Bira and its neighbour Kasuso, on the south-eastern tip of the peninsula. These proved to be the isolated buccaneer haunts we were looking for, and the hidden source of most of the nation's sailing prahus and their mariners. It was a good seven-hour jeep-lurch, even with Abu at the

98 A lowland Celebes family watches the world from the steps of their home. The women whiten their faces with rice paste to preserve their complexions

99 (over page) Looking to sea from the beach where the prahus are built

wheel, and for the last two hours we drove over a tyre-tearing track down a parched spit of land. We finally emerged on smiling white beaches, fringed with palms and the largest fleet of prahus we had ever seen. They hung at anchor, suspended over brilliant reefs, or lined the strand side by side, in preparation for departure.

Malaria was hyper-endemic by the beach, so the village had been built on the cliffs above it, near the fresh springs. A few brightly coloured pony-drawn traps, on twisted bicycle-wheels, meandered down the white-sand streets. The houses were meticulously painted and rose on ten-foot stilts above the ground. Their roofs were decorated with exotic pre-Islamic symbols of dragons and flying creatures, and even included wooden aeroplanes with wind-driven propellers. This was 'Bugisville' all right, and our arrival was accompanied by the usual howling horde of kids and adults who jostled us up the steps to the house of the Bupati, the government-appointed chief, where we had arrived to pay our respects.

'Get the hell out of here, you miserable wretches!' came a loud shout from inside. 'Be gone. Scram. Remove your horrible faces from my property immediately!'

It was a tall, thin, almost clownlike man with large destroyed teeth in a long mobile face who was the unlikely source of so commanding a voice; and it was a relief to find that it was directed not at us, but at our surrounding mob.

'Ha. *Ha!*' he exclaimed on seeing us. 'Englishmen! Ibu! Come and have a look at this, will you?'

Although he was the 'Keraing', the local hereditary chieftain, the government title of 'Bupati' actually belonged to his wife, who was the first woman in Celebes to hold the position. A broad and kindly lady of noble birth, Ibu (meaning 'mother'), as she was simply called, indulged her husband's eccentricities, constantly tidied up after him and clearly ruled the household and the village.

100 The well-built house of a successful Biranese sea-captain. The stilts rest on stones, a disadvantage in high winds, but the entire house can be picked up by the community and carried to a different location

100

98

'Perhaps they're not Englishmen,' she said; then, shaking us warmly by the hand: 'Please, don't be offended if you're not.'

The Keraing was a humorous, somewhat foppish extrovert, in complete contrast to Ibu, who stayed mainly in the background, signed the papers that mattered, and was acutely observant of everything that went on around her. But they got on famously together – and were to become our stalwart allies in a maelstrom of conflicting vendettas which were to unfold around us.

This seemed a far more promising environment, and we quickly accepted the couple's invitation to abandon our base in Makassar and move in with them in Bira, since it would clearly take many more weeks of negotiating before we could be sure of coming up with a prahu, *and* a crew, reliable enough to carry us eastwards.

That night, with our generator and four lightbulbs, we illuminated the Keraing's house and electrified the village for the first time in the thirty-odd years since the invading Japanese had withdrawn from Indonesia. As we sat down to the first of many repetitive meals of salted fish and ground corn, I broached the question of finding a prahu which might carry us as far as Aru.

'I own four prahus,' the Keraing stated by way of an answer.

'Three prahus!' his wife corrected him.

'Oh, yes, one of them sank. Well, I still *own* it, don't I, even if it is underwater off Java somewhere? Anyway,' he continued, 'two of them are in Borneo – and where's *Sinar Surya*?' he asked the general assembly of eavesdropping elders in the corner. They shrugged at each other.

'Laid up on the beach,' Ibu answered from behind. 'It will need a lot of work – beginning with a new mainmast!'

'If *you* can find someone who needs to send cargo to the Aru Islands,' the Keraing announced, 'then *we* can get the boat and a crew ready for you in a month, which is the last possible time for heading eastwards!'

Since there was no question of us being able to invest in a cargo ourselves, let alone afford to charter the empty vessel, our only solution lay in returning to Makassar and attempting to persuade our Chinese friends to raise the merchandise themselves and to send us along as its stewards and guardians. Yong's father was appalled at the idea, but was finally persuaded to invest in fifty tons of raw salt, to be used in the curing of the venison which abounded in the Eastern islands, as well as several hundred plastic chairs, and a quantity of spare diving equipment for the pearl-shellers who worked for the Aru branch of the Tan family.

We were ecstatic as we returned to Bira with the good news, but a closer look at the grounded *Sinar Surya* and the motley bunch with whom we might sail made it clear that our troubles were far from over. There was still an immense amount of work to do on the boat, not the least of which, it seemed to us, was replacing her rotting mainmast. The Keraing, however, had put the wheels in motion, and while *Sinar Surya* was being prepared for the sea, and the pirates were still arguing about where she might go, and with whom, Lorne and I spent the following weeks suppressing our impatience by exploring our surroundings.

101

101 Like Noah's Arks, up to 150 feet long, the Bugis prahus are built with wooden pegs, instead of nails, which swell and secure the timbers once the boats are launched

102 Beached on Bira, awaiting repairs. There are no drawn plans, the prahus are only built from the image in the shipwright's mind, so no two are the same

In the coconut groves by the beach scores of men were building prahus from scratch, some over 150 feet long. Their only tools from the outside world were the 'parang', the broad-bladed machete of the East, and a hand-drill resembling an oversized corkscrew, with which they could make all the other tools they required to produce these spectacular Noah's Arks.

Prahu-building is ruled by ancient deities, mediated by specialized shamans who choose the timbers by 'calling' to the trees and cutting only those which 'reply'. The boats thus grew from no clear design – but emerged organically, with asymmetrical spars, as if barely freed from the forms of the forest.

Precisely chiselled pegs of a different wood from the rest of the ship, which swelled and secured the timbers once they were immersed in the water, were used instead of nails or screws. At night the beaches flamed with bonfires lit to extract lime from the coral, which was then mixed with coconut oil to form the white cement with which the hulls were caulked.

Wherever we had been in the Celebes lowlands people would call out to us, 'Hello, meester!' – but in Bira it was always 'Hello, Inggeriss!' which assumed was simply because news of our true nationality had got around. But it was an elderly shipwright on the beach who explained that all foreigners were called that here, since the only other outsider to have lived in the village was an Englishman named Collins, who, it turned out, had spent many months here during the 1930s. He had had his own small prahu built, and finally sailed eastwards, leaving a strong imprint on the group psyche. There were even rumblings that we might represent a sort of Karmic return of this man – who had apparently shared our obsession for their sailing craft, as well as for Bira's surrounding wildlife.[11]

Fortunately, Collins was remembered with much affection, which, according to the old shipwright, was the only reason why the Keraing was going out of his way to help us.

'Ibu and the Keraing are good people,' he told us unexpectedly, during one of our many conversations sitting on the beach. 'Listen only to them. There are many bad people here, too.'

It was certainly true that now, when at last it looked as if we might have our prahu, an increasing number of extremely sinister nakodas were approaching us with offers to take us to the Aru Islands. Some already had their boats fully rigged and ready to go – but the temptation to leave immediately was easily outweighed by the transparency of their predatory motives, and our allegiance to the Keraing and his wife. It was Ibu who told us that her husband was terrified of the water.

'He can't swim,' she said. 'He used to travel in prahus as a young man, then a guru told him that one day he would die by water. Now you will hardly ever see him in a canoe. That's fine by me. He stays behind now with the old men, women and children while the rest of the village puts to sea for nine months.' For that was how long it took before the monsoon carried these men back home again. The odds on returning at all were fairly poor by the sound of it; for, according to Ibu, of the

ninety prahus which had left Bira the previous year, five had still not returned, and no word had been heard from their crews.

There was no doctor in the region, and Ibu reckoned that the three major causes of mortality were shipwreck, malaria and being killed by a python. This seemed rather extreme to us until we discovered that Bira was indeed one of the most heavily python-infested regions in all Celebes. We heard numerous stories about the pythons even entering the houses at night during the arid seasons when game is scarce. Nearly all our crew were to tell us harrowing anecdotes of personal encounters with hungry pythons – some of which had been measured at over twenty-eight feet long. They all wore serpentlike black coral bracelets as special protective amulets against snakes. Laba, who was later to become one of our shipmates, had been a fruit farmer and had only recently taken up sailing on the advice of the local shaman after a string of close calls with pythons.

Laba was quite a celebrity in the village, and from him we learnt just what it is like to be embraced by a really big snake. His fruit plantation had been a good four-hour walk from the village, and he was used to visiting it alone. He had found there the stinkingly obvious lair of a large python, a cave mouth which he stuffed with kindling which he then ignited. He was standing back to admire the conflagration when the full weight of its rightful resident landed on him from a bough above, where it had been watching. Flattening him to the ground and knocking the wind out of him, it had begun its killing process by throwing a few coils around the tree to anchor itself, and a few more round Laba, pinning his arms to his side. It doesn't squeeze very hard, Laba explained, but tightens its grip each time you exhale, making it increasingly harder to draw the next breath. It made no attempt to bite, but held its face close to Laba's, intently watching him while its forked tongue flickered around his nose.

'They just look at you very closely,' he told us.

It was at this point that Laba had effected the only feasible escape procedure for such circumstances, although it required a good deal of luck. In the coils adjacent to his wrists he located the python's cloaca and managed to give it one hell of a goosing. The astonished reptile released its grip just long enough for Laba to break free and stagger off down the track – with the serpent in hot pursuit apparently loudly vocalizing with the same sibilant barks which we were later to hear ourselves while filming a python hunt. The snake caught him again savagely round the legs with its jaws, but he managed to tear himself away and keep running until he finally passed out from shock and blood-loss. It was after dark when he finally regained consciousness with the jolting realization that the snake should have caught up with him. But it had not, and he managed to make his way home to safety.

He was still recuperating at home a few nights later when a rustling from the rafters above his bed proved to be yet another python which had entered the village and was lying in wait. It was then that the local shaman had suggested that unless Laba became a sailor he would probably 'die by python'.

Apart from some rudimentary agriculture, and the building and sailing of prahus, Bira's only other income was earned by the village's four intrepid python-hunters, led by Rindi, who sell the live snakes for their valuable skins to Chinese traders up the coast. Rindi was a shy and diminutive man of indeterminate age, whom we first met at the Keraing's house and persuaded to take us along with him on a number of occasions to record his unenviable working day or, rather, night.

The first was on the local islet of Likangloe, where the once abundant population of wild goats had recently been massively reduced in inverse proportion to that of the snakes which ate them, and where the resident family of fisherfolk had lost a sixteen-year-old daughter to a python only the year before. Since a python's skin begins to deteriorate in quality once it has grown to about fifteen feet the largest are left alone, which is just as well as each one must be caught at night, alive and by hand, with a lamp to attract them from their lairs, and at least four men to get them into the sack afterwards.

We followed the hunting team in the dark, stumbling across the scrubby terrain, heavily pitted with limestone fissures, until Rindi located a promising lair by cautiously sniffing its entrance for the distinctive aroma of a large reptile which doesn't brush its teeth. The hurricane-lamp was placed about twenty feet in front and pumped up to maximum brilliance while we lay sweating and mosquito-bitten in the shadows, fingering our cameras and the trigger of our temperamental Sun Gun, expecting that at any moment a curious snake would be drawn to the light from the shadows behind us, rather than from the cave ahead.

As we watched, a leathery doglike head began extending from the fissure on a seemingly interminable, peristaltically moving neck. When it was fully clear of the cave, three of the hunters then simultaneously seized it by head, tail and centre and held it straight enough to feed head-first into an open sack held by the fourth man.

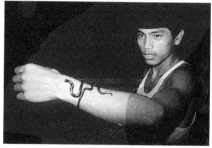

103

It was only about twelve feet long – a baby by local standards – but it hissed and barked and thrashed and stank until finally converted into a writhing sack of potatoes. The hunters had drawn straws for their positions of the evening, which in order of desirability were: sack man, head man, tail man and middle man. The head man could get bitten, the tail man could get doused with noisome excreta – and if they both missed their grasp, then the middle man got both bad ends of the snake coming back at him at the same time.

104

Although we were suitably impressed by the mere twelve-footer caught in Likangloe, the hunters promised that before we left they would take us into what was known locally as the 'Death Cave' to find the really big pythons. Lorne and I had often visited this particular cave in an attempt to film the Celebes Macaque, a baboon-sized monkey unique to the island, which nested in the giant tree which grew from it, but we had never thought of actually venturing inside.

Every sunset the apes would return from their day's foraging to sleep in the branches of this giant tree, and we were driven to distraction by our repeated attempts to film them properly in the few seconds after

103 Black coral serpent bracelets are worn as charms against attack by pythons and poisonous snakes

104 Bira's python hunter allows his son to play with a live snake, before selling it down the coast for its skin

103

they arrived and before the sun set. The monkeys themselves turned out to be a highly evolved and accomplished band of thieves, and were treated by the Biranese as a neighbouring tribe. Their history told of many wars and truces between the villagers and the 'men of the trees', and of how the monkeys would carry their dead down into those same caves which had served as a human burial-ground or, rather, burial-dump since pre-Islamic times.

The Keraing had told us that in the 1950s a military scouting party from Makassar had angered the village by entering the caves with special equipment and making off with a good deal of valuable porcelain — indicating it had also been used as a burial-chamber by early visiting Chinese mariners. It had been used more recently as well, during the Darul Islam revolutionary uprisings of the 1960s, when the bodies of execution victims were flung into the cave. For another ten years not a soul had dared enter it, until the snake-hunters steeled themselves to descend in pursuit of a python which had consumed a child in the dry season of 1969. On closer cross-examination Rindi confessed that since then he and his team had not entered the place until we came along. We were to understand why.

It was only a forty-minute scramble away from Bira through dry and spiny scrub before we could see the great tree looming far above any of the surrounding vegetation. But, on reaching it, it proved to be a good twenty feet taller than it appeared, for it grew from the floor of a protective circular sinkhole, perhaps forty yards across, and with vertical walls about twenty feet deep fringed by tangled thorny-vines and spider's webs. We cut our way through these and, following our python-hunters, who now seemed considerably less enthusiastic about the venture than they had been when they first suggested it, we slid down coconut ropes to the sinkhole floor and to the forbidding cobwebbed entrances which extended from its walls. It was quickly obvious why this was known as the 'Death Cave' — and, indeed, why the great tree had assumed such vulgar grandeur, for the stinking loam around its roots was thick with human bones. Skulls of goats and apes and people also littered the insides of the caves — where the air was chokingly rancid — and extremely large, spindly white spiders scuttled away from our lights. The loamy bat-dung crawled with poisonous six-inch millipedes, and at one point we automatically prostrated ourselves amongst them as a horde of disturbed bats swept towards us to escape. The deeper we went, the more clearly python tracks became apparent. Even the tracks smelt like pythons, over and above the surrounding stench, and football-sized bundles of bones were pointed out to us as the regurgitated remains of their meals. There was a passageway which ended with an abrupt vertical drop into darkness, but it had a conveniently adjacent stalacmite for attaching a rope.

Rindi, whose crew possessed only pressurized paraffin-lamps, asked to borrow our torch, and revealed with it a patch of silt floor a good thirty feet further down, as untrammelled as the bottom of the deep ocean trenches — except for the unmistakable tyre-tracks of several large pythons.

'See, Tuan, a whole other world down there. We had to go down there in 1969 following the snake which ate Denke's little girl. We got it and cut the baby out of it. We need ropes, Tuan. The snakes don't need ropes', he chuckled feebly, 'because they *are* ropes. Shall we go down?'

'Shall we?' I turned to Lorne, who was also having difficulty in breathing, and was quite aware of the idiocy of attempting a further rope descent (and hopefully subsequent ascent) with our equipment.

'Tell you what, Tuan,' Rindi volunteered. 'This is bad season for big snakes. They're not eating now, they're sleeping. Very easy to find, but very angry. Not easy getting up that rope with angry snake behind. Better we find you more big snakes outside Death Cave.'

We were not hard to convince. We already had a fairly impressive snake hunt on film from Likangloe, even if only a small specimen was caught, and the really big ones would definitely have to wait.

Although all this was entertainingly unpleasant, in Bira the most genuine threat to our lives came disguised in the quietest way, when we broke the cardinal rule of touching an unidentified creature. We had been snorkling together in the shallow reefs when we found the most beautiful octopus, barely a hand's breadth in size, which rhythmically glowed with vivid blue circles. Since eyesight requires that I do most of the close-up camera work, it fell to me to film the creature crawling slowly across Lorne's fingers. On our return to London, David Attenborough kindly came over to watch the rushes with us, and when he saw this particular episode he shrieked: 'You fools! That is a fully adult and deadly Moluccan Blue-Ringed Octopus!'

We had never heard of such a thing; and apparently it had only recently been catalogued, after a spate of Australian deaths on the Great Barrier Reef. It is particularly odd to watch that footage now, in the knowledge that a quick nip from that delicate creature would have sent Lorne into a coma in five minutes – and to the Pearly Gates, or thereabouts, shortly afterwards.

105

We were to witness a different and more promising sacrifice only after we had spent many patient weeks in Bira, when a white cock and a black goat were ritually slaughtered in *Sinar Surya*'s hull, signifying that at last we were about to depart. It was a messy sacrifice, since the shaman (the very same who had advised the Keraing to avoid the sea, and Laba to avoid the land) was such a trembling wreck that he could barely hold the machete and needed to be supported from both sides to avoid falling on his face.

'He's been shaking like this ever since he was sixteen years old,' the Keraing told us, 'when he first had the experience which made him take up the profession. He was fishing with his uncle, and they caught a large silver fish. As the fish died it changed colours like a rainbow, and he left his body and has never really returned to it. So he's the village shaman.'

'Is there always this much blood when he's on duty?' I asked.

'Yes,' the Keraing grinned at me. 'No prahus can put to sea before the black goat of stability and the white cock of courage have been sacrificed for a safe journey. But if you think this is bloody' – and he laughed his hacking tubercular laugh – 'our ancestors wouldn't think of

105 Bira's white sands have never seen beach mats, parasols or sun-oiled tourists

going to sea in a new prahu which hadn't first been rolled into the water over the living bodies of seven women in their first pregnancy! And, by the way,' he added, as if it was all part of the same subject, 'I think I've come up with the safest combination of captain and crew for your journey. You'll meet them tomorrow.'

Living with the Keraing and his wife was a very public affair; and, although they barked a good deal at the constant throng which invaded their household while we were there, they were traditionally in no position to deny them entrance, and each resident of Bira got his chance lengthily to observe our every blink and mannerism. When we were asleep, it had ceased to matter, but when we ate it still remained a bore.

Thirty pairs of eyes stared with unwavering concentration as I dipped my hand into the all-too-familiar breakfast of slightly sour rice and salted fish.

'Look, he's pushed the fish's head aside.'

'How can he live on such little mouthfuls of rice?'

The low running commentary on our every move was a familiar background to all our meals in Bira, but there was an added tension in the air today. They could sense our nervous impatience, and they were determined to remember everything very clearly, for it could be many years before they would again have the opportunity to witness such exotic behaviour. Today the big hairy visitors were leaving.

The crowd at the door parted to let through a gaunt old man wearing the black peci hat, symbol of Indonesian nationalism, faded sarong and a shirt with so many patches that it was hard to tell which was the original material. He took a seat in solemn silence and, uninvited, started to roll up some of the Keraing's tobacco.

The Keraing waved in his direction. 'This is Ladjang. In the days when I travelled in prahus he always went with me. We even sailed as far as Singapore. Never again! I'm sending him with you to make sure you have no problems. He is very stupid, but you can trust him and he knows more islands than all the crew put together.'

Ladjang's brow wrinkled as if focusing on some minor anxiety that nothing could be done about anyway. His mouth hung slightly open to reveal one enormous tooth dangling in solitary splendour from his upper gum and which wobbled alarmingly whenever he spoke.

He appeared to be an unprepossessing 'guardian' until you looked into his humorous and lively eyes. We had yet to learn that the 'problems' the Keraing was anticipating could come from our own crew, and that Ladjang's job as our intermediary with them was to call on all his diplomatic skills and moral courage.

At that moment the principal 'problem', Tandri Dewa, our captain-to-be, stormed in. Slight and in his mid-twenties, he moved with energetic nervousness, his sharp eyes darting in all directions, as if on constant guard against a knife in the back – a worrying habit which I have since come to associate with compulsive back-stabbers.

'Where are your things?' he demanded. 'We're late!'

In Europe such abruptness might have raised an eyebrow or two, but in Indonesia it was stunningly rude. There was a shocked hush, and then the Keraing, with a sly smile, told him that Ladjang would be sailing with us.

I had to sympathize with Tandri. This was to be his first independent command, and his status and authority were already threatened by our presence. Having to take Ladjang the 'elder statesman' along as well was a further humiliating blow. He tried to argue, but everyone in the room knew that the battle was lost before it had even begun.

We couldn't believe that we were actually on our way. We packed up our possessions and our battered pile of equipment, walked on air, despite our load, through the butterfly and lizard gardens to the high cliff overlooking Bira's deep-water harbour. The sea was dead calm and the coral a glistening treasure trove of vivid gems. Seemingly suspended in mid-air, and connected to this world only by their anchor cables, floated the prahus of Bira's magnificent fleet. That moment will remain forever crystallized in my memory. Whatever desperate or mundane disappointments might lie ahead, as we gazed down at those phantoms from another age I felt that we had become travellers in time. For more than a year Lorne and I had struggled towards this moment and, contrary to all the laws of psychology, we were finding that the realization of our dreams surpassed our wildest expectations.

Once aboard *Sinar Surya*, the idyllic image was shattered. Frenetic confusion reigned, as new rattan was hurriedly woven into cradles for her steering oars, rips in her old sails were frantically patched and last-minute adjustments made to her standing rigging. Canoe-loads of coral and sand were being ferried from the beach to fill her empty hold, for she could not sail against the monsoon to Makassar without ballast. To my inexperienced eyes she seemed still to be floating far too high in the water, and I doubted that we would get away before sunset.

However, in the midst of all that confusion, Bendra, the shaman, was calmly intoning Islamic and animist prayers, and making offerings on deck for the Nuang Ase, or 'leaving the land' ceremony. He, along with some of the older nakodas, had divined through omens and astrological portents that this was the last auspicious day for embarking on the seasonal voyage. If we were not away by sunset, there would not be another appropriate departure date for more than a month. We were not alone in our dilemma, for all the other prahus in the fleet around us were up against the same deadline.

The Keraing came aboard with his guests and family in colourful array. The Nuang Ase is the one day in the year when the taboo against women boarding the prahus may be broken, and they brought with them a feast, including the black goat of the earth and the white cock of the sky which had been sacrificed in our hull the night before. Even in that dead calm, the ladies turned green with sea-sickness. Etiquette demanded it, as a display of their femininity.

At midday an unseasonal wind began gusting from the east, and our calm anchorage was transformed into a choppy lee shore. Tandri Dewa decided that, ready or not, we must make a move, and the guests and grateful ladies were put ashore. Lustily chanting Bugis sea-shanties, our entire crew edged *Sinar Surya* directly into the eye of the wind and

106 On the day of our departure a farewell feast is consumed on the decks of *Sinar Surya*. It is brought by the women, who are allowed on board this one day in the year

107 Raising our anchor from the coral without benefit of winches is no mean task

beyond the reef. A safe distance from shore all sails were set and, with the last anchor hauled in, the mizzen and foresails were backed — the crew hanging far out over the deep-blue water to keep the booms at an angle that would force her bows around towards the south so that her mainsails could fill. Soon her hundred tons were brought to life as all eight sails pulled hard on her first tack of the season.

In the spreaders forty feet above us the agile topmen, Basso and Rasman, executed hair-raising victory somersaults before shinning down the shrouds with the rough wires grasped between their toes. We had only known *Sinar Surya* as a lumpish extension of the land — as dependent on it as a baby is on its mother; now she had come of age as she surged south to a thrilling new rhythm, new smells and new sensations. Every creak and groan was music to me, and the surge of each wave echoed through her entire frame and re-echoed through mine. Her crew danced to their tasks, and I understood for the first time the meaning of the Indonesian words for 'crewman' — 'anak prahu', literally 'child of the prahu'. With a shake of her eight great sails, she had become a mother in her own right, and we were all her children.

Our immediate problems were sorting out our living arrangements, for although it had been agreed with Tandri that we would occupy the ship's only excuse for a cabin we now found our things moved down into the hold. Rather bitter negotiations resulted in our final victory, and our stuffing our possessions into the windowless cabin astern and ensuring that our toothbrushes — significant status symbols — joined the only other two aboard in the privileged rack at the foot of the

106

mizzenmast. One belonged to the one-toothed Ladjang, and was shared amongst a few fastidious members of the crew; the other was Tandri's, to be used by no one, not even himself.

The east wind held firm, the blue waters parted, and we surged south along the fringing reef towards Tanjung Bira, the southernmost point of Sulawesi. At the top of its high cliffs is the sanctuary of the goddess Sampanena, protectress of mariners. Our crew's wives would already be heading there to make offerings on behalf of their husbands.

Beneath the point lies Krander's whirlpool, a notorious navigational hazard, powerful enough at times to drag down the smaller prahus, so most sailors steer well clear of it. For the people of Bira, however, it is a point of honour to scythe through the troubled gap between the whirlpool and the rocks.

The monster was at its most mellow that day, but still energetic enough to toss *Sinar Surya*'s hundred tons around in an alarming manner. Lorne was dangling over the bowsprit filming as I firmly held his legs, when he was taken off-guard by a violent lurch and dropped our wide-angle lens cap overboard. He howled with dismay at the loss and was to curse the incident many more times over the months to come. Old Ladjang, however, nodded his approval.

'That was a fine offering you made to Krander and Sampanena,' he remarked. 'Now our voyage is sure to be a safe one.'

We were part of a scattered fleet of Bira prahus. Two were headed south to Flores, one south-west to Bali and Java, and another west to Borneo. We watched them disappear into the dusk as we anchored at

107

the little island of Likangloe, where we had witnessed our first python hunt. Both wind and current were still unseasonably favourable for Makassar, but Tandri decided, probably wisely, that we would need more ballast from the beach at Likangloe. The cliffs of Sampanena were still in sight, but the required auspicious departure had been made.

The sun came onstage for its evening display of vulgar wealth, and Ladjang turned towards Mecca in prayer. I found a quiet corner of the deck to gaze up at the moonless sky. Those who have only seen the northern stars may not realize how much more dramatic are those of the southern hemisphere. I was absorbed by their brilliance, embraced by them, lost in them, and I slept.

From Lorne's Diary

Our cabin is barely large enough to accommodate both us and our equipment. We cannot fully stretch out in it, nor sit upright without cracking our heads on the decking above. It is four foot six inches wide, extending to a princely six foot six, but the forward end is so packed with our gear that there is barely enough room for our legs.

We share it with an unwelcome assortment of fellow travellers. Some are there to suck our blood, while others are content to compete with us for our meagre stash of private food. This morning a rat poked his nose in, but they usually seem to prefer the main hold. It's the insects that enjoy travelling cabin class. We don't see much of them in the daytime, but at night the bedbugs crawl out from under our mats, and we listen to the cockroaches munching away merrily in the food-basket between our heads, and to the brittle scrabbling of their feet on the ceiling a couple of feet above us. They haven't found their sea legs yet, and a sudden lurch can bring several of them raining down on our faces. It's hard to sleep with a panic-stricken cockroach clawing its way out of one's eye-socket!

At dawn we set sail due west along the southern coast of Celebes. The east wind, which had held all night, chose this moment to reverse itself, and the west monsoon blew relentlessly into our faces. At the end of every clawing tack we found ourselves back at almost the same place we had started; we began to learn the realities of life aboard a Bugis prahu.

Downwind or on a broad reach they are magnificent craft, but upwind sailing is definitely not their strong suit. Lightly laden, as was *Sinar Surya*, they are a disaster. Pointing, at best, some sixty degrees off the wind, and drifting downwind at an alarming rate, we made little or no progress during the next three days. The crew were kept occupied completing the many jobs that should have been finished before putting out. Nobody appeared to give orders, and everyone performed the tasks which most suited his mood of the moment.

There were only two whose work seemed never to end, and they bore the brunt of an endless string of the only direct orders we ever heard aboard. Amir and Mansur must have been about eight and ten years old. They were the cooks, washers-up, barbers, lice-pickers, deck-swabbers and general gofers at the bottom of a subtle pecking order that slowly revealed itself. This was their first voyage, and their labours were complicated by severe bouts of seasickness, through which they soldiered on valiantly.

At the peak of the hierarchy stood Tandri. Ah, Tandri! The very sound of his name makes my sense of humour evaporate. Every encounter became a challenge, a test of strength. For hours at night he held court immediately over our hatch, inches above our heads. His audience was the crew, and the language their own, but he knew we sensed the content of the canisters of venom dropped into our claustrophobic sanctum. Old Ladjang remonstrated with him quietly, but the others were silent, and we realized that our captain was infecting them with a subtle but poisonous hostility towards us. It was the beginning of what was to become the greatest and most dangerous hardship of our voyage.

Our immediate conflict was over navigation.

On the fifth dawn we hurried on deck to confirm my certainty that at last we had rounded the south-western point of Sulawesi, and had a clear run north to Makassar. The previous night we had been well on course for it. I checked and then rechecked our position before slumping down in despair. We were in precisely the same place that we had been in three dawns previously! My despair was caused not so much by the frustration of not reaching our destination as by the final shattering of my most cherished illusion about the Bugis.

Once amongst the world's greatest blue-water navigators, guided by wave patterns and the clues in seaweed and bird droppings, the Bugis had now lost so much confidence in their old ways that they had been reduced to coast-hugging, on the principle that if their ships sank they at least had a chance of making it ashore alive. It was a reminder of the early days of European seamanship, when captains discouraged their crews from learning how to swim so that they were more likely to sink with their ship than abandon their posts and struggle for shore.

Sinar Surya carried only an antique compass whose oil was so clouded with age that we could hardly read the rose. I doubt if it had ever been correctly swung, and even our little hand-compass was more accurate. The only chart was more symbolic than effective. Dated 1910, it extended from Singapore to northern Australia, so many of the islands on our route – let alone the hazards – did not even figure. The Bugis had fallen between two sciences, forgetting the old before they had mastered the new.

'Christ, these characters are bloody hopeless! We've got to do something,' I fumed.

'I still think we should let them try it their way and see what happens,' Lorne ventured. It was an argument that had been simmering for two days, and it was clear he was beginning to waver.

'Even you must be getting a pretty clear picture of what happens. Look at that bastard – there he goes again!' It was the bus that we had seen twice every day for the last three days, making its regular coastal run between Bulukumba and Makassar. We had both come to hate it and its invisible driver, whom we visualized as a smug glutton sleeping

108 Eastward bound towards the Aru Islands at last, together with a small fleet of Bugis prahus

109 Navigation is a community affair, with a chart which dated back to 1910 and was on such a small scale that most of the islands on our route did not appear

in a comfortable bed each night and stuffing his face with three square meals a day. So crazed were we becoming that I was sure that even at that distance we could spot the fiendish grin he directed at *Sinar Surya* floundering on the horizon each time he passed!

Lorne tried feebly to stick to his final defence. 'But, hell, they've been navigating safely to Aru for centuries.'

'Aru? You can forget about Aru. At this rate we'll be lucky to make it to Makassar before the next monsoon!'

We went below to plot our rebellious strategy. While waiting for them to reach the outer limit of their seaward tack, we fished for our enormous aviator's chart which was larger and more colourful, if little more useful, than theirs. Protractors, compasses, rulers, and any other impressive props we could think of – even a film-footage chart, and the monocular (or half a pair of binoculars) inherited from our stepfather.

Judging the moment, we exploded on deck with all our navigational 'tools' and I, usually the smooth talker of the family, went into action. Lorne tells me it was my finest hour – and my most shameless. Our objective was simple. It had become obvious that the east-setting current swirled strongest close to the headlands. We had to keep them heading out to sea as long as possible, so that we could fully clear it on our return tack.

I talked utter rubbish for hours, and on the few occasions that I faltered Lorne would break in and take over until I had recovered my strength. We never did persuade them, but for six valuable hours we managed to hold them on that course far out into the Flores Sea, until finally they came to their senses, noticed the distant and almost invisible shore, and hurriedly tacked towards it again.

We hadn't gone as far as we would have liked, and it was touch and go until the very last moment, but we just squeezed past the point between Tanakeke island and the mainland.

To us the white sands of Tanakeke looked inviting, but our crew were filled with apprehension the closer we got. Tasman, with the face and physique of a circus strong man, brought his largest parang on deck and glowered warily at the passing island.

'This is a bad place.'

'Spirits?' I asked.

'No, the people. They try to murder everyone who sails too close. Six years ago they attacked my uncle's prahu, killing him and everyone on board for their cargo.' Tasman understood such things. He had spent several years amongst the small Indonesian islands off Singapore. It was a period of his life that he would never talk about.

We left Tanakeke behind without loss of life, and spent the rest of the day on our well-earned broad reach northwards.

The next day we ghosted into Makassar on the faintest breeze. Amir and Mansur hung rapt from the rigging, transfixed by the slowly growing image of their future. Neither of them had ever seen proper shops, nor ice nor electric light – other than the bulbs which we had used with our generator to illuminate the Keraing's house in Bira.

I looked over towards the Pasanggrahan Hotel, and the balcony

110

110 A Bugis woman, unusually of Papuan origin

111 Riding high in *Sinar Surya*. Note the ship's sole water-barrel at the foot of the mizzenmast

from which we had longingly watched so many prahus which we could not sail aboard. It was a good feeling.

We were not even properly docked before Lorne and I leapt ashore and headed for our favourite Chinese restaurant. The solid ground rocked and heaved beneath us, but we were soon gorging ourselves on rich noodles and spicy chilled crabs and lobster – forbidden fruit while amongst our Islamic Bugis.

It was a busy four days. Yong had already put his cargo together, and we helped him supervise its loading aboard *Sinar Surya*. At his home his mother earnestly tried to fatten us up for our adventure ahead, as only the Chinese know how.

Yong lent us a precious scuba tank and a regulator to take with us, saying: 'Use it as you like, but please keep some air in it for Aru. You may need it to film my pearl-divers underwater, and to show them how it works. I've told them that I'm hoping to replace their old hard-hat helmets with this new scuba equipment, but they think I'm joking when I tell them they won't have any hoses to the surface.'

There would be no chance of refilling it; and one tank for four months through some of the world's most spectacular coral seas would call for superhuman restraint.

The cost of the charter to Aru had long since been settled: Yong would pay them half the sum now, and his relations would pay the balance once we and the cargo had safely reached Aru. But Tandri now came up with the bright idea of charging an exorbitant additional fee for every island we needed to call at *en route*. After a marathon round of negotiations, lasting almost a whole day, we managed to whittle it down, with Yong's expert assistance, to the equivalent of about twenty American dollars per island visited.

Neither Tandri nor Yong knew – and we were not about to tell them – that we no longer had enough money left to make a single call. Here, at the very beginning of the voyage we had come to Indonesia to make, we were completely broke. Werner came to our rescue with the loan of a hundred dollars, which would have to see us through the three or four months it might take us to reach Aru. Just how we were to get out and home once we had arrived there was a problem we still refused to think about.

We paid a final courtesy call on General Aziz, Werner's friend who had lent us Abu and his jeep to film the Toraja. He received us wearing a sarong and bouncing a six-month-old grandson in his lap. He gave us an official letter to show the military commanders we might bump into along the way, and sent one of his high-ranking aides down to the dock to see us off.

The immaculate officer stepped gingerly aboard *Sinar Surya* and failed to conceal his astonishment at our living conditions. He informed a grovelling Tandri that we were expected to reach Aru alive, and that if anything unfortunate befell us Tandri and his crew would find their lives very uncomfortable. It was of course pure bluff, and rank-pulling on a vulgar scale, but from then on the crew was to become almost irritatingly attentive to our safety, if not to our general well-being.

Our next port of call would be Bira again, which anyway lay directly on our course back eastwards, and where some unfinished business remained to be settled. Sailing conditions were perfect all the way, and we were back there again an unbelievable thirty-six hours later. The crew had one last night with their families, and the opportunity to share with them some of the advance they had been given by Yong. A good deal of Yong's salt, we also suspected, was off-loaded secretly that evening, to help tide the waiting families through the subsequent nine months without their menfolk.

The Keraing and his family came to wave us farewell from the cliff-top, and we sailed east into the gulf of Bone, and an empty blue sea. It was the last time we were ever to see him alive. Years later we returned to Bira to learn that the shaman's prediction that he 'would die by water' had come to pass in rather too literal a sense. He was hacked to death by one of his own people as a result of a long-standing territorial vendetta over water rights – on the very strand where we were to see him waving us off. His assailant did not come out of the affair unscathed. Having badly underestimated his victim's popularity, he had fled with his family to Makassar and boarded a large inter-island ship for Java. Two days out the ship foundered in a storm, and sank with everyone aboard.

Next day we were visited by a pod of dolphins which behaved as if they had escaped from a circus. They amazed us by leaping high out of the water and somersaulting two or three times before nosing beneath it again without missing a beat. We were only later to learn that these were the Spinner Dolphins, the most acrobatic of all their family.

Our ship's most vulnerable spot was the first four feet of her mainmast, which was heavily eaten by rot. This was considered serious enough by the Keraing to have supplied Tandri with the cost of a new mast which he had promised to have cut from the forest of Bouton, an island we knew nothing about on the south-east of Celebes, a two-day sail across the Gulf of Palopo.

The Bugis step their masts directly on to the deck rather than through it on to the hull floor beneath. A dismasting often means the dominoing of one mast into the other, down through the decks, cannoning the cargo through the hull below, and sinking the ship very quickly. This apparently not uncommon event provokes much mirth, but very little change in mast-stepping techniques.

Not even Wallace had been to Bouton, and we were unable to find any reference to it in the literature. Bau-Bau, the island's main town, revealed itself as a collection of neatly kept white stilt houses, nestling beneath jungled mist-shrouded hills. It even had a creaking dock at which we could tie up directly alongside.

Our crewmates warned us about the Biranese girls' reputation as practitioners of a dangerous form of magic which could trap a man on their island for ever; then they disappeared ashore into the backstreets. Going ashore ourselves, we soon realized that the girls' magic was of a very straightforward kind. Almost without exception, they were breathtakingly beautiful; their every movement a languid dance, and their smiles open and confident – so different from the shy tittering behind shawls that we had seen amongst the Bugis girls. Bau-Bau was infinitely more friendly than Makassar, and far less desperate than Bira.

It did not take them long to inform us that we had arrived with their traditional enemies, the Bugis. In the days when the great Bugis kingdoms had ruled the seas all the way to the Spice Islands they had been unrelenting in their determination to conquer Bouton. Each year the west monsoon would bring a fleet from Makassar, each prahu bristling with as many as a hundred warriors. No sooner had they been fought off than the east monsoon brought a fresh invasion from the kingdoms of the Moluccas. This constant cycle of warfare, involving fleets as mighty as the Spanish Armada, had kept Bouton in isolation up to the present day.

Despite our unsavoury choice of shipmates, our arrival was cause for celebration, and on the very first afternoon we were whisked away from *Sinar Surya* to stay in the comfort of the sultan's guesthouse, which was far more impressive than anything we had seen in Makassar.

We were surprised that the sultan had even noticed our arrival, but the young courier who had taken us up to the guesthouse laughed.

'Everyone in Bouton has noticed your arrival. Since World War Two only four other Westerners have been here before you.' He told us we would meet the sultan at his palace that evening for dinner.

Dinner turned out to be a royal-welcome banquet in the great hall, and it was quite literally a glittering affair. The sultan and his court wore locally woven sarongs and turbans shot through with threads of real gold and silver. The belts holding their ceremonial ivory-handled daggers were all of beaten gold, as were the jewellery and headdresses of the women. The walls were hung with elaborate textiles, and a small orchestra of metal gongs and drums played surprisingly watery music.

'I don't want you to think that we eat like this every night,' said the sultan with a smile; indeed, we had seen him earlier in the day wearing well-cut Western clothes. 'But I hear that you Europeans have very romantic ideas about the East, so I thought this might please you.'

We were sitting cross-legged on either side of him with a vast array of tiny dishes on finely worked brass trays stretching before us, and entirely lit by Aladdin lamps on specially wrought stands.

I wish I could describe the sultan's appearance but my eyes were elsewhere, for on my other side sat Sadria, one of his radiant daughters. In an island where most of the girls looked like princesses, the princesses looked like goddesses – and Sadria was no exception.

She dipped her fingers delicately into a dish and, to my astonishment, popped a morsel of food into my mouth instead of into her own. Sadria leant back on her heels, smiling at me expectantly. I shot a nervous glance at our host. He, too, was smiling, but with sardonic ambiguity, and my eyes shifted to his ceremonial dagger.

'Well,' he said, 'if you don't feed the poor girl soon, she'll starve.'

Not at all sure that I was doing the right thing, I fumbled towards the nearest dish for a finger-load of food, and turned to Sadria. The sight of those slightly parted lips was almost my undoing but, with the hollow

112

112 The girls of Bouton, who
danced for our greeting ceremony

117

feeling of a gambler who has laid out far too much on a horse, I plunged the titbit firmly into her mouth before my resolve could falter.

She chewed, oh, so delicately and reached towards another dish.

'This', said the sultan, 'is how we customarily feed our guests. It shows we trust each other enough to have no fear of being poisoned.'

Trust me enough! My God, I wasn't at all sure I could trust myself!

So the evening went. Each of my hand-fed morsels tasted different; indefinable combinations of spices and textures which were quite new and delicious to me. But my judgement may have been clouded. . . .

Over the days that followed their hospitality knew no bounds. They drove us as far as the mud roads would allow in the royal land-rover, and down to the bay where a pearl-oyster hatchery was being tried for the first time; and at night there were more festivities, and endless delectable maidens vying for our attentions. . . . On the fourth day they took us up to Wolio, the old fortress that sprawled across two hill-tops overlooking Bau-Bau. We had often seen its crumbling ramparts from a distance, and had assumed it was Dutch, but now learnt that it had been built by the islanders, long before the Europeans.

Only once we were inside did we appreciate the immense scale of Wolio. Its fifteen-foot walls, with occasional gun-embrasures and rusting cannons, extended a full five miles around the old palaces of Bouton, the great mosque and a vast and excited crowd. All of Bouton was there, while far below us small sailing craft packed with more celebrants were still arriving from the outlying islands.

Drums began pounding, and several seemingly frail old men launched into a frenzied war-dance, prancing and stabbing at each other with their kerises. At any moment I expected to see one drop with a cardiac arrest, but the sultan told us not to underestimate their power. They had been his father's personal bodyguards, ready and able to defend him with their lives, and once a year they still performed this fierce dance inside the mosque from sunset to sunrise without pause.

113

A more melodious music engulfed us as eight girls floated down the steps of the old palace. Their hair was entwined with golden cords, and their dresses, richly embroidered with beads, pearls and precious metals, flowed almost to the ground. With impassively inward-turned faces, they performed a languorous dance of infinite restraint.

'They have been in seclusion for eight days,' said the sultan, 'learning the secrets of womanhood. Today they resurface as adults, ready for marriage.' He chuckled. 'My grandfather was something of a scholar. He brought all his power to bear to force the women of his household to reveal these secrets. Despite his most terrible threats, he could extract nothing about what went on during those eight days.'

We asked the sultan what all these festivities were in aid of and he said: 'Didn't you realize this is your welcome ceremony? I'm sorry we couldn't do it the day you arrived, but it took a little bit of organizing.'

Every dance we saw that day had the flavour of a different influence. Some tasted of the parched winds of the Arabian Gulf; others of the exuberant tribal animism of the South Pacific; while others again echoed the ancient Hindu courts of Java and India. Even Europe was represented, in what was almost identical to a traditional flag-dance I had once seen in rural Portugal. I realized also with a jolt that the dancers were wearing a motley of costumes representing centuries of brief encounters with the West – from seventeenth-century Portuguese ruffles round their throats, down to modern trainers on their feet.

The sultan showed us the royal regalia which were secreted in the palace. The centrepiece was an exact replica of a Portuguese explorer's helmet. Finely made of solid silver from the local mines, it must have weighed twenty pounds, and was adorned with a shimmering cascade of golden plumage which Lorne at once recognized.

'The Greater Bird of Paradise feathers symbolize courage,' the sultan told us. 'Those who returned from Aru and New Guinea alive brought these as proof of their valour.'

115

113 The royal daughters and nieces, in sarongs of silver thread, from whom we could not tear ourselves away

114 A noble of the Sultan's court

115 Five miles of fortified ramparts, complete with rusting cannons, protected the isolated Sultanate of Bouton from pirate marauders

116 The former chief of the royal bodyguard, who had personally defended his sultan's life in hand-to-hand combat

117 Amongst the seafarers, the maidens of Bouton have the reputation of being beautiful sorceresses, whose magic can trap a man on their island for ever

118 A Boutonese baby wearing silver and gold jewellery made from the local mines

119

We left Bau-Bau very, very slowly.

The dock groaned beneath the combined weight of the town waving and singing goodbye to us in full ceremonial dress. Although a fair breeze was picking up from the south-east, the harbour was aquarium calm, and the poignancy of this departure from a fairy-tale kingdom in our pirate prahu was marred, alas, by making so little headway that an hour and a half after cast-off we were still within spitting distance of the dock.

Everybody hates a bad leaver but, whereas in the West you can usually close the door on a guest who has finally reached the garden gate, in the islands it is impolite to stop waving and chanting until he is either round a corner and out of sight, or else too distant to be able to see the whites of his eyes. Whether the people were assembled by order of the sultan or simply from the hospitality of their hearts, they gave barely a sign of diminishing the ardour of their farewell.

Only, perhaps, in the eyes of the sultan's exquisite daughters was a hint of boredom betrayed. Since our first arrival here, their Seductive Highnesses had flirted with us as consistently as had their father ensured that we were together only during public occasions. Now, from the instant a hawser no longer connected our prahu to their island, they had cast us unrestrained looks which said: 'At last, I'm all yours. Come and get me!' But, as time wore on, and the whites of our eyes were still clearly visible, the girls, without missing a beat, subtly modified their glances as if to convey: 'God knows we've tried, you heartless bastards.'

It took us eight very wet and almost windless days to inch our way up the ninety miles of the Bouton Straits before we could turn eastwards into the Banda Sea. Throughout the entire journey we saw perhaps six tiny fishing villages and one ugly landslide scar whose remarkable story we had all heard various times in Bau-Bau. Only four months previously the land had suddenly plummeted into the straits, taking with it a village of some eighty souls. The only survivors were one family who had been visiting relatives in Bau-Bau at the time. They returned in their outrigger at night to find no welcoming lights.

With just the ghost of a headwind, our only method of going about was either by dragging our bows round with ten men furiously paddling the dugout canoe, or simply by drifting into the opposite shore and poling our bowsprit off whatever fulcrum presented itself.

The Bouton Straits became progressively more narrow and sinister. Their dark waters, in places only a few hundred yards across, were met by vertically plunging forest, wreathed in mist, and for the most part deathly quiet. Only during the occasional bursts of sunshine did they begin to sing with birds and bugs. Once, they exploded with a sound so terrifying that it brought all of us below instantly out on to the rain-drenched deck. We had just cleared a jungle overhang, and slipped beneath it like a snail under a mushroom, when we awakened an enormous colony of giant fruit bats – the 'flying foxes' with a wingspan of over three feet. The first sound was a chilling quadraphonic chitter. We looked up to see the tree limbs rippling with leather and fur. The

119 A suspicious Boutonese court official with his silver-pommelled ceremonial Keris.

120 (over page) Our reception party in Bau Bau. Only three other Westerners had visited Bouton since the Second World War. The Boutonese headgear is influenced by China, and the ruffles and jackets by the first Portuguese explorers who visited the island in the sixteenth century

bats then erupted from their roosts like all the demons of hell, screaming, whirling and excreting partly digested fruit over the full length and height of the ship. Some caught in the rigging and thudded to the deck, spitting and baring their fangs at us before being hurriedly kicked overboard. Even our Bugis, quite familiar with flying foxes, paled at the encounter, but Tandri was not deterred from his hazardous method.

The drawback to poling a hundred-foot schooner with ninety-foot masts off vertical jungle was that there was no guarantee of reaching the tree trunks with our bowsprit before reaching their branches with our masts. To be locked inextricably in the overhang would have been nearly as disastrous as a dismasting.

When we finally reached the top of the Bouton Straits the rain had ceased as completely as the wind and it was only the current which carried us eastwards into the luminous open sea. For days we drifted within sight of land, beneath a high bright overcast sky which was mirrored perfectly in the polished water.

It was no longer so easy to remain an island of reason when every timber surrounding us had been magically selected; when our departure had been synchronized not with the weather, but with inner portents of another kind of time. Even the black goat and the white cock sacrificed in our hull for a safe and speedy passage now began to haunt us every bit as solemnly as did the ghosts of our investors in London.

As a parting gift the Keraing had given me a scale model of the prahu we were sailing in, which I had lashed to the hull walls facing backwards. One night I had a vivid dream that to correct this error would bring us the wind. The next morning Lorne filmed me cutting the model free and lashing it down again, facing forwards. The wind came so swiftly that within half an hour we were reducing sail, taking water over the deck, and beginning to lumber into a building seaway.

The wind we had waited for so long quickly rose to gale force, and drove us on a desperate roller-coaster ride for five days and nights. Our rotten mainmast began whipping sickeningly to and fro and required five men constantly clinging to its lee mainstay to cushion the strain. The prahu's very short timbers – designed to give flexibility – were now moving so violently against each other that the water pouring between them required the hand-pumps being manned round the clock.

Four men were needed to hold down the steering oars, which bucked in their harnesses like panicked elephants. Their supporting beams ran through our tiny cabin, and we could put our feet up on them and feel the entire ship squirming and stretching like the spine of a fish. Sails began splitting with the sound of gunfire, and with no spares they were sewn up *in situ* – an incredibly dangerous task in a full gale.

Our Bugis performed astonishing feats of skill and bravery. Unlike the clipper ships of the last century, our prahu had no guard-rails on the deck, and no rigging harnesses or proper ratlines, yet our crew scaled the masts barefoot to cling to the spars with their legs alone, like lemurs. From these thrashing heights they would then shin ninety feet down to the decks again on single frayed and rusting wires.

Despite the dubious seaworthiness of our ship, for the first few

121 A solid silver ceremonial helmet, copied from that of a Portuguese sea captain, sports the faded feathers of the Greater Bird of Paradise. The man holding it shows signs of inherited tertiary syphilis

days of the storm my sense of danger was eclipsed by the exhilaration of at last thundering in the right direction. My first real fear came only when I caught sight of Tandri's face watching his five strongest crewmen hanging miserably to the mainstay of our rotten mast. It was the first time I had seen him reveal any emotion in his face, and it had something of the intensity of grief. My fear was further sharpened when Tooth, the only practising Muslim aboard, stiffly emerged from below wearing his black peci hat, and proceeded to prostrate himself towards Mecca at hours not prescribed by Islamic doctrine.

Finally we limped into Ambon, former jewel of the Spice Islands, written of so glowingly by Wallace, but now all but denuded of trees. In the harbour lay enormous foreign freighters for carrying the timber away, exuding oil over the graves of what had once been the most famous coral gardens in the Far East.

It was normally polite, and expedient, to pay respects to the military commander of an area on first arriving, but this was the only time when we were actually frog-marched off to meet him before we had time to draw breath. He sat, rheumy-eyed and suspicious, behind an enormous desk in a crumbling office. He reviewed our ship's papers and letters from General Aziz at length, and then, finding that our passports were almost new and empty, he began rubber-stamping them viciously.

We were eventually released and returned to find some of the crew busily repairing the mainsail on the dock, while the rest, with Tandri and the officers, were being bullied by lesser officials who were nosing around the hold and demanding to see their personal possessions. Although we were terrified that they would find where we had hidden our film equipment, it was easier for us than for our crewmates to express our anger, and we blustered the officials off the ship.

That night we had a conference with Tandri for the first time.

'I told them *three* days before we can finish repairs,' he told us, 'but we can do enough tomorrow to hold us to Banda, if weather is good.'

It was an uneasy night, pondering the risks of leaving illegally, with a barely seaworthy vessel, from an island of which we had read so fondly in Wallace and had come so far to see.

The next dawn we had a better look. During the night two more timber tankers had arrived and anchored. It was the closest we had come to the outside world in nearly four months – yet they were responsible for the oil which glossed the harbour and had killed the coral. Behind the town, where Wallace had ecstatically rambled with his butterfly-net through glowing forests, the hills were bare.

Not yet halfway to our appointment with the Paradise Bird, each island was already proving to be a kingdom unto itself, and the power of our permits was clearly waning the further we travelled. Of our ship's company, only Tooth and Tasman had ventured as far east as this, and the waters ahead were equally unknown to all of us. Even if we could escape from Ambon with our cargo and wallets intact, none of us much cared to think about what receptions might lie ahead, as we approached the isolation of New Guinea.

5 To Haunts of Birds of Paradise

The night comes quickly. This sudden land
Never lends us a twilight strand
'Twixt the ocean shore and the daylight night,
But takes, as it gives, at once, the light.
           Punjabi Love Poem

As soon as it was dark we slipped gingerly out of Ambon and sailed softly south into the solitude of the Banda Sea. Any minute we expected to see an official powerboat bearing down on us with demands to return to harbour, but as the stars grew more brilliant and the glow of the town receded we were gradually suffused with elation and the closest thing to comradeship we had so far experienced with our Bugis crew.

The night was very gentle, and the dark transparent sea was cleft at our stern into two long green curtains of gossamer where our steering-oars ignited the bioluminescence. With our sails and psyches barely repaired from their ordeals, we now felt ourselves released into an ocean of unknown delights.

It was time to celebrate. With a light breeze behind us, the mainsail was at a ninety-degree angle to our hull, and provided a perfect light-screen for the projection of our slide-show.

The photographic image, even in newspapers and magazines, was as rare as electricity in the Moluccas at the time, and none of our crew had seen such a display of coloured light as we threw on *Sinar Surya*'s sail that evening. They all came to huddle aft of the mizzen, leaving only Tooth at the steering-oar and Tandri remaining aloof but nevertheless fascinated by what we might reveal of our world.

With our pocket-sized slide-projector, powered by the Honda generator purring away in the hold, we cast up the incongruous images we had hurriedly bought on our departure from Heathrow months before. There was Queen Elizabeth Trooping the Colour with the Coldstream Guards; the royal family waving pinkly and benignly from their balcony at Buckingham Palace. There were cockney barrow-boys in the markets of Soho, and their pearly kings and queens – the 'rajas of the poor people', we explained to their satisfaction.

'Those buttons', Tasman remarked, 'look like the mother-of-pearl shell which used to reach Makassar from the East.'

I agreed. 'They might even have been brought by your great-great-grandfathers from the Aru Islands, which once provided the world's finest mother-of-pearl shells.'

We had thought the photos of the Apollo moon landing would be our trump card, but they were greeted with the mildest interest. In our earlier attempts to introduce our crew members to the proportionate distances which separated Europe from Indonesia, they had become indifferent to the distances which separated the stellar bodies.

122 A fresh basket of Bandanese nutmeg. The fruit provides two spices, the nut itself, and mace, the red membrane which coats it

'So men go to the moon in rockets the way you two came from England in rocket planes?' someone asked.

'Why go to the moon?' Tasman enquired.

'Did the Queen go to the moon?' asked Amir.

'What's on the moon to go there for?' continued Tasman.

Some of them turned to regard the sickle moon which was rising over the Banda Sea.

'Are there still people living there?'

'Well, if no one lives there and there's only stones to bring back, why *go* there?' Tasman persisted.

Answering these questions taxed our ideologies as much as our grasp of Indonesian, and we hurriedly projected more slides of the changing of the guard at Buckingham Palace, until the show was interrupted by a shift in the wind, and our screen was close-hauled to keep us placidly moving towards the Banda Islands, barely a hundred miles to the south-east.

For its size, the Banda Sea is one of the world's deepest. It lies on the same tectonic fault-line which runs from the Aleutian Islands of Alaska, down past the profound ocean trenches off Japan and the Philippines, to the South China Sea. Far beneath our keel and the tropic heat meandered what oceanographers call the 'psychrosphere', that inky realm which permanently borders on freezing, and where we knew as yet uncatalogued creatures of the deep still swam.

Close to the centre of this luminous body of water lie the Banda Islands, which rise 22,000 feet sheer from the ocean floor to crest the surface with smoke and jungle. The ten islands are so small that they appear only as specks, if at all, on anything but a hydrographic chart. Their total land area is barely seventeen square miles, and the tallest mountain, forming one of the only three inhabited islands, is the 2,200-foot cone of the still-active Banda volcano. The unique conditions of climatic and volcanic alchemy make this the probable source of nutmeg, the 'gold' of the spice trade.

An early mariner had written: '. . . from far out to sea, we could detect the scent of paradise wafting from the hills of Banda'.

Since Banda's original discovery by the Portuguese in 1512, it has changed hands constantly between European powers vying for the nutmeg monopoly. Christopher Columbus had been looking for a shorter route to Banda when he had stumbled on America! Even Oliver Cromwell scrawled his signature on a Treaty of Banda in 1654, and after the Napoleonic Wars the island was exchanged for New Amsterdam, in the New World, which is now better known as Manhattan Island. But, since the Dutch withdrew from Indonesia, Banda has abdicated from history, and time moves past her as she lies forgotten, like a sleeping princess, gradually reverting to her primordial state.

On the dawn of the second day we discerned the smoke-wreathed cone of the Banda volcano perched on the horizon like a veiled Egyptian pyramid. The following morning it was close enough for us to begin worrying about our approach. While Lorne and I had been sparring with the officials in Ambon, our crew had been exchanging navigational gossip about Banda with the sailors on the waterfront, and they now produced three scrawled maps of the entrance to the island. On comparison each proved to advise a different approach, and despite the light breeze and calm sea we felt the tension mounting as we came to within two miles of the island without seeing a sign of habitation or a harbourage.

Suddenly a thirty-foot lombok – a sailing sloop resembling the Chinese sampan – emerged from behind the island and disappeared into the trees.

'There! There! That must be it!' we all shouted in chorus, and Tooth recklessly committed us towards what we sincerely hoped *was* a hidden entrance that would accommodate a vessel three times the size of the lombok. A channel appeared which divided the now awesome volcano on our right from a narrower island on our left called Bandaneira. Slightly curved, it meant that shortly after entering the channel our horizon was cut off behind us, as it was ahead by yet a third island, Lontar, and it gave us the impression of being not so much in the middle of a sea as in a glassy landlocked lake high in some mountain range.

The wind was now blowing some fifteen feet above the surface, catching our sails and pushing us through a water so unruffled that only our bow-wave disturbed it. Often mentioned in sailing literature, this experience is like being drawn through the water by an angel, giving the impression that the ship is no more under a mariner's control than the path of his destiny.

Nobody spoke. All of us were standing, Amir and Mansur wide-eyed and grasping the corners of the wooden stove on the foredeck. Apart from the sporadic cries of parrots which left flashes of the spectrum across the towering forest, there was nothing to be heard but the murmuring of our weigh against the hull. The light was eerily refracted through the wreaths of smoke curling from the volcano which plunged into its own reflection barely a hundred yards to our right. We had read that the depth and steepness of this bay were so great that the destroyers of the occupying Japanese had been able to tie up directly alongside the town. It was hard to believe that the bottom was still several thousand feet beneath our keel, while we could practically pick the fruit from the jungle on either side of us. With the thin strands of black volcanic sand, and flecks of what looked like gold-dust flashing in the pristine water, it was like slipping into paradise over a polished surface of obsidian quartz.

As we curved along the channel, the town of Banda came into view on our left, a nestling patchwork of white-walled colonial buildings with red-tiled and sago-thatched roofs. Draped above the town and half-consumed by forest, were the magnificent crumbling remains of early Dutch and Portuguese fortresses, their cannons still balefully eyeing us from the ramparts. The strand was zebra-striped with black and white sand, where a number of brightly painted local fishing boats and lomboks lay side by side. The only incongruity marring the scene was a large rusting motorized research-vessel anchored just off-shore, and flying a Pertamina flag to show that it belonged to the national

123

123 Approaching the smoking volcano at the heart of the Spice Islands. Christopher Columbus was looking for a shorter route to Banda when he stumbled upon America

124 (over page) Wherever we went hundreds of children welcomed us

petroleum company. It was the sole rather dour reminder that we had not entirely left the twentieth century behind us. Although it was clearly deep enough to moor directly alongside the town, Tandri, owing to innate Bugis caution, chose to anchor near the research ship, where a rising coral bank came to within fifty feet of the surface.

We immediately dressed in our rumpled best and had ourselves paddled ashore to make our obeisances to the Bupati, the local government official. We found him playing table tennis in the echoing ballroom of the former colonial governor's residence, which now served as the site of perpetual ping-pong tournaments. He was a stocky curly-headed man in shorts and shirt-sleeves, his fine features suggesting Arabic or Indian ancestry. He blushed with the astonishment of seeing us, and unhesitatingly gave us *carte blanche* to film whatever we liked. This was thankfully the most informal Bupati we had yet encountered.

'Where's your friend?' he asked us. 'I thought you were leaving today.'

'What friend?' Lorne replied. 'And we've only just arrived.'

He found it hard to believe that we had actually arrived in the prahu, and not in the rusting Pertamina ship which had also apparently brought the only other Westerner to visit the island in more than ten years just the day before.

'This *is* a year of coincidence,' said the Bupati. 'The first prahu to anchor here in five years arrived at the beginning of this year – Pertamina ships never put in – and now three "Orang Putihs" on the same amount of tides!' We gathered that the ship was due to depart at any moment and felt compelled to satisfy our curiosity concerning this other foreigner who had dared to trespass on Banda. After leaving the Bupati to finish his game with his barefoot opponent, we hurriedly returned to the strand and persuaded Mansur and Amir to paddle us over to the rusting vessel. A few yards from the gang-ladder we found the stranger wallowing in the sea surrounded by naked water-children. He was the first Westerner we had laid eyes on for several months. He had very blue eyes, and water-droplets festooned his bushy hair and beard, giving him something of the appearance of a Japanese Snow Monkey emerging from a bath in the hot springs.

I accosted him from the canoe with barely polite demands as to who the hell he was, and what he thought he was doing there – and discovered him to be the intrepid Lyall Watson, biologist, explorer and prolific author-to-be of books about the nature of mind and discovery.

His ship was due to depart in fifteen minutes, which gave us just enough time to accept his offer of a *refrigerated* drink on his afterdeck, and to hear his surprising explanation that his presence was due to the inspirational writings of one Alfred Russel Wallace. Lyall had been lent this vessel by the Indonesian government to reconnoitre the islands along the Wallace route to the Aru Islands, with a view to bringing the international cruise-ship *Lindblad Explorer* on her first Indonesian voyage here the following year. The difference was that Lyall had begun his journey at Wallace's destination, Dobu, and was heading westwards for Makassar, whereas we were doing the reverse.

There was barely enough time to exchange information about the islands each was about to visit, to learn that he had just completed his book *Supernature*[12] which drew on very much the same obscure source material that I had used in my doctoral thesis at Lancaster University. Independently, via our separate disciplines of biology and comparative religion, we had each been pursuing the same Ariadne's Thread of connections which led, we felt, to a radical re-examination of 'rational science'. It was only many months later, back in England, that I read the first review of *Supernature* and realized that the author was the same Snow Monkey that we had met in Banda Bay. A year later, after *Supernature* had become a bestseller, Lyall was to write a generous foreword to my own book – which helped it find a much wider market than it might otherwise have had. It seems strange that Banda – at the midpoint of the Wallace route – should have been the nexus at which our life-paths crossed. We were the first Westerners to reach the islands for many years; we had arrived independently and unknown to each other, and our stay here had overlapped by an hour!

Although with Lyall we had barely had time to shake his wet hand and exchange zoographical titbits, it was with a sense of excitement that we watched him steam out of Banda in his rusty vessel.

The following dawn we paddled ourselves from our prahu half a mile across to the island of Lontar, famed for its nutmeg, mace and cloves. The once neatly cultivated plantations had run wild, and now produced barely 5 per cent of what had been harvested at the peak of the Dutch colonial days, yet it was richly beautiful. With our inevitable Pied Piper's gaggle of pursuing children, we explored the aromatic forests of nutmeg and kanary trees, amongst whose roots we found the scattered gravestones of early Dutch, French, Arab, Malay, Portuguese and Chinese mariners. After the children had finally left us in solitude, we began to see the lilac-blue flashes of the nutmeg pigeon, *Carpophas concinna*, unique to the region and lovingly described by Wallace. A giant amongst pigeons, and with a voice like the horn of a Model T Ford, the vividly blue bird feeds exclusively on nutmeg – which reportedly gives its flesh a delicious flavour.

We befriended a young boy who was gathering nutmeg with the tool which has remained unchanged since long before Banda's discovery by outsiders: a lozenge-shaped basket of woven rattan on a long pole with a non-return valve, and twin fangs for hooking the fruit into the basket without having to lower it to the ground each time. He showed us how nutmeg provides two spices: the nut itself, about as big as an oval apricot, and mace, the blood-red filmy membrane which coats it.

The Bandanese are a very tidy people, beautifully dressed in some of the better imported Javanese batiks. Every household sported exotic pets, and especially brilliant and highly talkative parrots perched, often untethered, on carefully constructed parrot-stands with little roofs over them. Children carried pet Cuscuses on their shoulders, the morose arboreal fluff-balls with pouches and prehensile tails: now we had well and truly entered the domain of the Australo-Pacific fauna.

125

Apart from fruits and spices, Banda's main export now is tropical birds of numerous gaudy varieties which, like the fish beneath the sea, made one ponder again on the gaps in our understanding of the evolution of species. The fact that such baroque variations in design in no way overtly contribute to the survival of an individual is often ignored when discussing the 'survival of the fittest' theory. Such 'design above necessity' points to aesthetic or fanciful forces operating in the development of species quite independently of their need to survive.

This was shown most vividly beneath Banda's waters. For, as Wallace had correctly remarked (even without the benefit of mask and flippers), Banda's bay contains more species of fish than are found in all the rivers, lakes and seas of Europe. So astounding was the sight which greeted us beneath the surface that we decided to breathe half the compressed air in the single tank which Yong had lent us in Makassar, ostensibly to film his pearl-diving operation in the Aru Islands.

The black volcanic sand was ribbed with drifts of white, from which rose multicoloured castles of coral, with surreal turrets over thirty feet high. All our focal planes were shot through with drifts of fish interweaving with the tidal flow like the autumn fall of countless varieties of leaf. The coral crags were wreathed in plants looking like animals, and animals looking like plants, and with every grasp we could pick up the shells for which the Moluccas were named, and which from Renaissance times have been sought after by the shell-collectors of the world. On a dive such as this – in waters probably never previously dived with scuba equipment – a high degree of fear is constantly counterbalanced by a kind of sacred awe. Life, in forms as beautiful as it was grotesquely unfamiliar, was everywhere, above, below, within and without.

Apart from her living reefs and forests, the only surviving testament to Banda's place in history now lies in the disintegrating battlements of her fortresses and the crumbling splendour of her architecture. Perhaps the most nostalgic example was the palace building, where we had met the Bupati playing table tennis. It had been built by the French, as a magnificent governor's residence, during the brief Napoleonic period that they had colonized the island. It was an exact replica of the famous Opera House of Naples. Its floor and support columns were of white marble imported all the way from Italy, and it had been appointed with the European luxuries of the time. Now it was echoingly empty of all but the giant chandeliers, a battered ping-pong table – and a memorable piece of graffiti.

Scrawled on a window-pane with a diamond ring was the suicide note of Charles Rumpley, the last French governor of the island. I copied it down as faithfully as legibility allowed:

126

Quand reviendra t'il le Temps qui formera mon bonheur?
Quand frappera la cloche qui va sonner l'heure
Le moment que je reverais les bords de ma Patrie,
Le Sein de ma famille que j'aime et que je bénis?

CHARLES RUMPLEY, 1 September 1834

125 The nutmegs are hooked off the trees with a lozenge-shaped basket of bamboo and rattan in use on the islands for centuries

126 Charles Rumpley's suicide note, etched in 1834 with his diamond ring on a windowpane of the governor's residence. It has survived unshattered for 154 years, although this photograph barely survived Lawrence's fire

127 Dominating the island from every vantage point, Banda's volcano erupts about every hundred years

137

When will my happiness return?
When will the bells toll the hour
Of my return to the shores of my country,
And the heart of my family, whom I love and bless?

Immediately after writing this, Rumpley blew his brains out beneath the crystal chandeliers.

The note was visible only by focusing closely against the refracted light, as when examining a scroll of frost under a microscope, and we wondered if Wallace had noticed this poignant testimony to one soul at least who found the solitude of such strange beauty unbearable. In his darkest hour, Rumpley must have remained immune to the consolations of his surroundings, the rich and effortless harvest of life for its own sake, born through adaptation and survival of the fittest. He alone had failed to adapt, to release himself from memories of his past, to the dance of the present. This message, symbolizing all human loneliness, had so far survived for 154 years.

In the old Dutch church we found another, more personal message – and a hint that our own present, too, should be danced to the full. Although Banda is nominally a Christian island, the church is attended only by its verger, who opens its doors each day, and keeps it clean and bright. Lorne had been walking past it alone when the verger ran down the steps to ask him to translate the inscription written on a flagstone embedded in the church floor.

Lorne was in a strange mood when he returned to the prahu to tell me about it. The flagstone turned out to be written in English, and commemorated the death of a John Leod, an English midshipman who had died here in 1900. He had been exactly Lorne's age, to the month, and the same monsoon had been blowing.

128 Banda's only church, where Lorne discovered a sinister gravestone. The clock remains stopped at the exact moment of the Japanese invasion of the island in the Second World War

128

Lorne took this very hard and, although he didn't talk about it further, he was so withdrawn that evening that several of our crew asked if he was unwell. He was furious when I told them what had happened. They took it as an obvious omen for our immediate departure, and we might well have sailed on the tide, except that it remained for us not only to complete the repairs to our sails, but also, if we possibly could, to find and film the extraordinary 'laweri' fish.

Unique to the Banda Islands, the laweri was reportedly only eight inches long, but had eyes as luminous as five-watt bulbs. The Bupati had confirmed that two years previously a Japanese ichthyological research vessel had spent several months in the outer islands exclusively studying this anomalous creature, though they had never once set foot on shore. Since its eyes continue to glow fiercely for days after it has died, the locals use them as bait for night fishing. They were also used as bedside night-lights for Bandanese children afraid of the dark. How consoling, we thought, to awaken from a nightmare to the benevolent gaze of luminous eyeballs drifting in a drinking-glass next to one's bed.

Just as Bira had its small syndicate of specialist python-hunters, Banda had its handful of laweri experts. We were introduced to one of these by the Bupati: a slender upright old man called Ende, who was barely five feet tall. He agreed to meet us at the strand shortly after nightfall. We'd expected a slightly more elaborate expedition, but it was only Ende, his elflike young son, and their fragile and tiny canoe which awaited us. It was a moonless and cloudless night as we paddled precariously out in search of the laweri.

We retreated from the glow of the town into obsidian waters which vividly mirrored the stars above us. The dark cone of the volcano exactly matched its shadow in the water, so that we appeared to move into a great black diamond suspended in the spangled sky. For a long time we sat, adjusting to the night-blooming aromas and the roar of insects which poured to us from the shore. Then the child shouted to his father from the bow, and we began following what at first appeared as the faintest glimmer beneath the surface, and which quickly dissolved again into stellar reflections. We pursued this shimmering phantom for some time, to the left, to the right, disappearing completely, then re-emerging behind us again, leading us in circles like an Irish bog-fairy.

We had loaded our fastest film and set our cameras for maximum exposure but we were still preparing ourselves for a disappointment when the glow suddenly began rising beneath our canoe obviously from a great depth. Increasing in size and luminosity as it rose, it broke the surface around us with such brilliance that it challenged both our credulity and our ability to keep our balance. It was distinctly unsettling.

Like most schools of fish, the laweri moved as a fluctuating unit, but fibrillated with such intensity of light that it became difficult to keep our balance in the canoe, and quite impossible to film. Each fish moved so rapidly – though the school itself moved slowly – that it was impossible to focus on an individual before it had melted into something else. Lorne and I just sat there shouting at one another.

The experience was comparable only to my first and only sight of the aurora borealis over Alaska many years before – except that, rather than being distantly and dispassionately overhead, this was *alive*, much larger than ourselves, very bright, and not only moving all around us, but also seeming to 'contain' us in some way, as if we were being ingested into the belly of a luminous whale.

We were still shouting at the top of our lungs when the laweri ebbed back into their depths, leaving behind that feeling of having awakened from a very important dream which one cannot quite remember. Now, again, only the blessed immobility of the stars was reflected off its inky surface – and Ende and his elf-child were loudly laughing at our excitement.

We were silent for a long time as we paddled home to *Sinar Surya*. Then suddenly we both burst into an enthusiastic and quite impractical discussion about returning some day with highly specialized state-of-the-art equipment, to film these beings, perhaps holographically, from underwater. But we knew this was just talk, and that a night encounter with the laweri of Banda was a numinous experience which could never be adequately captured on film.

We were now keenly aware of how quickly the season of the west monsoon was drawing to a close, and with every day we risked losing the wind which could carry us to the islands of the Golden Bird. We were also painfully conscious of our diminishing film-stock. Knowing that our adventure could end abruptly at any time, we sought only to shoot footage which, if the worst came to the worst, could be cut into a coherent story of our voyage thus far. A vital ingredient still missing was

129 The cannons of Fort Rotterdam, built by the Dutch, jealously protected Banda's bay for 350 years

130 Tacking away from Banda in the dying breezes of the west monsoon

131 The Cuscus, a pouched, tree-dwelling fluffball indigenous to the islands east of the Wallace Line, makes a popular meal – but an even better pet

129

131

130

footage of *Sinar Surya* under sail, shot from beyond her. And it was for this purpose that we had arranged to borrow the Bupati's motorized launch so that we could cover *Sinar Surya*'s departure from Banda the following morning before climbing aboard her. This plan was nearly our undoing.

We had agreed on a precise time and place, and even double-checked that the launch was in the right spot on shore before we bunked down. We told Tandri and the crew under no circumstances to get under way until it was clear that we were in the launch and the motor had started. At dawn we had ourselves paddled ashore. An hour later we were still frantically lugging our equipment up and down the shore searching for the now-vanished motor-launch and its promised pilot, when we happened to notice *Sinar Surya* sailing out of the channel towards the open sea.

We almost stopped breathing as we remembered Tandri's individualism, and Werner Meyer's stories about the Bugis weakness for 'losing' their passengers, particularly if they happen to be the owners of the cargo being carried.

Would they come around at the point, and tack to and fro waiting for us? Clearly not. She kept right on going, all sail pulling. The awful truth began to dawn. How easy it would be for Tandri to explain to the Tan family in Aru (if that is, indeed, where he was headed!) that the two Orang Ingeriss sent their regards, but had decided to go their separate way somewhere *en route*!

We had only the clothes we quaked in, and all our cameras slung about our shoulders. Lorne planted himself like a furious concrete pillar, silently trying to hypnotize Tandri back through his monocle. I flapped back and forth like a chicken, not quite allowing myself to scream at the distant vessel. There were a number of fishermen readying their boats who fully took in our predicament. Without being asked, and with no mention of money, several of them immediately offered to paddle us out after our mutinous pirates.

Now, *Sinar Surya*'s dugout canoe was fifteen feet long and yet so precarious that we had always avoided carrying all our camera equipment in it at one time; rather, we had joked, as the royal family avoids travelling in the same aeroplane. The Bandanese canoes, such as the one we had chased the laweri in, are half that length, far slimmer, and people of our relative bulk require the equilibrium of parallel-bars specialists to stay upright in them. Just slinging a camera from one shoulder to the other caused these canoes to lurch violently.

However, we thankfully accepted a canoe each, to spread the risk of camera loss, and lay quivering with anxiety in the sopping scuppers, while urging our Bandanese angels to paddle for all they were worth. I was powered by a frail fifty-year-old and his perhaps thirteen-year-old but wiry assistant, and Lorne by two young bloods in their prime but paddling a less seaworthy canoe. With a light breeze behind her *Sinar Surya* was now rounding Bandaneira island and moving out of sight. The swell began building as we approached the same point, fully expecting to see *Sinar Surya* miles ahead of us, but she was still in view.

Had Tandri's nerve cracked? Had she hove to to wait for us? But, no, as our boatmen remarked, it was only a sudden lull in the wind which had stopped her.

Our paddlers were fully aware of our distress and, if anything, needed encouragement to reduce their exertions. They were soaked with sweat and rasping deeply for breath when we finally caught up with our ship, but adamantly refused any of the rupiahs which we so thankfully thrust at them.

The decks were lined with the grinning crew as we climbed stiffly and furiously aboard – but we were beginning to learn to conceal our anger. Tandri greeted us like long-lost friends, which he had certainly never done before, but in every other respect behaved as if nothing was amiss. Tooth was looking shaken and uncommunicative, as if finally crushed by the group soul. Some of the crew came up to touch us gently, as if to signify that they had only been following orders, and had played no part in the decision, but it was Amir and Mansur who confessed that they had overheard the heated argument between Tooth and Tandri, and the final decision to abandon us if they could.

Most of the crew appeared genuinely relieved that we had joined them again to share the long haul ahead, through the Banda, Ceram and Arafura Seas towards our still-distant destination of Aru. But all too soon they were to start muttering superstitiously amongst themselves again, for now we were dismally to confront the dwindling tail of the west monsoon. Was this already the start of the 'pancaroba' – the 'change of the monsoons', when the winds die, or else fitfully revolve around the compass for one long month before the great east wind begins blowing from the opposite direction? The lull in the wind which had reinstated us as 'anak prahu', 'children of the prahu', and had come as a heaven-sent blessing, persisted until it began to seem a curse.

A puff would come from any quarter for a short period, then release us again. Four dawns later the Banda volcano was still clearly visible on the horizon. When we lost sight of it we were still drifting helplessly far north of our course, close to the coast of the head-hunting island of Ceram.

This was the deepest and emptiest quarter of the Banda Sea. For days and nights on end there was no wind to fill our sails, nor any fish to take our vertically dangling hooks. Morale and supplies quickly dwindled as we lay as still as a painted ship. After three days of eating only ground corn flavoured with salt, some of the crew went over the side to scrape barnacles from the hull to make soup with. It tasted like seawater. Our Bugis turned out to be appallingly unsuccessful fishermen, hardly landing a thing even when we had been at anchor.

We donned our masks and fins, and swam uneasily in this deep sea, to taunts from the crew of 'Big fish! Big fish!' – they meant the man-eating variety. We dived along our hull, the centre of our universe, and were comforted to find it was also the home of other marine creatures: crabs nesting in the crevices, and tiny fish too agile to be caught.

During the day there was nothing else to be done, except to throw buckets of seawater over the cracking decks to protect them from the

133

134

132 *Sinar Surya*'s top-heavy dugout
canoe was no fun to carry filming
equipment ashore in, but it made the
driest sleeping-place on deck

133 Using the prahu's 'convenience'
over the steering oars could be
disconcerting at night in a high sea

134 A final puff of wind, before
being becalmed for six agonizing
days and nights

equatorial sun. As time passed, the crew began murmuring and eyeing us from crouched groups on the foredeck, seeing us through narrowed eyes, as if for the first time, as harbingers of ill fortune and a blight on their habitual ways. In an attempt to defuse the tension we would play their favourites from our tapes: selections from Joni Mitchell's *Blue*, Crosby, Stills, Nash and Young, and particularly the haunting strains of Neil Young's track 'Helpless, Helpless, Helpless', which still reminds me of that first realization of just how vulnerable were our seagoing ancestors through those centuries of sail.

We were getting hungry and anxious, and our will was being subtly weakened by knowing there was no feasible contingency plan in the event of a 'worst-case scenario' – which seemed already to be upon us with the 'pancaroba'. The ship's wildlife began getting totally out of hand. The rats which had so far only visited our tiny cabin singly and infrequently now took to visiting us regularly in groups, led by tour guides. Our inquisitive super-roaches surfaced by the score, and began marching over us in the daytime as well as at night. While the rulers at the top of the food chain wilted, and in my case began feeling as if they were on the way out, life at the bottom end, in numerous unsuspected forms, seemed to be bursting, parthenogenetically, from between the timbers. Living things were beginning to twitch and multiply in our drinking-water barrel at the foot of the mizzenmast.

An exhausted seabird made an unwise touchdown, and disappeared down the forward hatch in a cloud of feathers and grasping brown hands. We got a foot each. Tandri, looking leaner and harsher, remarked: 'Very good, Tuan! Still alive, eh! Many vitamins in foot – bones, skin, under fingernails!' Enjoying our discomfort, he went on to discuss the butchering techniques required for the rats which we would shortly be eating if this kept up.

It was during this desperate languid emptiness one night that we saw something we couldn't explain. Our shipmates could, but I still find myself completely at a loss.

All hands were sprawled listlessly on deck, beneath our great dead sails which veiled half the Milky Way. Lorne and I were lolling aft, next to the ever-vigilant Tooth at the tiller.

We were all familiar with orbiting satellites, which were clearly visible in these latitudes, and we had even become bored with pointing them out to each other shortly after leaving Makassar. But this was not one of those. I saw it reflected in the water first, and stood up just as Tasman and two others in the bows did the same. They pointed and shouted back to us all.

'Look! Look! A number two!'

Only a few other people bothered to get to their feet, but we all looked. High in the sky ahead of us a white light arced downwards, too slowly for a meteorite, too fast for a falling satellite, came to a halt, changed to a bright green, then ascended again in a different direction at immense speed before abruptly vanishing. On its final streak it was occluding, leaving the impression of a course of vivid green stitches covering a good third of the sky.

'What's that?' I asked.

'That was a good one, wasn't it?' Tasman replied.

'A good what?' I persisted.

'Mericarocket,' several of them chimed in (we had learnt it was their word for orbiting satellites). I hotly disputed that this was a 'Mericarocket', on the grounds that satellites do not behave that way. But Tasman was quite clear about it.

'No. There are two kinds of Mericarocket,' he said, raising one finger. 'Number one is slow steady traveller, and number two' – and he raised two rude fingers as if I were a three-year-old – 'is very fast, wild traveller, like firefly, and sometimes changes colours, too.'

'Yes, Tuan,' Tooth assured us authoritatively from his cross-legged post at the listless helm. 'That was a number two. Not so many as the number ones. My grandfather saw those, too, before there were any number ones to be seen. He called them good luck.'

On the sixth day the wind did pick up again – with a vengeance. It drove us towards the Watubello reefs, through which we gingerly picked our way with the topmen shouting directions from the masthead. From here we ghosted into the Ke Islands, the last landfall before our destination. This was not the ideal port to find succour and sustenance. This was a rough and hardy community of isolationists, where Westerners seemed not to have set foot in living memory. We had further arrived during major political manoeuvrings for power amongst the various chieftains, with an angry jealousy prevailing against the very young and eccentric Bupati, to whom we dutifully tottered to pay our respects and to cadge a good meal, only to find ourselves his weakened and unwilling captives. Here, too, they dwelt in wooden stilt houses, eccentrically constructed of driftwood, on flat coral sand, thicketed with scrub and low forest, and we met the Bupati waiting for us at the bottom of his steps, surrounded by an unnervingly quiet but attentive crowd. To our amazement, and to the evident disapproval of the citizenry, he was a 'sixties groover' of the first water, a taste he claimed to have acquired while a student in Jakarta, where his father was evidently influential enough to have inflicted his son on this distant island as its government-appointed top dog. He looked too young to have gone to university, and too insane to be on the streets. Instead of wearing the white shirt and peci hat characteristic of his office, he met us at the crowded foot of his steps in a coronation T-shirt emblazoned with the Union Jack, and a moth-eaten Beatles wig on his head. He was also quick to introduce us proudly to the mortally poisonous banded sea-snake which he kept as a 'pet' in his water-barrel.

'But it's dead,' I impolitely pointed out.

'Oh, yass! Oh, yass!' the Bupati yelled. 'The Grateful Dead, Year, Year!' And he rocked and rolled for a few minutes, to the scowling disapproval of the none-too-friendly onlookers. Tandri, Tasman and Tooth, who had accompanied us thus far, now cannily chose this moment to slink back to the ship, without waiting for the almost universally accepted greeting gesture of a cup of coffee or tea.

135

135 Mahommed, the eccentric young chieftain of the Ke Islands, with his Beatles wig and his deadly pet seasnake

We had explained we were ravenous but, as time and talk droned on, and the Bupati revealed his roles of clown, man-of-the-world, excitable anglophile and power-wielding bully, it still remained out of the question to invade the kitchen, the sanctum of the women, and forage for a nibble.

After many hours a bowl of tepid water and a brace of pop-eyed fish-heads were placed before us, and a handful of most welcome bananas. Our merciless host then refused to permit us to sleep anywhere other than as his guests that evening – an invitation accompanied by thinly veiled threats of what might befall us and our crew should we be so foolish as to refuse.

Lorne and I were placed, protesting weakly, in the bachelor Bupati's matrimonial bed of honour, which was infested with vermin and barely big enough for one of us. Throughout the night a throng of muttering onlookers pressed their faces against the mosquito netting, scrutinizing our every toss and turn. Our host, as far as I could make out, spent the night in a chair in the corner, constantly talking to the non-stop stream of visitors about his netted captives.

The following dawn, pretending to take a wee walk, we scuttled uneventfully and unpursued back to the strand where (and here, for the first time, our shipmates really came through for us) Basso and Rasman were waiting with the dugout, paddles poised, ready immediately to push off. We reached and boarded our blessed vessel in one swift movement, just as her anchor was hoisted on deck. All the sails were frenetically close-hauled, and we were out of there like America's Cup contenders, to make the remaining hundred-mile dash across the Arafura Sea to Dobu in the Aru Islands. The whole superlative operation was anticipated and commanded by young Tandri, our 'Hood' of the high seas, like a professional pirate. I thought I even detected a glint of pride – or was it companionship? – beneath his hard lively eyes as I leapt aboard.

The last gasp of the west monsoon proved to be a major exhalation which carried us before it almost as furiously as had the gale in the Banda Sea. We were trailing fishing-lines, as usual, baited with silver foil, when Tasman gave a great cry and hauled in first one magnificent dolphin fish – the first we had caught during the entire voyage – then another! And at once, for no accountable reason, the crew were hauling in dozens of these great rainbow-hued creatures, which accumulated on the deck in far greater piles than we could consume. Many of them were still thrashing when we finally raised Dobu dead ahead. Aru was flat and jungled, like the Ke Islands we had just left, so that Dobu's wooden and sago-thatched houses blended almost indistinguishably with the background, and it was only the sunlight glinting off the tin onion roof of its mosque which gave its position away. We had left Asia behind us and entered Australasia – and the dolphin fish seemed to know just where the borderline began.

Our overwhelming relief at our arrival was tempered by the trifling detail that this was Friday, 13 April – just nine months after we had flown into Jakarta, and the very day that our Indonesian visas expired. From now on we qualified for a prison sentence. Although we had our plane tickets back to London from Australia or Singapore, we had been warned by Yong before leaving Makassar that there was no feasible way of getting out of the eastern end of the country, unless one could reach Port Moresby, seven hundred miles away in Papua New Guinea. Our mother in London, and our backers, Ringo Starr and Hillary Gerard (Ringo's assistant and our co-producer), had heard nothing from us for nine months. We realized that by now our mother must be as interested in our welfare as the other two would be about their investment. More worrying still was that we had of course been unable to view a single foot of what we had been shooting, and there was the distinct possibility that our film was by now so exposed to heat and humidity that we would have nothing to show for ourselves but fogged frames and tall tales!

As we approached the harbour we spotted a people-crammed motor-launch putting out to greet us. We suspected it might be the full contingent of the local constabulary, already forewarned of the arriving criminals, but it was the much-relieved welcoming party of the Aru contingent of the Tan Hans family, which had been anxiously expecting us for a number of weeks. They even greeted our astonished crew with

136

136 A mosque in the sandy streets of Dobu represents the easternmost reach of Islam

affection, though they did have a quick rifle through the hold to see what was missing. Apparently there was a good deal missing, but they were very inscrutable and polite about it at the time. We were taken back to their sprawling wooden home, where a brand-new room had been freshly added on for our arrival, and for several days Tans of all ages nursed us back to strength with enormous meals of their greatest delicacies: antler-marrow stew; the basted claws of the giant Cassuari bird; shark's fin soup; and 'tripang', or 'bêche-de-mer', the gelatinous protein-rich sea-slug with which, together with pearl-shell, the Tans were to make their fortunes.

Aru was a perfectly integrated society of numerous ethnic groups. Most of the population were dark-skinned frizzy-haired Papuans, like the New Guinea and Australian aborigines to the east and south of us. They were a much more self-revealing people than the Bugis: quick to laughter, extrovert and far easier for us to communicate with. The local Bupati, whom we now had legitimate reasons to fear, was extremely pleasant when we formally presented ourselves to him as illegal aliens.

He seemed a man of the world, yet his office and home were the simplest of timbered huts, again raised on stilts, and his desk a rickety driftwood table, perforated with shipworm holes and stained with ink.

He went straight to the visa expiry date in our passports, and asked with a grin: 'Not only are you illegal, but how do you propose to get out of here?' To which Lorne mumbled something about our having indeed pondered this problem at length over the previous three months, but having failed to come up with a solution. There was an uncomfortable pause, and I launched in with my best Bugis-accented Indonesian.

'It was the Cendrawasi, sir, the Bird of Paradise, which drew us here. For years she has haunted our dreams. Her glow, like the sun, has been too bright for us to think of how we might leave her island afterwards.'

'You have two weeks', the Papuan Bupati replied, 'before the next inter-island ferry-boat arrives which can take you west again to Ambon and then Makassar, where you can catch your plane to Jakarta and out of the country to Singapore.'

This was financially and legally out of the question, of course, but we thanked him all the same.

The 'pancaroba' would now last a good four to six windless weeks before *Sinar Surya* could head eastwards for home again, and even then she might not reach it for a further couple of months! There had to be another way out.

We walked back to the Tan Hans family through sandy streets glistening with shards of mother-of-pearl shell. Tethered in people's yards was the occasional tame Cassuari bird, looking like a nasty version of one of Jim Henson's Muppets. Amongst the more exotic of the local pets was a species of tree-dwelling kangaroo – no larger than a fat tabby – which hopped about the branches and came when their owners called them.

Tandri and the crew were draped along *Sinar Surya*'s deck, looking sleek and contented, having been paid by Yong's uncle, our host, Tan

137

137 A selection of Aruese delicacies: sea-slugs, bird's nests and the claws of the giant Cassuari bird

138 Aru marks the meeting-point of many different races, from the Malay Bugis of the Moluccas to the Melanesians of New Guinea

139 The chief treasure of Aru is the Golden-Lipped Oyster – source of the world's finest mother-of-pearl shell

138

139

Hans Chui, the balance of the money they had been promised on delivering us safely to Aru. Basso and Tasman were flirting with three Aruese girls, and finding themselves distinctly out of their depth, for these forthright amorous Papuans were a far cry from the demure and male-oppressed womenfolk of home. Mansur and Amir were goggle-eyed at the wealth of new experiences, and Tooth sat crouched in his usual position by the helm. Moored next to *Sinar Surya* was the Tan Hans family's bright orange and yellow *African Queen*-type pearling lugger to which we transferred our belongings to embark for the north of the islands to survey the pearl reefs and, if we could, the haunts of the Birds of Paradise. It was captained and crewed by Tan Hanses, and carried three Aruese divers.

The divers were still using a compressor and dented copper helmets clearly marked as made in Boston in 1910. Lorne had planned to make his maiden descent in this hard-hat equipment to film the pearl-shellers at work, but he changed his mind on discovering that the compressor ground to a halt at least three times a day, exposing the divers to the hazards of the bends as they were rushed to the surface from an average depth of a hundred feet. Many of the old professionals we had seen in Dobu were doubled over with this crippling curse of the pearl divers, and there was a high annual mortality rate. We were glad to have nursed Yong's scuba tank across the Moluccas, and to have breathed but half its precious air in the waters of Banda. We now lovingly attached it to its regulator and turned on the valve – but there was only a brief hiss of air, then silence. We were appalled to find it completely empty, having probably been tampered with by curious rodents in the hold. Once we had overcome our indignation, it was clear that Lorne would be obliged either to twiddle his thumbs or to free-dive.

Of Lorne's various accomplishments, his efforts on this occasion rank high on the list. Our knotted plumb-line confirmed that the divers were walking the reef all of ninety feet down. The teeming organisms from the rivers of New Guinea – just eighty miles further east – make these waters amongst the richest pearl-shell reefs in the world, but they are murky and current-torn. Yet Lorne somehow managed repeatedly to pan past the divers at their own level simply on desperate lungfuls of air, while I remained on deck opening, emptying and resealing our leaking underwater camera housing every time he burst to the surface with it, his eyes popping like a gargoyle's and water sloshing ominously against the inside of the housing window.

His footage shows the shadowy forms of the divers running a desperate slow-motion race, dragged behind the fast-drifting lugger and buffeted by the current. They must grab whatever pearl-shells come within their reach in their headlong rush along the bottom. Should they lose their footing, they are mercilessly dragged through the coral, until hoisted upright again like marionettes by the linesmen above.

They hunt the Gold-Lipped Oyster, provider of the finest nacre, but with a yield of only about one pearl in every fifty thousand shells. That pearl, however, can be a pink, black or golden-yellow monster. Whereas the salaried divers turn the shells over to their employers, any

140

140 The pearl-shell catch belongs to the boat's owner, but occasionally a monstrous pearl is found, which then belongs to the crew

141 With such ancient equipment pearl-diving is a hazardous career. This helmet was made in 1910

pearls they may find belong to them alone, and can make them disproportionately wealthy overnight. This arrangement adds the spice to what is otherwise a gruelling and hazardous pastime.

We spent five or six days diving off the reefs, and exploring the mangrove-shrouded tidal inlets for the tiny stilt settlements to enquire about the Birds of Paradise. We were told that their mating season was unusually late that year and that few birds had yet been sighted in full 'coat and tails'. But we also realized how slow the locals were to talk about the birds at all, and particularly about their special 'dancing trees' where the birds came to show off. For, though the birds were now strictly protected by law, their careful harvesting had for centuries been the prerogative of the Aruese, whose expertise in such matters was self-evident; otherwise the birds would have long since become extinct.

Captain Tan later explained that their reluctance to talk was due to many of them still pursuing their hereditary profession of carefully culling the birds for the international black market.

'We'll have better luck with our trading friend Achmed, further up the coast,' the captain said. 'We can pearl-dive in the morning and spend tomorrow night with his family ashore.'

Achmed was a bristly-headed Falstaff of Arabic–Aruense extraction. He ruled over a splendidly rustic hamlet, and joyfully welcomed us up his gang-ladder to his tilting treehouse of a home. The community thrived off a magnificent monument to eco-technology which they had built in their tidal estuary. It was an intricate fishing trap about a hundred yards long, of vertically planted stakes interwoven with different fibrous grids for selectively filtering the catch by size and shape. Its fruits were surely more impressive than any fisherman could hope for. In addition to the usual gaudy cornucopia of tropical fishes, the trap regularly revealed sawfish, shark, manta ray, crocodile and even dugong, the Asian sea-cow whose protuberant breasts first inspired the mermaid myths, and whose tears are collected throughout Indonesia in special little bottles as powerful love potions.

The captain, Lorne and I were to spend the night with Achmed, listening to animal and bird stories until the lamp-wicks died. We slept after he had agreed to send us the following morning with two of his Aruese forest guides on the six-hour hike to a 'dancing tree' and back. It was also apparently nonsense that the mating season was late that year, and a number of the birds had already been seen in full plumage. This overwhelmingly good news was tempered by the titbit that the birds only danced at dawn or sunset, for about ten minutes, before evaporating back to not even the Aruense knew where. This was fine from the technical standpoint of lighting, but it meant that half the journey, either there or back, would be along wild game trails through dense forest in total darkness.

It seemed we had barely slept for ten minutes before the two Aruese guides arrived. On sea-weakened knees we lurched after their dim shadows padding ahead with their bows and arrows slung over their bare shoulders. On a number of occasions they repeated their advice about showing no lights. A disobedient illumination of my torch revealed why, for I was instantly surrounded by clouds of chittering insects, quickly followed by bats swooping in to eat them, and found myself the centre of a vortex of unpleasantness.

'Quicker and quieter by dark, you see,' our guides said smugly.

It was the Greater Bird of Paradise, symbol of transcendence and immortality – to say nothing of plain good luck – which had drawn Chinese mariners to the Aru Islands in antiquity. The Aruese would sell the bird skins by weight – minus their legs. So the first specimens to reach Europe were legless, and it was assumed that the bird never landed, but mated and hatched its eggs on celestial clouds beyond the firmament, and thus came straight from heaven. Carolus Linnaeus therefore named it *Paradisaea apoda*, the 'footless bird of paradise'.

The Birds of Paradise generally are most remarkable for their sexual inventiveness, of which their plumage, which made them the objects of such human desire, are only part of the story. The Bower Birds, for instance, construct such astonishingly intricate 'casa chicas' to attract their lady-friends that early ornithologists refused to believe they were not man-made. Other species go to the trouble of stripping a strategically placed hole in the forest canopy so that they can dance in their own personalized shaft of sunlight.

Echoes of all I had read or heard of this bird family moved through my numbed brain as I sweated on through the darkness.

Of the Greater Bird, Wallace had written:

> . . . at the time of its excitement . . . the wings are raised vertically over the back, the head is bent down and stretched out, and the long plumes are raised up and expanded till they form two magnificent golden fans, striped with deep red at the base, and fading off into the pale brown tint of the finely divided and softly waving points. The whole bird is then overshadowed by them, the crouching body, yellow head, and emerald-green throat forming but the foundation and setting to the golden glory which waves above. When seen in this attitude, the Bird of Paradise really deserves its name, and must be ranked as one of the most beautiful and most wonderful of living things.[13]

Not just a pretty face, the Greater Bird of Paradise is, paradoxically, both similar in size and closely related to the crow – with which it shares much of its inventive precocity, as well as its raucous voice. We had always been amused by Wallace's transliteration of its mating cry: 'Wank-wank-wank-wok-wok-wok-wok!'

When we actually heard it with our own ears calling through the darkness ahead we were totally unprepared for the accuracy of Wallace's onomatopoeic description. The sound was loud, urgent and hauntingly plain – with a hint of self-parody and something of the Disney Road Runner character's nasal 'Beep beep'. But these voices utterly belied the quivering fragility of the beings themselves. For when we actually *saw* them they were so sensationally exquisite that we forgot our professionalism for a long moment and simply gaped upwards. We knew they were going to look good, because even dead ones were pretty splashy, but it was the way they moved and vibrated and flirted with the light that was so hypnotic.

The birds always return to mate in the same tree in which they were conceived, and it was to one of these secret 'dancing trees', guarded by the family for generations, that we had been led. The bark of the great tree glowed a birch-tree silver as the light gathered, and when the first shafts knifed through the canopy the highest boughs suddenly ignited with what seemed to be a kind of St Elmo's fire of shimmering gold. There were perhaps sixteen birds, about eighty feet above the ground, and barely visible through our telephoto lens which by now had become wall-eyed with internally growing fungus.

And they danced, in this gathering dawn in a distant jungle. They danced, fibrillating their tails, then freezing like open flowers of sunlight, before quivering again and hopping about their drab hens, enticing them with simulated ravishings of handy gnarls and protuberances on the branches.

We even got a few blurry shots, and eyed the surrounding climbable trees for possible locations for building a blind where we could film them from their own level, hopefully the following day. For now that we had found what we were looking for we planned to visit this 'dancing tree' as often as was required to get the birds really in the can.

The hike back was through the first real jungle I had actually seen since being a teenager in southern Mexico, and it was a wonder of iridescent beetles, moths and science-fiction flora. There were giant ferns and fan-palms, and trees which towered from roots which arced out of the ground, as if growing upside down from their branches. We could walk beneath them like ants beneath the legs of monstrous spiders whose racinous limbs bristled with orchids and bromeliads. We were astonished to see enticing sea-shells of numerous sizes and varieties festooning the branches high above us. Had they been transported there, we wondered, and nailed down as love-bait by some inventive and un-catalogued Bird of Paradise? It was only later that we learnt that these fine shells are inhabited by Aru's singularly athletic and fussy species of arborial Hermit Crab!

I remember returning through this magic forest effortlessly buoyed by an immense sense of well-being, and overflowing with gratitude to Achmed for allowing us to glimpse his Family Tree, and to the Tan Hanses, all the way back to Makassar and beyond, and down through their generations.

Several hours later, when we staggered back to the hamlet, Achmed and Captain Hans took us aside.

'Look,' Achmed said, 'come down to the strand and you'll see. Shortly after you left an Australian fishing boat anchored just five hundred yards offshore here. We've sent the crew over to tell them about you.'

'You see,' our pearling captain added, 'a glimpse of the Cendra-

142

142–3 The Greater Bird of Paradise. The most spectacular, prized above all others for its golden tail, is found only in the remote jungles of Aru

wasi's golden tail always brings good fortune. This may be your very lucky day. Very sad you may leave so soon, but perhaps it's safer this way, if it works.'

Within half an hour, two Australians had put ashore in their Boston whaler, and were striding up the step-ladder into our host's wooden hut to sniff us out. Though strongly built, they seemed barely out of their teens, but they warmly boomed their names at us, and clasped our hands with the grip of crocodile jaws.

'Well, gooday, gooday!' the skinnier one observed, taking in our general appearance. 'Yer not missionaries, and yer not anthropologists, or you'd be fatter and cleaner on both counts! So what are you "wingeing poms" doing so far from home?'

'Desperately trying to get out!' I replied feebly, and went on to explain our predicament.

Their craft was the last of a handful of foreign boats, the first in years to have been granted experimental prawn-fishing rights in the region for a limited period. They explained that they had finished their survey, that their visas expired in a few days' time, and that they had simply been putting in for some coconuts before scarpering back home to Darwin, 500 miles south-south-east across the Arafura Sea.

Certainly they would take us with them, they told us, but only if we could leave immediately.

'Right now?' we enquired.

'Yes, immediately!' the fatter of the two said, making me wonder whether perhaps their visas had not also expired.

'What about your captain and crew? Shouldn't we settle it up with them first?' I asked.

'We *are* the captain and crew, mate,' the other one explained. 'Oi'm the crew, 'e's the captain and orficers.'

Sure enough, these two owned and operated what to our rustic eyes was a spectacularly futuristic vessel. Between them they handled the seventy-foot, steel-hulled, diesel-powered deep-sea trawler, ranging with her for many hundreds of miles beyond the nearest shipping lanes or navigational radio beacons. To us these beer-drinking warm-hearted Aussies were the wizards of their time, 'push-button' piloting their Star Ship *Enterprise* deep into unknown waters.

In Dobu we had the briefest opportunity to take our leave of the Bupati and the Tan Hans family, who had treated us as their own children, and whose effusive farewells were no doubt partly fuelled by their realization that they would not have to do so indefinitely.

We pulled slowly out of port, and purred past *Sinar Surya*. She lay low in the water with her new copra cargo, looking her sleekest best. A brand-new if slightly twisted mainmast was in place, Tandri having evidently learnt that purse-pinching was the lesser part of valour (when it came to prahu 'penisi' sailing). Amir and Mansur crowded out from below decks to dance and shout their goodbyes. Tooth stood up and waved. Tandri and most of the rest of the visible crew remained listlessly in position, coldly observing the waving foreigners on their departing space-ship. Was there no honour amongst thieves? I thought, distressed that one should be so abruptly regarded as enemy aliens again, having shared so much together. We were only to learn the true story, and the outcome of their voyage home to Bira, many years later, when it was confirmed that our shared adventure was very much a part of the tales they were telling their children and grandchildren.

We butted out into the Arafura Sea, towards Darwin and safety. The consolation of our richly stocked refrigerator was offset by appalling sea-sickness. After the maternal loping motion of *Sinar Surya* in all but the highest seas, this muscular vessel was a nightmare for the inner ear and, quickly revealing ourselves as 'wingeing poms', we wretchedly accepted their offer to rig the stabilizers, even if it reduced our speed and added to our fuel cost.

When they learnt that our chief remaining concern was to contact London as soon as we reached Australia, they said: 'Let's give 'em a bell now, then, mates!' And within minutes we were talking to our mother in London on the radio telephone. She was grateful for the call, since she had reported us missing to the British consular authorities in Jakarta three months previously.

Ringo was out, but our co-producer Hillary was there, as clearly as if he were in the next cabin. 'Where the hell have you boys *been*?' he shouted. 'Don't you get any newspapers out there? Big changes have been going down. Apple's being divided up at the moment. We can't guarantee your post-production any more, I'm afraid. So don't hurry back. You might as well carry on swinging in your hammocks out there until the dust settles.'

So what if it was all a professional fiasco, and we no longer had the security of a post-production job to go back to? We had sailed with the pirates and seen the golden bird, and sensed something immense and mysterious still waiting to be discovered in that harsh fairyland. We would wait, like buddhas, for the next wind. If we could raise money by 'phone, then we might still give ourselves that long-planned holiday we had been promising ourselves in Bali, which I had still never been to. After all, there was a good chance that all our so carefully nursed film was completely spoilt by heat and humidity. Maybe it was all just a dream, we thought, in those first languorous gluttonizing weeks in our motel room, then we began to focus more closely on Hillary's words to us: 'Apple's breaking up . . . film's post-production is cancelled . . . swing in your hammocks.'

We picked ourselves up, climbed on a plane in Darwin and flew back to the thick of it in London.

Apple had not quite gone bust. Hillary threw his arms round us in greeting, and Ringo leant on his silver cane in the background and made appreciative Liverpudlian sounds about his pirate and flying-saucer movies, which he had apparently forgotten all about. Not much of our footage had spoilt after all and, in time, everything gradually came together and the films saw the light.

But that bird, dancing on film, is still to me but the palest reflection of those bursts of gold which I actually saw, for a moment, that dawn in the jungles of Aru.

6 Life Amongst the Men of Wood

Paper wraps stone,
Stone breaks scissors,
Scissors cut paper . . . sometimes.

The Bugis, too, have their 'Boogie man'.

The Aru Islands represent the easternmost limit of the Bugis' traditional monsoon trading cycle, for beyond them lies the 'Belakang Tanah' – the dark and dangerous 'Ends of the Earth'.

The Bugis venture into the muddy shallows of the Arafura Sea only in legend and nightmare, or if driven there by storm, for the sprawling mangrove swamps of west New Guinea are the domain of a people they fear as a tribe of skull-toting man-eating monsters. 'Monsters' is a rather harsh description of the Asmat tribe of cannibal headhunters, for they seldom reach five foot eight, but they're nevertheless an impressive lot, as we were to discover. . . .

The Asmat are a wood-age culture, living amongst the estuaries of the world's largest and least-accessible alluvial swamp. The rivers which snake through their mangrove forest daily rise with the tides to submerge the entire area for up to a hundred miles inland; and daily withdraw again to expose nothing but mud, roots and crawling things – without a stone to be found. For the pre-Stone Age Asmat, rocks are a vital magical ingredient for certain rites, and are obtainable only at great risk through trade with the highland tribes. The value of stone is exceeded only by that of steel, an almost mystical substance which occasionally reaches them in the form of hooks, knives or axes.

The word 'Asmat' means 'Tree' or 'Wood' people, for they are the same word and, like their totemic creature the praying mantis, they are the forest itself come alive. Legend tells how their creator, Fumeripits, carved their first ancestors from trees which he then drummed into life, standing back to watch them dance.

The Asmat also carve trees into which they drum the spirits of relatives killed in battle with neighbouring villages. These spirits can only be released through a vengeance killing. The carving of these

145

144 Even the bravest warriors are vulnerable to psychic attack, so this man sleeps on the skull of his father as a counter-measure

145 The bis poles, inhabited by the spirits of warriors killed by enemy clans, stand over the village until anointed with the blood of revenge victims

spectacular twenty-foot 'bis' poles is part of an elaborate ritual which ultimately requires the killing, beheading and eating of at least one retaliatory victim from the offending village or clan. 'Inhabited' bis poles may stand in a village for weeks or even years until anointed with the victim's blood which then releases their residents to eternal rest in the land of ancestors, so the poles can be discarded to rot. More than mere carvings, inhabited bis poles are 'living beings' about whom the entire Asmat religious ecology of revenge and regeneration revolves, but to museums and collectors around the world they rank amongst the most valuable and coveted examples of contemporary primitive art.

Nowadays it is rare enough either to be a bona-fide headhunter *or* a cannibal, but to be both simultaneously is – at least to a snooping anthropologist – a singular accomplishment. The Asmat were to achieve world fame in 1961 when Michael Rockefeller, son of the late American Vice-President, disappeared off their coast. He was last seen swimming strongly for shore from his drifting open boat towards the nearby village of Otjanep.

Michael Rockefeller was a child of the Steel Age: heir to the most powerful clan of his nation, which had risen on the tide of oil and US Steel. He studied ethnology at Yale and in 1961, aged twenty-two, made his first trip to Indonesian New Guinea (now called Irian Jaya) on a collecting expedition sponsored by the New York Museum of Primitive Art. A few months later he made his second – and last – trip to expand what was already the world's finest single collection of Asmat art, (now at the Metropolitan Museum of Art in New York).[14]

From his base at the mission and government post at Agats, on the New Guinea coast east-south-east of Aru, Rockefeller made bis-spotting sorties to outlying villages, where he would bargain for the poles in the 'encouraged' currency of tobacco and steel fishing hooks, paying half of it down and the balance on delivery of the poles to his base at Agats. The method worked perfectly for all the villages except Otjanep – an isolated community of warrior master-carvers where Rockefeller found no less than seventeen superb upright bis poles. The Otjaneps wryly accepted both the bargaining process and the healthy down-payment, but they never delivered the poles. Rockefeller was only to see them again by chance, on the last day of his life.

Since he had vanished without a trace, the international press had a field day. Some theories insisted he was drowned in the strong currents before reaching shore; others that he was eaten by a shark or a crocodile. The one that caught the public imagination, however, was the suggestion that he was eaten by the Asmat themselves.

None of these theories was more plausible than another, since no further evidence came to light until thirteen years later, when Lorne arrived with two colleagues to film the Asmat.

They were to be the first outsiders actually to live in Otjanep, and were to spend many weeks naked amongst the villagers, becoming the adopted sons of their war leaders, and finally being exposed to what most probably happened between Michael and the Men of Wood. The resulting film, in which individual accounts by the war chiefs of Otjanep

146

are juxtaposed with their neighbouring villages' versions of the events, is an interesting exercise in determining who is telling the truth. The trail of clues which led Lorne and his colleagues to the bizarre circumstances of Rockefeller's last hours are recounted below.

From Lorne's Notes

I first arrived in New Guinea with two old friends, the American and Belgian cinematographers Bill Leimbach and Jean-Pierre Dutilleux, to make a film on the relationship between Asmat art and their head-hunting and cannibalism. I had longed to film the Asmat ever since I first saw New Guinea's distant mountains from the pearling reefs of Aru. I was in Los Angeles when Bill called me from London saying he had just paid a flying visit to the missionaries at Agats, and had won their general approval to shoot a film there. We had decided on the village of Otjanep because it was by far the most notoriously resistant to outside interference with its traditional way of life.

The best precaution against being beheaded and eaten by one's all-star cast is to do some fairly thorough research before attempting to live with them. The trouble here was that no government or mission post existed in the region until the 1940s, and no white men had visited Otjanep itself until 1956. Subsequent contacts were few: some brief visits by armed Dutch colonial officers (the area was still a part of Dutch New Guinea until the 1960s), a few unsuccessful missionary attempts at soul-salvaging and, in 1959, a brief visit by the French film-maker Pierre-Dominique Gaisseau, who made the memorable documentary *The Sky Above, the Mud Below*. After forty-eight hours in Otjanep, the rising agitation of the villagers caused the nervous supervising Dutch official to order Gaisseau and his team back to the safety of the mission post at Agats. Two years later Michael Rockefeller was to make his brief bis-pole bargaining visit to Otjanep. But, a few months later, Otjanep was the only village in the region which the massive party

146 The unpredictable Kurum, Lorne's adopted father, repairs his monitor lizard drumskin with a glue of resin mixed with blood scraped from the leg of one of his wives

147 At high tide there is no dry land
for up to a hundred miles inland

148 Agats, the remote government
and missionary outpost, from where
we set out for the notorious Otjanep

148

of foreign and national intruders vainly searching for the vanished Rockefeller failed to reach, for its sinuous river (its sole means of access) proved to be massively and expertly barricaded with newly felled trees. Neighbouring villages suggested there was very good reason for the Otjaneps to lie low, for they knew *exactly* what had happened to the young white man.

The accusations made little sense to us for a variety of reasons. First, there are many instances of innocent but frightened people barricading themselves against outsiders; second, Rockefeller was already known in the region as a bearer of tobacco and gift items; third, the Asmat were known to include outsiders in their vengeance cycle only if previously attacked by them, and nowhere in Otjanep's slender history was there evidence of the white tribe having earned such inclusion. Only later did we discover that our assumptions were ill-founded.

Cannibal jungles are supposed to be pretty inaccessible, and the great southern swamp of the Asmat is no disappointment. It could only be reached by single-engined missionary Cessnas, flying the full breadth of the world's second-largest island, over Indonesia's highest mountain range. We took off from Jayapura, the northern capital of the Indonesian half of New Guinea, and had only been airborne for ten minutes when the crackling voice of another pilot came over the radio warning that the weather in the highlands was turning nasty.

'Shit!' exclaimed our young American mission pilot. He was less concerned with religion than with accumulating flying hours as a New Guinea bushwacker to earn himself a chance at flying for a major international airline.

'Sorry, folks,' he howled above the engine. 'Looks like we'll have to try again tomorrow. There are three different weather zones between here and Agats, and they've all got to come up like lemons on a fruit machine to make it through. We can't get these little crates high enough to clear the mountain-tops, so we gotta work our way down through the deep valleys. Not the nicest neighbourhoods to come down in.'

He expertly spat the end of his cigar out of the open roaring side-window, and shouted back to us.

'One of the Protestant planes flew into the wrong valley the other week. By the time they realized they'd blown it, the valley was too narrow to turn round in. . . . Wham! The rescue 'copter found out they'd survived the crash but not the reception party. They ended up on the dinner menu! We could push ahead anyway, if you like.'

The three of us chorused that trying again the following day would suit us just fine.

It was only after another four days of abortive attempts that we finally found ourselves soaring over the high Baliem Valley and the huts of the Dani tribe, whose thriving community had remained unknown to the outside world until the 1930s. I thought of Rockefeller, who had been there with the Harvard–Peabody Expedition filming the last great tribal war of the Dani peoples, shortly before he went on to his death in the Asmat swamps.

166

Far to the east and west of us we could see snow-capped peaks, and by the third hour of flying the terrain was becoming progressively wilder. We entered deep gorges with furious white rivers rushing through them far below, and perpendicular walls of jungle rising to disappear into the mist above us either side of our wing-tips. We were savaged by updraughts, our aileron cables creaked and popped, and our pilot chomped his thirtieth cigar almost in half as he wrestled with the stick. Only J.P. was enjoying himself. Bill looked rigid and green, and I was feeling very uneasy about facing danger without the security buffer of a camera lens to look at it through. At one point we passed within three hundred feet of a high ridge, at the same altitude as ourselves. It was topped by a community of circular huts. Outside, so close that I could almost distinguish the expressions on their faces, a group of some forty naked men, women and children stood poised to perform some solemn ritual, as if frozen in time, as we careered onwards through the angry air.

'Uncontacted!' our pilot yelled. 'Crazy, eh? We pass 'em every few weeks. They can see we're people of sorts inside this bird. But they don't smile much, do they? Never seen 'em wave, either. We drop them stuff, sometimes, the old-fashioned knives and mirrors mainly – just in case we have a flat tyre round here. . . .'

We turned a corner in this chasm, and abruptly the mountain wall was behind us, and we dropped from eight to one thousand feet over the sprawling southern swamp. Flat and horizonless, because of the heat haze, its only features were occasional wide rivers, which snaked lazily back upon themselves, each loop taking several miles to return to a point a few hundred yards from where it had begun.

'Done it again, boys!' our pilot screamed above the engine, with alarming enthusiasm. 'Agats is only about another hundred miles on the nose. But best not to count your turkeys, eh?' And he foraged in his multiple pockets for another cigar – I hoped not his last.

The squelching landing-field, raised just a few feet above the high-tide mark was a two-hour boat-ride downstream from Agats. We had been in radio contact with the missionaries since leaving the mountains, so a rusty old riverboat was waiting by the landing-patch for us.

In Agats, the tiny administrative and missionary nerve-centre of the region, sun and rain beat furiously on the rusting iron roofs of crumbling stilt shacks connected by rickety boardwalks. These boardwalks were exceedingly dangerous. A friend of ours had recently walked and canoed half the length of New Guinea without mishap, and had finally reached the safety of Agats only to fall through the boardwalk and break his leg. So it was with caution that we hauled our daunting mountain of equipment from the jetty towards the nearest house in town – the mission headquarters. This was my first look at the Asmat, and it was a depressing sight. They seemed like aliens in their own swamp, and their faces reflected their anguish at being gradually brow-beaten into the Christian work-ethic. In Agats they were forbidden to appear naked, and so had to work for two weeks to earn a pair of shorts which might last them four.

149

150

149 These nosepieces, intended to give the fierce appearance of a tusked boar, are made from carved nautilus shells. They are forced through the cartilage between the nostrils

150 Flotsam from distant freighters makes welcome ornaments. Note the arrow scar on his chest

151 A beauty-scarred Asmat maiden

152 An Asmat woman in full and splendid plumage

We were met by a lay brother who led us to our airy cells, telling us that the bishop and several of the fathers who were in town from their outlying posts would be joining us later for dinner. I was prepared for a social ordeal, but they turned out to be an articulate and hospitable bunch from Holland and the American mid-west, who came here to save souls but discovered that their first priority was to save bodies. One of them, an elderly fine-faced man, boasted of having made only two conversions in all the seventeen years he had been here. Their Crosier Order was clearly at the liberal end of the Catholic spectrum, and their bishop was a tough compact man in his mid-forties, with an unexpectedly earthy sense of humour.

'This might seem kind of a one-horse town to have a bishop,' he told us on meeting him, 'but it's considered a high-risk post. Murdered bishops attract more attention than murdered padres, which means more donations to our Order's collection box if anything goes wrong again. So they've given me the world's smallest bishopric in terms of population, but probably the largest in land area.'

'When I first arrived,' he recalled as we sat on his veranda

151

152

overlooking the swamp, 'there were a lot of strange things to get used to. For instance, it's customary for important men to greet each other by firmly grabbing the arm with one hand, and the testicles with the other! It can be a painful experience if you're not expecting it.'

'And hardly less so', one of the others added, 'if you are!'

Now that the after-dinner wine was flowing freely, they admitted to having enslaved the Asmat with tobacco – to which they are completely addicted – and excused it on the grounds that it was the only available leverage they had over them for suppressing headhunting and cannibalism.

'Piet, here, once manoeuvred his canoe between two war-parties,' one of them said, pointing at the older man who had made only two conversions. 'He shouted, "If you fight, there'll be no more tobacco," and everyone went home.' The old priest blushed at our laughter.

'It didn't work so well the second time, did it, Piet?' someone else continued. 'You had a little trouble, didn't you?' And, to the general merciless merriment of his brothers, the old priest was required to raise his trouser leg to show us the large purple scar-tissue either side of his leg where one of his excitable flock had loosed an arrow right through it. The time seemed ripe to broach the subject of Michael Rockefeller.

'You'll hear all kinds of wild stories, but as far as I'm concerned he either drowned or was eaten by a shark.' The bishop spoke lightly, but with finality, and we knew we were going to get nothing further out of him or his subordinates on the subject. It was clear, however, that they were none too keen on our choice of making Otjanep our headquarters.

The known story so far was that on the morning of Saturday, 16 November 1961, Rockefeller left Agats bound south for Basiem, a village with a small mission outpost. He was aboard a makeshift catamaran, made of two canoes lashed together and powered by an eighteen-horsepower outboard motor. With him were two mission boys, Leo and Simon, and a Dutch anthropologist, Renee Wassing. When their outboard was swamped near the mouth of the Sirets river, they began drifting out to sea. Leo and Simon promptly made a swim for shore and help, leaving Wassing and Rockefeller to drift throughout the night, wondering whether the boys had succeeded in reaching land. The following morning, with the coastline still just visible, Wassing was unable to dissuade Rockefeller from attempting to swim for it himself. He stripped to his shorts, tied his steel-rimmed glasses round his neck, and with two empty petrol-drums for added buoyancy struck out for shore in what was now the general direction of Otjanep.

'I think I can make it,' were his last words to Wassing.

By the time Wassing was rescued from the drifting outrigger twenty-four hours later, Michael's father (then governor of New York) and his twin sister, Mary, were already winging their way towards New Guinea in a chartered jet. Twelve Neptune aircraft scouted the open sea; Dutch naval and missionary boats combed the estuaries; an Australian Air Force Hercules flew in a cargo of helicopters; and the United States Navy offered the services of an aircraft-carrier. The astonished Asmat, who did not immediately flee the onslaught of outsiders, accepted immense tobacco bribes to mount a search-party of more than a thousand canoes. After ten days the search was abandoned; everything returned to its sleepy primordial state, and all that remained were a few vague rumours pointing the finger of guilt at Otjanep.

We had not come with the intention of unravelling the Rockefeller mystery, but we decided it would be wise to delve deeper into the matter before leaving Agats. I began cautiously digging around in the mission archives for clues, where I found an official record of events which contained this startling entry: 'April 1958. A government patrol, investigating headhunting reports on the Cassuarina coast, killed four warleaders in Otjanep. This may have led to the death of Michael Rockefeller three years later.'

Searching further I discovered that just a few months before Gaisseau's arrival the Dutch colonial government was attempting to eradicate a headhunting war between Otjanep and the neighbouring village of Omanasep. In Omanasep the Dutch patrol burnt down all the longhouses, destroyed all the canoes, confiscated the weapons and arrested eleven men. When the patrol reached Otjanep, where news of the sacking had preceded them, they met with fierce resistance. The nervous Dutch officers opened fire on the Otjaneps with pistols and sub-machine-guns. The full body-count was not recorded, but amongst the dead were four important war-leaders.

This suppressed skeleton in the Dutch cupboard, which provided an excellent motive for including the 'white tribe' in the Otjanep revenge cycle, was a disquieting discovery to make so shortly before setting out with the intention of living in the village. The only changes known to have taken place there over the preceding thirteen years were that Otjanep had split up into two warring factions, Upper and Lower Otjanep, separated by a few miles of gently flowing river, and that all attempts to establish missionary schools in either of them had resulted in the terrified flight of the teachers.

Aboard the mission post's dilapidated launch we chugged down the Cassuarina coast towards Basiem, the closest mission post to Otjanep and Rockefeller's original destination when his outboard was swamped. Here we found the Asmat wore the same sad faces we had seen in Agats, and all of them feared going anywhere near Otjanep. To reach our destination we would have to wait until the Otjaneps came to Basiem to trade for tobacco.

The very next day five canoes came surging up the river, packed with standing warriors chanting ferociously as they thrust on their long paddles. Feathered headdresses fluttered with their exertions, and the sun glinted on their bone knives and shell nose-pieces, highlighting the red and white markings on their otherwise totally naked black bodies.

They were no less fearsome at closer range. Behind each imposing nose-piece was a face of rugged individuality, stamped with the scars of a lifetime of naked warfare in the swamps. Although we were later to become friends with each one of them, we now had very mixed feelings about placing ourselves at their mercy. Having at last found them, we were no longer at all sure we wanted anything to do with these people.

'Don't worry,' one of the missionaries had told us before we left Agats. 'If they *did* kill Mike, then the whole thing's settled now. One death is enough to avenge a hundred. The Asmat believe in revenge, but they don't expect an eye and a tooth for *every* eye and tooth.' It was a kindly remark, because all of them, even the bishop, had gently attempted to persuade us to film anywhere except Otjanep.

The course of events overcame our discretion, and it was not long before the three of us were balancing our filming equipment on our knees in the unstable canoes and gliding through the very waters where Rockefeller had made his fateful swim.

Then suddenly the same thought struck Jean-Pierre and myself simultaneously. 'What . . . ,' he shouted back to us.

'Yes, what if they *didn't* kill him?' I completed his sentence for him. We looked at Bill, by far the whitest of the three of us, and made a few anthropophagous jokes at his expense to suppress the sombre thoughts that, first, there had been *four* Otjanep warlords killed by the Dutch and, second, if they had *not* eaten Michael, then it was still their turn to settle the score regardless of how many victims they chose to do it with.

153

153 The people of Otjanep referred to the neighbouring tribe, who were the first Asmat to be contacted and acculturated, as 'the edible ones'. The Edible Ones now walk the rickety boardwalk at Agats with confidence

154 (over page) The Asmat setting out in their war canoes for a traditional greeting party

171

The jungle sounds closed in around us as we turned into the narrow Etwa river towards Otjanep. A King Cockatoo – an enormous black parrot with a saffron-coloured beak – lumbered noisily overhead, and the drumlike call of a Cassuari bird, as large as an ostrich, echoed through the undergrowth. Far ahead something slipped quietly into the river. As we drew level with the subsiding ripples one of our paddlers leapt into the water, grabbed a four-foot monitor lizard by the tail with his left hand and knifed it fiercely with his right. Pandemonium broke loose as the violent side of our hosts' nature welled to the surface and the dead lizard was savagely battered by everyone within range.

We arrived, rather shaken, in Otjanep to a fanfare of bamboo war-horns. The villagers, who had already been alerted to our arrival, greeted us in their most resplendent finery. We were appalled. They were covered in the filthiest of rags – old shorts tied together with rattan, disintegrating T-shirts worn as pants, pants worn as T-shirts. They had obviously dressed in the appropriate garb for white men.

There was only one thing for us to do: we stripped. There was a moment of stunned silence, then a series of war-cries and hoots of delight as the villagers gazed at the first nude pink flesh (or was it?) of their lives. The ice was broken. We were to live naked for the rest of our stay, with our only clothes being 'Asmat boots', as we called the dried mud which caked our legs to above the knee at low tide, and soon most of the villagers returned to their natural state as well.

Close to the banks of Otjanep's tidal Etwa river stood the Leu, the single large longhouse behind which ranged the row of small stilt huts which served as individual family homes. The Leu is the Asmat equiv-alent of the gentleman's club, and consisted of one enormous room with a number of evenly spaced hearths. In common with its Western counterparts (which themselves seem to be on the way out), it is a refuge from the harangues of the wife, the din of the children and the perturbations of nubile females, as well as a sanctuary in which to swap salacious stories and to plot wars.

Living in the Leu we found ourselves thrust straight into the Asmat daily routine and were surprised at how comfortable life in the swamp could be. They were impeccably solicitous hosts. We had, after all, brought a small fortune in the pernicious black tobacco 'of their choice', as well as knives and fish-hooks, which required the wits of Solomon and a certain amount of physical courage to distribute even-handedly. But I suspect they were also intrigued by our presence. They were endlessly amused by these strange creatures who seemed to match none of their previous conceptions of the white man, and who now swam in the river with them, went as naked as they despite their revoltingly pink-coloured skins, and took a childlike delight in their finely wrought rattan armbands and shell and dogtooth necklaces – and didn't even mind eating their food.

We had brought rations to last us for two months, but we ate so well on the local fare that we ended up giving most of them away by the time we left. Having no cooking utensils, they roast or toast or steam their food in leaves directly over the embers. Their 'staff of life' is sago, the chalky starch extracted from a palm tree, neither nutritional nor tasty, but excellent for cushioning the short sharp bursts of highly varied protein plucked directly from the environment. We lived on fish, shellfish, monitor lizards, wild boar, arborial marsupials and a host of rarer delicacies, including a form of leaf-steamed plankton, which I remember as one of the most delicious meals I have ever eaten.

Their efforts to make us feel at home were not always as altruistic as they appeared. Few of them spoke intelligible Indonesian, but the most adequate interpreter was Kukoi, the young government-appointed chieftain who had been to mission school at Agats. They had noticed our ineptitude when having to squat in the mud for the call of nature, as they did, on the public riverbank, so Kukoi decided they would make for us a device which he had seen at mission school – for the pink people's 'convenience and comfort'.

155

155 We thought it wise to dress correctly. When in Rome. . . . Jean-Pierre is on the left, Lorne is behind the camera

175

156

With much shouting, laughter and drumming they dug a pit and then laid two raised, closely adjoining logs across it as a foot-rest when squatting. The only catch was that this thoughtful structure was excavated on a slight elevation a few yards from the Leu house's front balcony, and in full view of most of the surrounding family dwellings. For the rest of our stay, our most intimate moments could be enjoyed by the entire community.

One day I was approached by Kurum, a notorious war-leader with a battered prize-fighter's face and a muscular body streaked with spear and arrow scars. I had been avoiding him since watching one of his uncontrolled rages over some minor incident which was forgotten within minutes. Kukoi had told me that Kurum had once nearly killed a missionary for trying to pressure him into sending his children to school up the coast, and the general claim that he had tossed one of his babies into the fire because it 'cried too much' was not denied by any of his present three wives. I was cross-legged on the Leu-house floor, watching the burning embers, when Kurum rushed up to me, his nautilus-shell nose-piece trembling with excitement. Shouting in eager Asmat, he thrust a leaf-wrapped gift at me which, being conditioned to expect such packages to contain succulent morsels, I eagerly opened. Kurum howled with laughter as I nearly dropped his precious gift of a pile of bloated squirming thumb-length sago grubs. The missionaries had mentioned them as the local delicacy, the larvae of the obscenely big Capricorn Beetle, which they 'raise' by cutting down an appropriate sago palm, honeycombing its centre with enticing holes, 'seeding' them with pregnant Capricorn Beetles and returning some weeks later to harvest the wriggling treasure-trove of grubs.

Kurum squatted down by the fire next to me where I was examining the gift, removed a grub from the quaking leaf, placed it on the embers for barely a few seconds and popped it into his mouth. His rugged face dissolved into an expression of such tender contentment that I was emboldened to follow suit. Once I had it in my mouth, there seemed to be nothing to do but bite down. An explosion of hot rich fatty protein was followed by a sensation of a jolt of energy rushing through my system, as if I had swallowed a potion of some sort. Then my teeth crunched on its little black head, and I was instantly converted into a sago-grub addict. We were shortly joined by Bill and J.-P., who, after an initial reaction similar to mine, shared this bizarre feast with the same delectation as Kurum and myself.

Kurum spoke no Indonesian, but was highly communicative nevertheless. He pointed to the few remaining grubs, and banged his skull a number of times with his fist. He repeated this until he recognized from my stunned expression that I understood what he meant, then he burst out laughing again. He was telling us that sago grubs are the next best thing to human brains, which they closely resemble, and with which, as I knew, they are closely associated in Asmat rituals.

The simple effectiveness with which the Asmat solved the problems of food and shelter left plenty of leisure time for art, games, story-telling, and of course warfare. In fact they met all the fundamental criteria for an 'affluent society' – without even having reached the technological level of the Stone Age. They drew from their surroundings only what they needed. We also discovered that their swamp, rather than being the hellishly inhospitable 'white man's grave', was actually exceedingly comfortable so long as one didn't attempt to dress or behave like a white man.

One morning we followed the warriors deep into the swamp to find a mangrove tree with a buttress-root suitable for the carved phallic extension essential to every bis pole. They took turns with the village's sole metal axe and hacked at the chosen tree as they would at an enemy. When we returned to the village with it the women were waiting for us, lined up on the bank brandishing their husbands' weapons and screaming with rage. They began shooting arrows and throwing spears at us, then clubbing the men as they tried to struggle ashore.

It took us a while to realize that this assault was all part of the *bis pokumbai* ritual and, although the men are often seriously wounded, the women's targets are the jungle spirits which must be driven from the trees before the carving begins, otherwise the dead soul would have to share space with another resident. The fact that Rockefeller was ever able to 'buy' and make off with standing bis poles was because the unavenged spirits simply vacate the 'export' poles and move into the new ones which are promptly carved again by their living relatives.

Over the following weeks this and other trees gradually took on the shapes of personalities so forceful that it was hard not to imagine someone living in them. Carved with prim pursed lips, or fierce open mouths with sharklike teeth, these human and animal figures stood on, or clasped, or squatted upside-down on each other in an ascending lattice of interconnected bodies. These distinctly erotic, filigreed totems included the creatures most closely associated with the victim whose souls they harboured: there were fruit bats, Cuscuses, King Cockatoos,

158

156 The tangle of creatures extending from the bis pole's navel depict the genealogy of the dead soul inhabiting it

157 The elaborate decorated skulls of dead relatives are immediately distinguishable from the crushed and blackened craniums of enemy victims

158 A stabbing-dagger made from the shinbone of a Cassuari bird

157

and the ubiquitous praying mantis, which for the Asmat not only is the 'forest come alive' (like themselves) but also has the additional endearing characteristic of eating its own kind.

None of the master artists carved in quiet solitude, but elbow to elbow, loudly praising or criticizing each other's work as it took place. Precious shards of carefully worked metal tipped their tools: a quarter of a pair of scissors, a tin-can top, a broken chisel. All the poles for a given vengeance rite were worked on together, and carefully stored in the Leu during those periods when a little hunting and gathering became necessary. Then, well fed and siesta'd, and on no apparent pretext, a great shout would go up and the poles would be brought down for a communal carving session on the riverbank. Those who were not carvers donned their finery, gathered round and beat out long rollicking riffs on their hourglass-shaped drums. The rest of the community danced around them, and sometimes the carvers would lay down tools and join them as well.

To start with, we steered well clear of the subject of Michael Rockefeller, and never once broached the subject of who *these* poles were intended to avenge. But it was also clear that 'spies' from other villages occasionally crept amongst us to observe the proceedings. They were in no hurry to finish the poles. It was all part of the process of giving the guilty village plenty of time to contemplate what would, at some unexpected moment, most assuredly befall them. This lackadaisical approach to meeting a completion deadline is an essential part of their martial etiquette. But not only the bis poles must be finished by the time they launch the raid. Entirely new canoes, spears, shields and war-horns must also be intricately carved just for the occasion. The Otjaneps were having such fun that it was hard for us to grasp that they were actually preparing for a killing.

The more fascinated we became by what they were doing, the stronger the bond seemed to grow between us, quite regardless of the absence of a shared *verbal* language – except via the narrow conduit of Kukoi's mission-post Indonesian. We became so confident of this that we began to film long interviews with them, guided by the rhythm, cadence and emotion of their stories. When we later played back the tapes to a mission father in Agats who was fluent in the regional dialect, he explained that we had captured the Asmat equivalent of 'Nixon's missing twenty minutes'.

There was an occasion Kurum, the hot-tempered war-chief who had brought me the sago grubs, was having difficulty in getting through to me. As he continued to ask me for something which was obviously very important to him, his customary scowl grew increasingly more menacing, until I thought it wise to call for Kukoi's verbal assistance.

'He want you be son,' the young chief said, and the penny dropped that Kurum had decided to adopt me.

The Asmat have two ways of forming alliances outside their clan. The first is through a solemn wife-swapping rite, for which, being wifeless, I was (I thought rather unfairly) ineligible. The second method was through adoption. There was a spontaneously sunny and endearing side to Kurum, despite his dangerous unpredictability. My readiness to accept his invitation was based, I suspect, largely on vanity, for it is not every day that one gets a chance to become the child of a cannibal headhunter. I was also surprised by his offer, since only the previous day we had indulged in a flaring row over some tobacco that I had refused to give him. It was the sort of exchange which the Asmat seem frequently to enjoy, in which you stick your face a few inches from the opposition and work yourself into a howling rage, using the language of your choice. It's a method of discourse which has a surprisingly refreshing after-effect. Kurum had failed to get the tobacco out of me, so perhaps his motives for adopting me were no more honourable than my own for accepting him. He knew, however, what the rite required. . . .

He rushed delightedly off to his hut and reappeared again with his three embarrassed wives in tow. One was a ripe teenager with a baby on her hip, another was a world-worn thirty-year-old, and the third was a charming shrivelled lady – indeterminably older – with skin like the Piltdown Man. Kurum pointed at their breasts and made earnest sucking gestures with his lips. To my horror I realized that if he was to be my father, then his wives would obviously become my mothers.

Bill and Jean-Pierre chortled at my discomfort but, being better-mannered, I ignored them and leant dutifully towards the eldest lady first and took a half-hearted peck at a dangling rock-tipped dug, and began to move on.

'No! Both! Both! Suck! Suck!' was the obvious meaning of their impatient husband's shouts as he hopped up and down, becoming more and more angry. The eldest wife tenderly lifted the second pointed piece of anthracite for my attentions. Things could only look up from here on, and I was getting into the stride of things by the time I got round to the youngest. But here there was a shock in store. I should have thought of the baby on her hip! How strange it was, after all those years, and in that setting, to sense the taste of my earliest childhood flooding into my mouth again. Jean-Pierre was later adopted by the master carver and humourist Agope, but he insisted on inspecting his future mothers by peeping through the slats in their hut before he deigned to accept the high honour. When Bill's turn came to become the son of another warrior chieftain, he had sixteen nipples to get past, and he moved so slowly that we virtually had to prise him off the poor youngest before gangrene set in.

By now we felt bold enough tactfully to broach the subject of Michael Rockefeller, whose fate had now become much more interesting to us. The three most tenable theories (in the absence of the suppressed Dutch information) were that he had drowned in what the press had reported was a six-mile swim to shore, or that he had been eaten by a crocodile or a shark.

We had established that salt-water crocodiles are fairly rare here, and the Asmat said they seldom saw them. Sharks, on the other hand, were plentiful, but there was not a single known incident of them attacking humans. This was confirmed by the Asmat women, who spend many hours a day netting fish while standing on the muddy sea-

159 (over page) Seven poles for seven dead warriors are ready to stand and dance the dance of revenge

179

bottom which slopes so gradually that they can be up to a mile out to sea with the water still only reaching up to their chest. The only danger, they told us, was of stepping on stingrays, so they shuffled along the bottom without lifting their feet.

We had also noted that in the tropical haze this low-lying mangrove coast was no longer visible to the naked eye at sea-level much beyond three or four miles – which was therefore probably the maximum distance Rockefeller would have had to cover before reaching shore. In fact, from as much as two miles out a swimmer could already begin touching the muddy bottom with his feet and would be able to wade the rest of the way. We were now fairly certain that Rockefeller had succeeded in reaching land.

Sitting in the Leu with Kukoi one evening, I asked him what he knew about the event. Although only a child at the time, he remembered the excitement well.

'There were many planes and boats everywhere,' he said, indicating low-flying sea-planes with expressive hand and arm gestures. 'All the other villages said we killed him. We were afraid and blocked our river with trees so that all those people wouldn't come up here.

'Later, when the padre from Basiem came and asked us what had happened to the white man, the elders were afraid to tell him. But what Ajam and the others who did it told *me* was that they were fishing and they saw this white man floating in the water. He was floating there, and he floated away to sea, and that's the truth. But everything is all right now because afterwards, when the village split up, we killed Ajam and the others. So it's all finished.'

Old Bertaham, a much-respected warrior, spoke less ambiguously. He is an adopted son, rather than a native of Otjanep, with a wife and children there, but he has wives and children in other villages, too, and no particular axe to grind for any of them.

'Ah, yes, I have killed many men!' He grinned. 'And I ate them all. Delicious!'

But when asked about Rockefeller his attitude changed to one of blunt authority as he began naming villages.

'Omanesep didn't do it. Amanamkai didn't do it. It was Otjanep and only Otjanep.' He explained that Ajam and the others were returning from fishing when they found Rockefeller lying in the mud, breathing heavily. Two of them were related to the chiefs killed by the Dutch police, and an argument broke out. They speared him there in the mud and brought him back to the longhouse and cut him up.

'They used a bamboo knife, like this one of mine, used only on people. You cut off his head, like this: his arms and his legs like this, and then you cut up here.'

Bertaham traced a line from his groin up his side and made a gesture of breaking his ribs and ripping open his torso.

'Then you pull his body back, like this, and throw him on to the fire. Everyone eats, but only the important men get to eat the brain. The government won't allow us to do this any more,' he added wistfully.

The skull of a revenge victim whose blood has been used to anoint a bis pole becomes an important trophy – necessary to the initiation rites of young boys. Rockefeller's skull and steel-rimmed eyeglasses were two bits of hard evidence which we knew could back the villagers into an incriminating corner. We hesitated to ask about them, but kept our eyes peeled, particularly when the pole-carving was completed and the village adornments were brought out for display. There were now seven superb standing bis poles gazing formidably down on the drumming relatives. But no one would tell us who they were for specifically. Nor had we yet asked. For weeks we had shared with them the fun and excitement of the poles taking shape, and had grown forgetful of the harsh reality that the souls being drummed into them would give them no rest until avenged.

We wondered whether on this occasion the Otjaneps would merely fulfil the symbolic rather than the murderous obligations of the rite, and I felt, too, that they themselves were unsure.

A steady rain began to fall, and although they barely faltered in their drumming and dancing I now sensed a subtle unease pervading the village. Then the sky blackened and released a furious thunder-storm. All night it raged around Otjanep, as only a tropical storm can do. Lightning stabbed the mangroves, briefly illuminating the bis poles' grotesque faces. Nobody slept. Bill, Jean-Pierre and I tossed in our hammocks that night without closing our eyes. Our hosts huddled over the embers; their occasional attempts at song were desultory and short-lived. They muttered amongst themselves in tones we had not heard before, and they periodically cast hard glances in our direction as if *we* were responsible for the elemental anger. They were afraid. And for the first time since our arrival in Otjanep we were afraid of them.

The following morning we packed up and left. They seemed relieved to help us on our way, out into the open Arafura Sea past where Michael had made his last swim, and down the coast to the mission post at Basiem.

By the time we reached Basiem's river, everyone's spirits had revived. We paddled upstream with them as warriors should: standing on the gunwales of our violently rocking canoe, Cassowari-bone knives tucked into our rattan armbands, dog-tooth and nautilus-shell neck-laces jangling and egret-feather headdresses billowing, roaring the simple war-chants our friends had taught us. It was only when we saw the resigned worldly-wise face of the welcoming missionary father, that we became fully aware of how distant we had become from the twentieth century during our barely two months in Otjanep. We realized we had completely overlooked the fact that, apart from our tribal finery, we were as naked as the day we were born.

Lorne returned to Otjanep a year later, and on that occasion I went with him. We arrived as lecturers aboard *Lindblad Explorer*, which was the first passenger-ship to venture into the region. The waters were so shallow that the 2,500 tons of steel (the most precious of Asmat substances) could anchor no closer than nine miles from shore. Thus

160

161

160 The missionaries complain that if the Asmat are left to themselves they spend all their time drumming, dancing and plotting wars

161 The women of Otjanep wore our safety-pins years before it became fashionable in Europe. For the more conservative, the quill of a Cassuari bird through the nose will do

183

Explorer appeared to the Asmat as a kind of 'close encounter of the First Kind', where the superstructure of another dimension was visible only as the smallest spot at the edge of their horizon.

Lorne was persuaded to lead us into the twin villages of Otjanep, but it was to turn into a tour guide's nightmare. We walked into a war.

I found myself piloting eighteen rich, pink and elderly passengers eight miles through the pre-dawn mist to an unseen shore, in a fragile rubber boat powered by a stuttering outboard. We were a ragged train of four such craft, and quickly lost sight of each other, so I glued my eyes to the compass course given by *Explorer*'s captain while maintaining a constant running commentary based on the little I knew of the Asmat, to prevent my canny protégés from suspecting my unease.

After several hours the mist lifted to reveal that we were all within a few hundred yards of each other, and already entering the mouth of the Etwa river – or so we could only assume, since it was indistinguishable from any other opening in this now limitless mangrove forest which sprawled as easily over the sea as upon the land, concealing beneath its many legs just where the one met the other.

We had entered the river and rounded the first bend in a tight convoy of slowly puttering and heavily laden Zodiacs, when from the mangrove roots behind and ahead of us surged some thirty canoe-loads of howling, painted, naked warriors. Paddling with enormous strength and speed they swept round us with inches to spare, while flourishing their genitals at the horrified day-trippers as they passed. They towered over us, ten standing men to a canoe, grasping the narrow freeboard with their prehensile toes, as we cringed in our floating rubber mattresses, four hours distant from our mother ship.

This was the traditional Asmat greeting, a ferocious show of strength, which they performed with a vengeance, fully aware of the impression they were making, for they cracked not a smile – until they recognized Lorne, piloting the lead Zodiac. Kukoi leapt excitedly aboard and shouted that they had been waiting all night since spotting *Explorer* on the horizon the previous evening.

With Lorne at our head we were escorted most dramatically upriver. He had warned us of the rivalries existing between Upper and Lower Otjanep, and had insisted that we should take gifts and passengers in equal amounts to both of them to avoid friction. On reaching Lower Otjanep we dismounted into mud up to our knees – those of us, that is, who were prepared to dismount at all, for there were several who now voiced the opinion that, though they had flown twelve thousand miles to catch a ship for two thousand miles to take a Zodiac ride for hours to see the Asmat, they were already well and truly satisfied. Although we planned to stay here two hours, they refused to budge from their protective rubber sheaths tethered in the mud. An illusory protection, alas, for they sustained a blitzkrieg from midday mosquitoes from which the rest of us, milling about in the smoke-filled Leu cheek by jowl with our excitable hosts, were quite immune.

Lorne was surrounded by a pawing throng, and was quite the man of the moment. Kurum, his adopted father, ran out and greeted him

162 Egret feathers and sago paste make an Asmat greeting party virtually indistinguishable from a full-scale attack

163 The 'forest spirits' dance with the villagers before being driven back into the jungle where they belong

162

163

warmly, showing him a baby born shortly after Lorne's departure the previous year, and named after him: Tuan Satu or 'Mr One'.

'A bit paler than most, isn't it?' one of the passengers commented drily.

'All Asmat babies are light-skinned for a start,' Lorne hurriedly but truthfully explained. But this plump symbol of new life was mixed, as we soon discovered, with the spectre of death, for when most of these Lower Otjaneps had come down to greet us at the rivermouth the warriors of Upper Otjanep had seized the opportunity to attack their village and, while we were being proudly shown baby Tuan Satu on the riverbank, behind the Leu a loud commotion was taking place where Kukoi's elder brother was still lying in the mud with a fatal arrow through his throat, surrounded by wailing mourners. Young Kukoi was distraught. It seemed a bitter irony that this pain was being borne by the one member of the community who was genuinely committed to its evolutionary change. Kukoi touched Lorne tenderly in greeting.

'It was Ari who killed him,' he wept, 'war-leader of Upper Otjanep. Always makes trouble. Now this.' Perhaps it was the carelessness of grief which made him suddenly blurt out: 'It was Ari, you know, who helped kill the white man.' We both stared at him in amazement.

'And did they eat him?' Lorne asked. Kukoi looked him directly and sadly in the eyes.

'Yes, they did. If you go up there, he will kill you, too.'

Now that the passengers were beginning to appreciate what we had got them into they were no longer enjoying their little outing so much, and were even becoming somewhat rebellious. But Lorne seemed far more concerned with the broader equilibrium than with the immediate welfare of us pinkies, and was still determined to go to Upper Otjanep. Since it was clearly unwise to take any of our passengers further upriver, and out of the question to leave them unattended in Lower Otjanep, Lorne would have to go alone.

'It's quite OK,' he whispered to me. 'I'm just as friendly with that lot as I am with these. We went to a lot of trouble last year to divide our attentions between the two of them so they wouldn't get too jealous.'

'Yes,' I put in. 'It's worked wonderfully!'

'Ari shouldn't be any problem,' he said. 'Keep everyone calm, show them the art, and the babies, and keep them away from the corpse. If I'm not back in half an hour, take them all home to the ship and come back with some serious help.'

You may know what it is like: there is nothing one can say.

I watched him slip down to the bank, make some soothing sounds to the mosquito-blistered stick-in-the boats, liberate one of the empty Zodiacs and disappear up-river with it behind a rooster-tail wake.

From Lorne's Notes

I reached Upper Otjanep to a scene of such turmoil that my arrival was almost unnoticed. A wailing crowd on the bank surged around a fallen figure. They paid little attention to me as I climbed ashore and joined them. At their feet lay a teenage boy – the second corpse I'd seen in fifteen minutes. His head had been partly severed by an axe blow to the back of the neck. He had joined the raid to Lower Otjanep that morning and been killed with the village's sole metal axe (the miracle of steel!). His mother was violently breaking up his shield and weapons, and together with her relatives and friends was screaming and moaning and rolling in the deep mud. I remembered Ari as combining the powerful physique and slow wits of the stereo-typical circus strong man with the unexpected ability to speak almost as much Indonesian as Kukoi. Ari spotted me first, and instantly left the agitated group of warriors he was standing with and came running purposefully in my direction. He was also in a high state of excitement, and Kukoi's warning was very fresh in my mind, but Ari's embrace was warm and strong, and I knew I had nothing to fear from him.

'Did the white man taste good, Ari?' I asked him, only dimly aware that the offensiveness of my greeting must have sprung from the defensiveness of my inner feeling.

My brashness took us both off-guard, but after a moment Ari began to laugh. It was a laugh from the heart and belly – as only the Asmat know how – so infectious that I began laughing, too. We clung to each other, howling with the sort of release which comes from extreme tension. That shared mirth, with the tears streaming down our faces, was to me more convincing than any verbal confession.

Back in Lower Otjanep, I was wondering if I really *would* take us all on the four-hour journey back to the ship if Lorne failed to reappear in thirty minutes. I consoled myself with the hope that Kukoi had told the truth about Ari eating Rockefeller, and that there were no further hidden outstanding debts between our tribes. To distract Kukoi from his grief, I encouraged him to sit with us and interpret questions and answers between the visitors and their hosts, and soon both sides relaxed a good deal and were communicating loudly and unself-consciously with each other through imaginative sign language. I was sitting with Kurum, Lorne's adoptive father, who still cradled the baby they had named after him. It was coming up to the half-hour, and I was in no mood for hedging my questions. With Kukoi's help, I now asked Kurum not *whether* he had eaten human flesh, but how it compared, say, to pigs or fish. The answer was either a leg-pull, or else startlingly well informed.

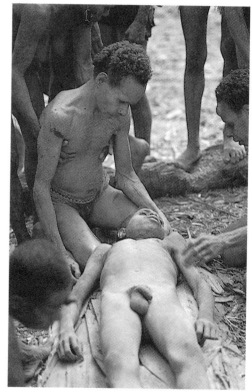

164

'Our own flesh is too tough, the Malay's is too sweet, the white man's too salty – but the Chinese is perfectly delicious!' Howls of laughter all round, which became quickly mitigated by a certain sheep-ish realization that we were not alone, and that the joke might be a touch close to the bone. They had momentarily forgotten, it seemed, that they were now surrounded by several dozen of our white brethren to whom, strictly speaking, the Otjaneps now owed a few heads of their own. It was this guileless sensitivity to their own joke which most convinced me of their honest guilt, and of Lorne's case for the prose-cution. I promised my own tribe that I would translate the joke later.

164 The fourteen-year-old warrior killed in his first battle on the morning of our return to Otjanep

165 When the men return from
cutting the trees for the bis poles,
their women launch a mock attack to
drive the jungle ghosts from the trees,
so the souls of the warriors to be
avenged can take up residence

An hour later, we had already been waiting in the Zodiacs for twenty anxious minutes before we heard the steady drone of Lorne's approach.

'Anyone need a lift?' he announced, and we spread the load with some of the other near-mutinous passengers. 'I've got a good story.'

Our train of rubber pods, laden with blanched explorers, puttered slowly down the winding estuary. We were escorted, but only for a short distance, by the still boisterous canoe-loads of Lower Otjaneps farewell committee. Lorne dallied at the back of the line, exchanging news for a few precious moments with the friends who kept up with him in their canoes. There were tearful goodbyes on their part when they stopped, watched us, then, suddenly swift and silent, headed back to their village. We reached the rivermouth and set our course for the long haul over a glass-calm sea towards the steel dot on the horizon. When I looked back, the Etwa rivermouth had already vanished into the drawn ranks of the mangroves; there was not the slightest sign that another soul might live beyond them, or ever had. We had moved through a chink in the space–time continuum, like Alice through the looking-glass, and the door had vanished behind us as we headed for our floating cocoon of time present.

The full impact of Rockefeller's fate only came home to us several years later in New York, when Lorne and I met the director Pierre-Dominique Gaisseau, who in 1959 had been filming the carving of bis poles in Otjanep when he was ordered out by a nervous Dutch police officer.

'You know,' Gaisseau told us, 'it almost happened to *us*. I'm now sure that the poles they were carving included those intended to avenge the war-leaders massacred by the Dutch. Who knows what would have happened to us if they had been completed while we were still there?'

He then astonished us by remarking that he and his team had managed to buy and *take away* the unfinished poles! This was a most significant missing clue in the chain of events.

Rockefeller had reached Otjanep on his brief buying expedition two years later, and recorded in his diary that he found there no less than seventeen spanking-new bis poles: '... these poles', he wrote, 'resulted from a bis pole ceremony which appears to have taken place some time *after* P.-D. Gaisseau visited the village in 1959' (my italics).

There is no record that Rockefeller was aware of the outstanding blood debt existing between the Asmat and the white tribe, so he could not foresee that perhaps included amongst the seventeen poles he arrived to bargain for were some which still harboured the unavenged spirits of the war-leaders killed by the Dutch. These spirits had simply vacated the poles which were bought by the French team, and had taken up residence in these newly carved ones to await their liberation to the land of ancestors.

The irony is that Michael Rockefeller had bought, and half-paid for, the omens of his own destruction. From the heights of millionaire-dom on the other side of the world, he had been lured by these totems to the swamps of New Guinea to become the sole sacrifice on behalf of the white tribe of Steel to settle a score with the People of Wood.

166

7 An Island of Dragons

For millennia the Komodo Dragon slumbered on its secret volcanic island protected by dangerous seas, breathing only in dream and myth, before finally awakening to science in the early years of this century.

The story goes that a pioneering Dutch aviator was attempting to island-hop in an early aircraft down the Indonesian islands to Australia, when engine trouble forced him to land on the desolate beaches of Komodo. He ultimately succeeded in repairing his engine and taking off again, but was to report that his efforts were seriously hampered by large prowling reptiles, unlike anything he had ever seen, which repeatedly forced him to retreat to the safety of his cockpit.

This, together with other stories from local pearl-divers, filtered back to Java, a thousand miles further west, and inspired an adventurous Dutch military officer named Van Steyn to reach the island in 1912, shoot a couple of specimens, and bring their putrid remains back to the Bongor Zoological Museum in Java, for the eager scrutiny of its curator, Van Ouwens, who was the first person to identify it correctly as a type of monitor lizard which had grown absurdly big for its boots. He named it *Varanus komodoensis*, or the Komodo Dragon. With twenty wickedly splayed, griffinlike talons, and layers of serrated backward-slanting teeth like a shark, the lizard is a land-dwelling amphibious carnivore, fast on its feet, and reaching eleven feet long with a weight, fully fed, of over five hundred pounds. Though also found on the eastern tip of Flores, and on a few neighbouring islets such as Rinja and Padar, the Dragon's central domain is the island of Komodo.

Though separated from her larger neighbours of Flores and Sumbawa, to the east and west, by straits little wider than the English Channel, the fury of those waters renders Komodo as isolated as if she were in mid-Pacific. For it is just here that the deeply shelving Indian Ocean which stretches uninterrupted to Antarctica meets the sprawling shallower waters of the South China Seas.

My first of many subsequent, more solitary, visits to Komodo was aboard *Lindblad Explorer* where for several consecutive years Lorne and I were employed as staff lecturers and guides during the vessel's annual six-week cruises through Indonesian waters. Owned and operated by a Swedish travel company based in New York, the vessel was a luxuriously appointed 200-footer, which carried high-paying passengers and scientists to inaccessible parts of the world for brief encounters with peoples and creatures so off the beaten track that they would otherwise require a special expedition to reach. The ship sailed continuously around the world, unloading and renewing her complement of passengers at international airports along the way. People for the Indonesian cruises were usually taken aboard in Bali, and deposited again in Port Moresby, Papua New Guinea, nearly three thousand miles further east. It was a total contrast to our usual way of exploring the

167

166 The giant monitor lizard, the Komodo Dragon can reach eleven feet long, and preys on goats, deer, and even man if they can get him

167 The memorial to the Swiss baron who in 1974 became the first known Westerner to have been eaten by a Komodo Dragon

168 (over page) A view towards the other neighbouring islets where Dragons also roam

islands, immersed in the environment, cut off from our roots and unconstrained by time. But aboard *Lindblad Explorer* we were now in the ambiguous position of experiencing the contrast between East and West far more dramatically than we might have done on our own, for she was a floating microcosm of everything Indonesia was not, where the world of the present was rigidly ruled by the chronometer, and divided from that of the distant past only by a two-inch hull of steel.

Luxuriously appointed, with laboratory facilities and an impressive library of films and reference books, her galley was stocked with the finest international foods and wines. The passengers included the nobility of the Western world, scientists and Vanderbilts, diplomats and captains of industry.

We were immensely fortunate with our staff colleagues, who were the pick of the world's experts in their respective fields. At the nightly lectures they would enthrall us all with their encyclopaedic knowledge of the natural world. There were the celebrated wildlife cinematographers Des and Jenny Bartlett, the couple with an almost supernatural ability to locate and anticipate the behaviour of wild animals. There were Ron and Valerie Taylor, the Australian shark and underwater specialists, who blithely finned their way amongst creatures which most of the rest of us would rather observe only from a helicopter. There was also Sir Peter Scott (son of the Antarctic explorer, and President of the World Wildlife Fund) who came along as a world authority on birds, lectured us on the Loch Ness Monster, but actually revealed himself to be a ranking expert on tropical reef fish, and would bubble for hours along previously undived reefs with our ichthyologists, happily scribbling long Latin names for each other with their wax pads and pencils.

The dark horse amongst us was the inscrutable Sutan Wiesmar, the only Indonesian aboard and our official government ombudsman for smoothing our way, where necessary, with local chieftains. Although he had certainly travelled more widely in Indonesia than Lorne or myself, we had the edge on him when it came to knowing the general background information, and the approaches to the wilder islands in the Moluccas. Thus finding ourselves the privileged one-eyed kings, we were disproportionately influential on the course the ship took, and we sometimes felt almost as if we were in command of our own high-tech superyacht, replete with the finest company and cuisine, cruising amongst the world's most fascinating waters.

There was a night when we were purring down into Indonesian waters from Hong Kong, bound for Bali, while our passengers slept peacefully below, and the phosphorescent waters glowed down our sides. Lorne and I joined the Swedish captain and his first officer on the bridge, which glowed like the cockpit of a 747, as Lorne unfolded his photocopies of the antique maps he had so assiduously collected over the years in maritime museums ranging from Greenwich to Manila.

'I'd rather you kept it under your hat, Captain,' he announced.

The captain scratched his bald head. 'Sure, sure. Go on. Where do you think this wreck is, then?' And we began comparing the photocopies to our ship's modern hydrographic charts.

It had been a long-cherished project of Lorne's to locate and dive on a singularly richly laden sixteenth-century galleon which had foundered during a typhoon somewhere off the island just twelve miles to the east of our present course, and which we believed no one else was aware of. He had discovered the first clue by sheer chance, amongst the disintegrating parchments in the deepest vaults of the Philippines National Library. But it was only with the technology of a vessel such as this that we stood a chance of actually locating the site of the wreck.

'See, Captain' – Lorne now flourished photocopies of elegant but almost illegible calligraphy – 'middle Spanish. It's a bitch to read. They're the only eight existing reports by survivors of what happened and where. If we can match their reports to the actual island, rather than the charts, we might be able to nail the wreck's location.'

The captain pondered through his magnifying glass. 'A lot of these underwater surveys haven't been repeated for sixty years, and weren't too reliable in the first place – but let's go and have a look, shall we? But keep it under your hat. The ship's owners in New York would go bananas if they knew of a little jaunt like this.' Lorne and I exchanged triumphant glances.

In the small hours, while our important personages dreamt below, we veered off course by a good ten miles to cruise slowly down the fifteen-mile shoreline of the suspected island, using our sophisticated sonar and radar equipment to plot each rock, and variance in distance between the shore and the edge of the reef, comparing them to the descriptions in the survivors' reports. One spot emerged which matched all the co-ordinates, and the captain neatly pencilled it into his chart with a tiny cross, and we marker-penned it on our old photostats with an overt skull and crossbones.

By the time our five-course breakfast was being served in the dining-saloon, we were back on course for Bali again and making up for lost time, with no one any the wiser – except, of course, for the four of us, who now suspected ourselves as being the only people in nearly three hundred years to know the probable location of perhaps the most spectacular sunken treasure-galleon in the Eastern Seas, and lying in only two hundred feet of clear water.

Aboard *Explorer* I also doubled as the 'zoo curator' and sheltered creatures which the naturalists deemed fit (or sometimes not) to bring aboard as instructive props to our nightly lectures. At one point I simultaneously shared my eight-by-twelve-foot cabin with a bucket of bizarre fish with unpronounceable names, a jar of coral with a blue-ringed octopus (which promptly gave birth to about five thousand minute and perfect replicas), a punctured hat-box of several rare and colourful spiders and beetles and a hideously large, but common, centipede which quickly ate his companions to remain the sole (and none too popular) star of our 'Entomological Evening'. There was also a splendidly red Bandanese parrot which quacked, and a Cuscus from Celebes, a marsupial, teddy-bear-like, fiddly-fingered charmer, much in demand for the pot. Being, like myself, both arboral and nocturnal, we got on well together, and after I had smuggled him triumphantly back

169

169 The young Cuscus which I rescued from the pot, and which became the engaging resident of our roof rafters in Bali

home to Bali with the Bandanese parrot he lived contentedly for many years in our rafters, frightening the geckos. Being indigenous to islands only east of the Wallace Line, they attracted great attention for miles around, and Cuscuses and Red Parrots became part of the painting and sculpture of the region. The Red Parrot made an even deeper impression. It quickly snipped its way to freedom, and for weeks reports would filter back from miles around of sighting its red flash and hearing its distinctive mocking quack. Then nothing for months, until the word began circulating that a new type of parrot, a pinkish colour, was now inhabiting the forests near Bedugal – and adding to Bali's rich repertoire of sounds an increasing orchestra of plaintive quackings.

It was not all exotic piracy aboard *Explorer*, however, and we were both kept very busy. In addition to having to give our nightly lectures our duties included writing the log, navigational assistance, diving instruction, and piloting Zodiac boat-loads of people with expensive cameras over uncharted reefs on to wave-swept beaches, and safely back on board again. In addition to guiding the ship to islands we already knew it was a unique opportunity to take her to places entirely new to us all – a gamble which was not always a success.

In one instance we lobbied for *Explorer* to pay an unannounced visit to a small island in the Watubella group at the north-eastern corner of the Banda Sea, about which none of us knew anything except that it was supposed to be populated with the descendants of former master boat-builders and animists.

The island was craggy and dramatic, and at the foot of its jungled cliffs we could see what appeared as an elegantly built little town, glinting with tin roofs, and lorded over by the great burnished and dented balloon of the inevitable mosque. We had no sooner anchored than I headed for shore in the Zodiac with Wiesmar and Lorne, to check out the scene, alarm the Bupati and ask if eighty-odd foreigners could put ashore for a few hours to snoop around.

Weismar carried a revolver in his belt on such occasions, more as a symbol of authority than of murder, but he nevertheless displayed an embarrassingly bossy attitude towards the cowering Bupati and his elders when we surprised them on their porch gambling with dominoes.

'I come from the government,' he shouted at their bleached faces. 'These are important friends of the President,' he went on, pointing magnanimously at Lorne and me. 'They're the first of many tourists who may come here. Make you all very rich. *Then* you can gamble. Now, what can you show us? Why would these rich people *want* to visit your miserable island? We'll be coming ashore in one hour to find out.'

The leaders of the community crouched in shocked silence, and I began shifting my weight from foot to foot and making placatory sounds, which Wiesmar instantly froze with a fierce glance.

When the Bupati finally regained his power of speech he stood up, bowed, and used it eloquently.

'Yes, General. Our island is at your, the President's and the rich foreigners' disposal. Come back in one hour and we shall treat you to our traditional welcome.'

Wiesmar strode back to the Zodiac; we shambled uncomfortably after him. 'Got to get these types moving,' he said to us, 'put a python up their arses, or they'll never make it to the twentieth century.'

'Yes, but what are they going to *show* us? Shouldn't we go back and find out?'

'No, never go back, lose face. We'll come back in two hours – which is what *one hour* means. Don't worry. Greeting ceremony better than nothing. It gives a chance for other people to sniff around.'

We returned aboard to announce that after our elegant lunch and a small siesta we would be received on an island which had never seen a Westerner in living memory. Two hours later we dutifully ferried our passengers ashore and were conducted with them to the village's broad square in front of the mosque. It was neatly arranged with benches to accommodate all eighty of us, which were surrounded by a silent throng of unsmiling citizenry – elegant, angular, sharp-faced people, tightly saronged, rather pop-eyed women, oddly hushed children with pinched, scrubbed faces. The event itself was to prove more disturbing.

The Bupati opened the proceedings with a long and obsequious welcoming speech in Indonesian, which was followed by a few dozen neatly attired young men in peci hats and white shirts assembling in quiet ranks before us and closing their eyes. A young leader stepped forward with his eyes open.

'What do you reckon, a dance or a speech?' I whispered to Lorne.

The Bupati then formally handed the front-man a glass of water.

'Probably another boring speech,' Lorne replied.

But with a loud shout and a triple pirouette he tossed the water in the air, and began munching on the glass and swallowing it. His companions now began shaking and shouting, too – entering what we suddenly realized was a full-on trance. Several were actually breaking Coca-Cola bottles with their teeth, and chewing and swallowing the pieces. Others were sticking bamboo barbecue-spits through their cheeks and pectoral muscles. A few were darning their mouths closed with needles and thread, while vibrating with a sort of St Vitus' Dance.

Our assembled protégés in their straw hats and Hawaiian shirts were aghast. Some fainted, others began staggering indignantly down towards the Zodiacs. I approached the Bupati as tactfully as I could. 'The visitors aren't really understanding this,' I said. 'They don't like the blood. Is there any way you can stop it and do something else for us?'

'Under*stand*?' he shouted at me above the hubbub. '*Nobody* understands it – and nobody likes the blood. Besides, there *isn't* any blood, or not much. This isn't *our* decision, Tuan.' He went on more calmly: 'Our traditional greetings are performed by the spirits through us. *They* chose this for you, and we certainly cannot stop them once they've begun.'

After a while older members of the community intervened to slap and embrace the participants out of trance and the atmosphere thankfully quietened down. Some began helping the performers unstitch their mouths, starting with biting the knots at their corners, like a Dracula's kiss being administered to standing epileptics, and then drawing the

170

170 The seated man in trance showed no signs of injury, despite repeated blows to his back with this enormous boulder

thread out of numerous bloodless holes round their lips. But this proved only to be the first act, and the star turn was yet to come. This required only five men: one shirtless hero, two people to hold him, and two others to wield and repeatedly slam a boulder against his back.

For a horrible impotent instant I shared with many the chilling suspicion that we might be about to witness an execution as testimony of their seriousness to entertain us. At first he stood upright, but he was shortly bowed over on his knees, presenting an arched spine to the blows. A terrible glottal sound was driven out of him each time but, far from fractured vertebrae and gaping lesions, his skin remained completely untarnished, if slightly darker. When he was finally embraced out of his trance, he opened his eyes with the same misty, enquiring expression of one who has returned from a great distance – from much further away than we ourselves had come.

It was a fascinating example of pure animist possession in the guise of orthodox Islam, but it was not appreciated as such by many of our passengers, even when I perspiringly attempted to interpret it for them at my interrogation that evening. Wiesmar, who had long since abandoned any attempts of his own to bridge the cultural gulf between the two worlds, was tickled by my efforts and sat smugly in the back row irritatingly grinning at my efforts to explain why it was all perfectly all right and absolutely fascinating, even if not what you'd expect on the croquet lawn.

'The Whizz', as we called him, was the son of the last Sultan of West Sumatra, and national turmoils had led him to become almost the Indonesian equivalent of a French Foreign Legionnaire – with the same sort of lurid past. He had been a colonel on the wrong side of the Sumatran war of secession and then, dabbling in politics, he had achieved the powerful position of chairman of the National Union of Students. When the tide of power shifted again he took the position of a VIP roving agent for TUNAS, the National Department of Tourism, also doubling as an intelligence-gatherer in the nation's outlying regions.

Though he looked like a portly sloe-eyed baby, he was deceptively rugged and alert. It was not merely the fact that we could speak the same language and share the same jokes, but the three of us met on deeper common ground midway in the no man's land dividing two profoundly different worlds. We were later to share much of our hazardous five-month trek with him into the heart of Borneo (see Chapter 9).

The Whizz's sense of adventure was perpetually stoked by his hope of finding clues to hidden treasure which, as everyone knew, still lies throughout this frontier land in many forms waiting to be discovered. It was this which had inspired his present position, as well as those he had held as official ombudsman for some of the earliest foreign sorties off the beaten track permitted since national independence. It was Wiesmar, too, who had been the government representative aboard the TUNAS vessel in 1976 which was the first to carry a whole shipload of sightseeing Europeans to Komodo – including the unfortunate Swiss baron who was to become the first known Westerner to be eaten by a Komodo Dragon.

It was only a year later, aboard *Explorer*, that I now paid my first visit to the island, and it was no less impressive than visiting it alone on subsequent occasions.

The night before arriving, Wiesmar sat enigmatically in the back row of the lecture lounge as our zoologists prepared us for what lay ahead. Their usual tendency to dispel misguided notions of threats posed by certain animals was absent from their discourse on the Dragon that evening. It was unanimously agreed that stalking the *Ora*, as it is locally called, required the utmost caution. Remarkably little is still known about the reptile. What *was* known at the time was that there were at least six well-documented human fatalities attributed to them since their discovery barely sixty years earlier.

At the heart of the arid Lesser Sunda Islands, Komodo is only about fifteen miles long by five miles wide. The *Oras* rule supreme at the top of a precariously balanced food-chain, but are hard pressed to thrive on the slender population of wild pigs, deer and goats which form their staple diet. They are also not averse to the odd buffalo and even feral horse, which they dispatch, like all their victims, by sweeping them off-balance with a thrash of their powerful tail, then directly opening their stomach with a single can-opening bite, and gulping down the spilled intestines before the animal has had a chance to die. The following morning we were to make a significant increase in the ratio of available warm-blooded flesh on the island by unloading some sixty succulent, slow-moving and heavily scented additions to the Dragons' larder.

Approaching the island in the pre-dawn darkness I was awakened as our 2,500-ton ship began tossing around like a rowing boat, and I quickly joined the captain and officers on the bridge. They were poring over charts, but the information provided by the Nautical Almanac stated that there was no predictable pattern to the sudden birth of powerful whirlpools and ripcurrents which could race around the island at a terrifying fifteen knots.

As a child I had read with fascination David Attenborough's *Zoo Quest for a Dragon*,[15] and the scaly denizens, which he had gone to such trouble to capture, had inhabited the imagination of my formative years; but I was not prepared for the charisma of the island itself.

It is the jagged congealed heart of a sleeping volcano, protected by a raging moat. Its forbidding escarpments towered against the dawn like the walled castle of the Prince of Darkness. The sun sent thin long fingers of gold down into mysterious valleys of prehistoric vegetation, while the ramparts above were silhouetted with Borassus palms, looking like lollipops with Afro hairdos seventy feet high. This seemed precisely the setting of Conan Doyle's *The Lost World*, written more than thirty years before the Dragon was discovered.

At the edge-seam of the world, in no one continent and in no one sea, Komodo was nevertheless to reach out in disguise to touch our Western imaginations. For accompanying the early American expedition to the island in 1926, led by the big-game enthusiast W. D. Burden, was a young pioneering cameraman named Willis O'Brien. O'Brien was so deeply affected by the island's prehistoric atmosphere, and the

171

171–173 Komodo's only village, whose four hundred souls are all descended from transgressors of the law banished to Dragon Island from neighbouring Bima. They live almost exclusively off the sea, catching squid from their twin-sailed catamarans. They fear the prehistoric landscape behind, as 'where dragons be'

173

174 The whole island is the
shattered remains of an immense
prehistoric volcano

struggling human community which barricaded itself against the prevailing monster, that he subsequently went on to make a timeless piece of film called *King Kong*.

We pulled into quieter waters, over the pearly coiling surface of Slawi Bay. Whales and manta rays heaved out of the water, in such rich varieties of species that our marine biologists were nearly falling over the rails with excitement and shouting identifications to each other in boisterous Latin.

Not a soul or footprint marred Komodo's crescent beaches, but the shells and marine flotsam would have made a malacologist's eyes water.

Three miles to the south squatted the only village on the whole island – a sorry-looking clutch of lean-tos on stilts with a population of some four hundred impoverished souls clinging to life at the edge of the sea. They are all the descendants of former subjects of the kingdom of Bima, on neighbouring Flores, whose sultans had gradually banished them, over the centuries, to Dragon Island. It has even been suggested that when the Sultan of Bima declared Komodo and its *Ora* a protected sanctuary in 1915 (only three years after it had been classified by science) it was less an enlightened gesture far in advance of its time than an effort to retain the 'teeth' in his penal-colony policies.

The village's precious few domestic goats and chickens are corralled beneath the houses during the day, and gathered up the vertical steps into their owners' homes each night. Their graveyard is encrusted with cairns and coral heads to prevent marauding Dragons from exhuming and eating the corpses. Their only fresh water must be painfully milked via a polyvinyl hose from one minute and unreliable spring.

They wrest their living almost entirely from the sea – their staple diet being the squid which are netted from their elegant twin-masted

174

catamarans. They fear the Dragons, and by and large keep their backs firmly turned to the forbidding crags and primordial glens behind them. Only a few enterprising villagers venture inland as nervous guides for the occasional outsiders.

On this, my first occasion, with a pile of passengers and a tight schedule, we chose the safer of two promising sites for Dragon-spotting, a 'short walk' to Loho Liang, barely a mile inland to a ten-foot observational ledge overlooking a dried riverbed. Here the reptiles might be observed from the safety above, and an adjacent tree extended its branches to the ledge providing a direct means of descent to stake the slaughtered goat used as bait to the ground. Alternatively, we could have made a four-hour 'long walk' up to Poreng, and the open savannah land where the Dragons could be encountered, if at all, on their own level, and where the offering of a sacrificial goat, as putrid as possible, was even more essential for distracting their gastronomic attentions from their observers.

We had often been amazed by the degree to which animal sacrifice still held sway throughout Indonesia. The two Brahminy Bulls, for instance, buried beneath the futuristic concrete dome of the Subud ashram in Java; the 200 water buffalo, and our own boar, at the Toraja funeral; the black goat and the white cock slaughtered in *Sinar Surya*'s hull – all these seemed inextricably part of the human order, and unavoidably beyond the reach of animal rights. It was droll to find that even *Lindblad Explorer*, microcosm of the enlightened West, was itself no less free of the need to supply sacrificial goats! And here in Komodo, with the sophisticates of my own tribe, we were nailing another beast to the deck – and waiting.

I had seen Komodo Dragons before: a couple of stuffed ones in various museums, and a few dispirited five-footers in the zoos of San Diego and Jakarta. Both dead and alive they lay on their bloated bellies, their atrophied legs drawn close to their sides. They gave no hint of their wild cousins who now stalked down the riverbed towards our bait. These held themselves fully clear of the ground on thick and muscular legs, moving from their hips with the slightly stilted grace of Olympic weight-lifters. The two large ones in the lead were about eight and ten feet long, and their long orange forked tongues (with which they scent their prey) flickered in and out over the ground like flames – giving a strong impression of the fire-breathing dragons of legend.

They also smelt of death. Their mouths carry a virulent bacteria to which there is still no known antidote. It is their singular evolutionary adaptation which maximizes the use of their barely seventy square miles of territory, for a victim who may escape an initial attack with only a slight wound will within a few days fester and stink so strongly that it is easy for other Dragons to sniff it down with their forked tongues and polish it off.

The languidly approaching leading monster froze about ten feet from the bait. It raised its head higher still, then rushed and thrashed the goat once with its tail, before efficiently opening its belly with a single slash of its murderous jaws and swallowing down its intestines. A writing free-for-all ensued, with moments of extremely swift movement as the smaller Dragons nimbly sought their scraps, while avoiding the jaws of the cannibalistic superiors. The larger Dragons effortlessly sawed through spine and bones, engorging enormous wedges of meat. After each awful swallow they would look briefly and contentedly around them as if waiting for applause, before resuming their meal and finishing off hoofs, horns and polyvinyl rope with equal delectation.

It was long assumed that the Komodo Dragon was a scavenging carrion-eater, rather than a hunter, and that like most reptiles it was solar-powered, and inactive in the shade or at night. Both these myths were exploded by Walter Auffenberg, the enterprising herpetologist from the University of Miami who, between 1969 and 1971, made the most exhaustive study of the creature so far.[16]

He lived here for thirteen months with his wife and child, firmly establishing that the Dragons are both hunters *and* active round the clock, for it was after dark that his camp was raided and his family driven from their tent while the notorious male, which he labelled 34-W, feasted noisily on their clothes and sleeping-bags. Auffenberg also records observing his son being systematically stalked by two Dragons on the beach – and his exhaustive analysis of the island's eco-system clearly reveals how quickly the Dragons would have become extinct had they been mere scavengers – rather than true predators. From my first glimpse, they certainly stalked with the confidence of predators.

The following day I visited the riverbed again with another bevy of passengers and two experienced naturalists. Shortly, a large Dragon had no sooner appeared than it lifted the entire goat, tethering-stakes and all, out of the ground and made off with it. This was after the staff had been briefed that there had been customer complaints about being

175–177 Dragons enthusiastically devouring a dead goat

175

176

cheated of their rightful spectacle by Dragons that preferred to eat in private. One of the naturalists, the quick-thinking Robby Hernandez, now stunned us all by shinning down the tree, grabbing the trailing rope and yanking the bait from the astonished Dragon's jaws. Two of our local Komodo guides then scurried to help him stake the goat back in place again in full view of the passengers, while keeping the temporarily confused reptile at bay with long forked poles. I was much impressed by this selfless devotion to customer satisfaction, and Robby, still shaking, confessed he had been inspired by seeing another naturalist do the same thing on his first visit.

Six weeks later, when the ship returned with fresh passengers flown in to Bali on the second of her annual Indonesian cruises, I found myself leading my own party of about thirty people on the short walk to Loho Liang's dried riverbed. With us were Des and Jenny Bartlett who were coming along to film. We had waited for some time and were beginning to worry, when again perhaps the same large and solitary Dragon arrived, immediately uprooted our goat and disappeared behind the undergrowth with it. Sensing a chance to show off and liven things up a bit, I shot down the tree in hot pursuit. Out of sight of the others, I came across the stake and its nylon rope at the point of vanishing beneath some bushes. I gripped it and was dragged powerless into the full-body embrace of a thorn tree.

Held fast, like Gulliver, by every part of my body, I had a few still moments to contemplate the proximity of the unseen Dragon ahead, before realizing that barely twenty yards away behind me an entire gang of late-coming lizards were fast advancing. I debated the merits of tearing myself loose and leaving my skin hanging on the thorn tree, but despite my convulsions I remained firmly transfixed.

177

My act of showmanship had gone awry and, pilloried on this cross of briars, I howled for help. Eventually one of the Komodonese guides reached me and unshackled me, like a maiden in distress, barb by barb.

Des Bartlett, in the mean time, had descended and approached the opposite side of the undergrowth, where he had accurately located the thief, fooled the goat from its jaws, and marched back to the cheering crowd holding it triumphantly aloft, like Jason returning with the Golden Fleece. I am glad to say his heroic pose was short-lived, for hurrying up behind him on one side came the now distinctly irritated first Dragon, and on the other the guide and my bleeding self, hotly pursued by a swollen throng of hungry giant lizards. It was no longer a matter of how to stake the bait down again, but of who could get up the tree first – and it wasn't a pretty sight.

The advantage of this short walk to the riverbed at Loho Liang over the long walk to the elevated plains of Poreng was that the Dragons could be observed from the safety of a vantage-point above them. It is the longer walk, though, which really takes one into the heart of the island, and a fairyland of prehistoric beauty. The trees swarm with six-inch flying dragons, *Draco volans*, the lizards which unsheathe their wings and glide through the air. Beneath the towering Borassus palms, spreads a diorama of exotic vegetation, which is more reminiscent of the dry savannah lands of Africa than of Indonesia, with grasses and ferns and prickly palms, and the absurd Kapok trees, their shiny synthetic-looking trunks sporting clustered pouches bursting with fluffy white cotton. Bizarre butterflies flap through the slanting light of what looks like a museum display of the Cambrian age. Megapodus birds can be seen fussing with the thermal controls of their enormous incubating mounds. Green jungle fowl and drongos add their cacophony to that of Sulphur-Crested Cockatoos – the pure white parrots with vivid yellow retractable crests, which fetch well over a thousand dollars apiece on the open zoo market.

After a serpentine climb 800 feet to a ridge, the grasslands sweep down again to Poreng, the open valley where Dragons and their observers meet, if at all, face to face. Or perhaps posterior to face, as in our case, when filming alone on a later occasion; for the Dragons are drawn to the bait from all points of the compass and, while concentrating on the feasting Dragons ahead, others, unannounced, came upon us abruptly from behind. Some, not unnaturally, concluded that *we* were the source of the putrefying aroma – and it was tree-climbing time!

Once, on an independent expedition to the island, we found the two guides who accompanied us on the long walk almost as worrying as the Dragons. They had been so forcefully warned by the authorities of the consequences of losing another visitor to a Dragon that their fear of the beasts was hysterically contagious. At one point Lorne was prostrate on his belly, and at last had a superb monster in his viewfinder approaching him to within fifteen feet, when both guides cracked and, with the forked sticks they carried as an ineffectual discouragement to charging Dragons, began beating 'the one-eyed one' and his camera into the ground instead – much interfering with his usual good temper!

178

179

178–180 Escorting visitors from *Lindblad Explorer* to view the Dragons from a safe vantage point above the dried river bed

On the ridge overlooking the descent to Poreng stands the cross which marks the spot where the baron who had been on the first expedition accompanied by Wiesmar met his unpleasant end. The inscription reads:

IN MEMORY OF
Baron Rudolf Von Reding Biberegg
Born in Switzerland the 8 August 1895 and
Disappeared on this island the 18 July 1974
'He loved Nature throughout his life'

The precise circumstances of his 'disappearance' are tastefully absent from the inscription, on the principle that the whole truth is not necessarily good for tourism. The full irony of the baron's epitaph is only apparent on discovering he was a pioneering wildlife conservationist of considerable repute and, much as he demonstrably gave his life to nature, so, too, in the end, nature returned that love with a totally Darwinian devotion.

Wiesmar describes the tragedy as resulting quite simply from breaking the cardinal rule about never leaving the group.

'More useful,' he would tell us, 'if this cross say "Always stick together . . . then nature no love you back!"'

Although Wiesmar had been accompanying another group on the short walk to Loho Liang at the time, he did take part in the subsequent days of combing the island for the baron's remains, and he told us the story as he knew it. The baron's party had apparently reached the ridge and was about to descend the mere quarter of a mile to the valley below when the baron, breathing heavily, had insisted that the others go ahead while he rested and waited for them on the way back. He was clearly in view of the party at all times, and vice versa, until suddenly he was not.

Despite the extensive search, which turned up a good many aggressive Dragons, all that was ever found was close to the spot where he had last been seen, and where his cross now stands – his hat, his camera and a bloody shoe.

Though the baron is the most celebrated victim, he was far from the first, and no longer the most recent, human to be devoured by the Komodo Dragons. For, though they were late to awaken to science, they have not been dimmed by its light, and stalk their now protected island with, if anything, a swelling confidence in their immortality. Something of this self-confidence, and the razor's edge between it and my own, was vividly revealed to me only three months ago, when I returned to Komodo for the first time in years.

We were on a brief visit with a small film crew and our producer, David Fanning, to reshoot some final connecting sequences for our television series. The main purpose was to get more of Lorne and myself on camera at the same time – *with* the Dragons. I had looked forward to it for months, but the encounter itself was not as planned.

We island-hopped to eastern Flores and chartered a wooden motor-vessel with its local captain and crew to carry us through the riptides and whirlpools to Komodo. It was the captain who broke the disconcerting news that the island now boasted the 'Komodo Safari Hotel', built with the support of the World Wildlife Fund and inaugurated by the Indonesian president a few years previously.

The establishment rose from the beach just where the path for the 'short walk' to Loho Liang began. Approaching from a distance, its five elegant barnlike structures looked menacingly modern and opulent, and we could visualize it harbouring Margaritas and swimming-pools. But on closer inspection it proved to be a crumbing façade, and the sole inhabitants were the hungry and extended family of the management itself, who were overjoyed to see us.

We were led to a splendid-looking bungalow, on high stilts, which had disintegrated so rapidly since it had been built three years previously that it was far more dangerous than sleeping in the bush itself. The veranda, its main attraction, spread out twenty feet above the ground on rickety support-posts as a platform presumably intended for observing, drink in hand, a Noah's Ark of wildlife cavorting across the dustbowl below. Its planking was so rotten that we were in constant fear of plunging right through it, and its gaping holes suggested that other unquenchable nature-lovers had already done so. The Safari Hotel was clearly but a symbol of preservation – and had been built more as an offering to an idea than as a permanent edifice.

'And are there still Dragons?' we enquired of our eager toothy *maître d'hôtel*. 'Ah, yes, indeed,' he replied. 'Many more than tourists, nowadays. Try Loho Liang tomorrow? Many Dragons. Take a goat!'

'If there are many Dragons, why must we take a goat?'

'Better take a goat. Take this goat, only twenty dollars!' He pointed out a particularly rickety-looking beast from his gaggle of bleating billies scavenging beneath the tables of what passed as the dining-room.

We had known from previous experience that with a little time and care it was by no means necessary to kill a goat to find a Dragon. Circling birds of prey frequently revealed the site of a recent kill, their regular runs and dens are readily identifiable – and anyway they usually find you first. We had a few days, and decided we would try the dried riverbed without a goat.

The 'short walk' was no longer a narrow scrub-fringed game-track, but a tidy tended path sporting periodic signposts in jocular accurate English such as 'This way to the Dragons' and 'You are now entering Dragon territory'. The accuracy deteriorated as we progressed past humbler signs marked, in one instance, 'DRUGONS HAIR', as if the mysterious sign-painter had increasingly lost his mind the further he had receded from the coast. There were, however, only five of us, plus our two young guides from the Safari Hotel filing past the peeling paint, amidst as rich a profusion of life and sound as ever.

I began to feel unwell – nauseous and dizzy. Too little sleep, perhaps, too much excitement, or maybe I was over-confident, after so long an absence from Indonesia, about going hatless in the midday sun. The shrubs had grown, the topology changed, so I did not at first recognize the riverbank, where we had so often come, alone and with others, with and without goats – sometimes, but not always, seeing

Dragons. Our suddenly hurrying guides made so quick a turn that before we knew it we were through a metal gate and inside a barbed-wire enclosure which now squatted on the riverbank. With us in our pen were a row of wooden benches with sago-thatch sunshades and a concrete screen, marked 'Laddies and Genitalmen', with not so much as a hole in the ground behind it.

Extending over the bank was a carefully constructed little hoist with a pulley and tackle dangling a meathook.

We were regarding this with worried disbelief when we realized that up on the bank with us, leaning against the wires of our enclosure, at least seven goodly-sized *Oras* were quietly observing us. A few more now rustled stealthily out of the bush, and flicked their scent organs between the wires at us in fingering flames, drenching us with their foul breath. In the riverbed, directly beneath the mechanical goat-crane, at least nine more Dragons were awakening with interest from what had clearly been a long and patient sleep. I had never seen so many at one time, and behaving in such a curiously low-key fashion.

181 The graveyard of Komodo is fortified with cairns and chunks of coral to prevent the human remains from being unearthed and eaten by the Dragons

181

In this wild spot, where we had once seen Dragons in their pit below us, we were now caged ourselves – and surrounded by them. Visiting ships now brought goat-bearing visitors four or five times a year, and the Dragons were waiting to be fed. We had deigned to approach their lair empty-handed of an offering, and *we* were now *it*. Maybe it was because this was so *real* that I felt ill. Some part of my subconscious had finally caught up with me about the ridiculous way we had chosen to make a living.

We required two shots – one of myself descending the tree to within a few feet of the riverbed, and the other of both of us walking amongst the Dragons on their own level. We were anxious not to disappoint David, our producer, whose first visit this was to Indonesia, and who was so undemanding throughout that it was hard to avoid going down that tree.

I hung in the branches, as close to the ground as I dared, with the world swimming. Three healthy *Oras* immediately got to their talons, ambled over and salivated at me with a sickening stench of excitement. The largest sidled up, cocked his head a few feet beneath my boots, opened his mouth, and embalmed me with a rising miasma of suppuration. They say that few intelligent animals will look you directly in the eye. Dragons can certainly be added to that short list, for long and hard he held my bleary eyes with a chillingly knowing malevolence.

Those Dragons wanted my insides first, and then the rest of me, to *eat*, and as I hung there above this ravening gang my mind and weakening fingers gripping the tree very nearly released it all to them.

Eventually I managed to crawl up to the safety of our enclosure before collapsing into the shade.

'Great stuff!' David shouted encouragingly. 'Now let's have the real "ora-show" we came here for. We just need that shot of you two walking with them like Daniels in the riverbed.'

'Sprinting past them, you must mean?' Lorne queried. 'We've never seen so many together, and they're not their usual selves.' I heard this dimly through my sun-drenched brain, and knew I would still need another half-hour before I could even crawl effectively.

Carefully choosing our moment, we scampered out of the gate past the more sleepy sentries leaning lasciviously against our enclosure, and reached the riverbed via a circuitous route, to find the Dragons there had been fully aroused by my dangling meat. We trespassed towards them over the riverbed like a couple of tip-toeing cartoon coyotes, hoping to God our team was already filming us from their set-up on the other side. Lorne, who is not famed for his sartorial propriety, wore flapping safari-shorts – which sorely tempted the little Dragons to take a provisional peck at his exposed pink shanks. This was to be avoided, since the virulence of their bite is in no way diminished by their size. My own scent seemed instantly recognizable to the large Dragon I'd been baiting earlier on, and he advanced purposefully, flanked by his cronies.

The shrieked warnings of our guides from the bank above were hardly necessary. We were not anxious to have our stomachs opened and vacated like tins of Heinz spaghetti. But the Dragons converged and began circling and trying to cut off our retreat, angling their tails around in preparation for throwing a few leg-blows to knock us off our feet. We retreated back up the bank. Again and again we tried to walk amongst them for the shot we needed, and each time we were driven back again. The only reason the *Oras* didn't pursue us up the bank was because each time, at the last moment, they were drawn back by some magnetic charisma which appeared to be emanating from the dangling meat-hook. For a moment I wished it held the rickety billy-goat we had shunned at the Safari Hotel. When the Dragons got too close I comforted myself by picking up a large stone in either fist with which, endangered species or not, I intended to make at least one of them look like a panda if they made a determined lunge for me. Our guides must have enjoyed this little ritual enormously, for they later told me that even hurling huge rocks has not the slightest effect on a Dragon which has really decided to go for it.

We were beginning to despair of getting the shot we had come so far for and staked so much on, when out of the blue, off a local boat, appeared a young Irish couple, attractively fresh-faced and improbable, with a guide – and a goat! At the last moment our sacrifice had been brought for us – by two far-wandering unknown members of our own tribe. From a film-making point of view, it was as fortuitous as Abraham's discovery of a sheep in a bush. From a personal point of view, it was also a singular relief, for we could now approach to within five feet of the Dragons as they gorged and clawed and fought each other over the rapidly disappearing carcass.

But it was disturbing to find how much these animals seemed to have changed since we had first visited them, both as glorified tour guides and as independent film-makers. Rather as David Attenborough describes them on his 1950s zoo quest, they had been fairly difficult to locate, solitary hunters which, once found, tended to be shy or instantly ferocious. But now they appeared to have undergone a sinister evolutionary transition. They had become communal half-hearted welfare citizens, lurking lazily for months on the fringes of these spots where they had learnt that, sooner or later, dead or living food would come to provide their next free meal.

Back in the village of Komodo, the headman was to confess what the manager of the Safari Hotel had denied: that there had indeed been several human fatalities in recent years, one of them a young French tourist. He also reported that for the first time in decades Dragons had begun entering the village in the daytime, and only a month before one had taken a goat from beneath the houses at midday. Whether there were suddenly more of them, or whether they were simply more brazen, he couldn't say.

In that Dragon's eye which looked into me, as I hung precariously above it, I realized I had seen how old and strong is the Dragon's history – and how much of its history is mine. For long as we may have been humans, and Tarsoids, and mammals and fish, our longest dream was as reptiles.

Komodo lies there to remind us, right now, wherever we are.

8 Dance of the Warriors

South of Komodo, lying alone in the Indian Ocean well apart from the main chain, is Sumba island. About two hundred miles long by seventy-five miles wide, it has only one potholed track connecting the east to the west.

Early British charts still mark Sumba as Sandalwood Island – for the aromatic forests which once covered its hills. During those centuries when the privileged wore silks and damasks, sandalwood clothes-chests were valuable items – but the greatest demand for the fragrant timber was as incense in temples, mosques and churches from China to Europe.

The rolling grasslands left after the forests had been felled allowed Sumba's other great natural resource, the unique 'Sandalwood' horse, free rein. Small, feisty, nobly proportioned, resistant to tropical heat and disease as well as spectacularly sure-footed, they were much in demand by the cavalry regiments of colonial days. In Britain, specially designed ships were built to transport Sumbanese horses back across the Indian Ocean to India and South Africa as mounts for the Raj. These traders, however, dealt mainly with coastal merchants and feudal chieftains at the arid eastern end of the island, since the wild and desolate coasts of the west presented few safe anchorages.

183

Although the Dutch had claimed Sumba as their own for centuries, they made no attempt to colonize it until 1901. Eleven years later they declared that they had tamed the more blatant expressions of slavery and human sacrifice. During the forty years of Dutch rule, only a handful of administrators actually deigned to live on the island, and after the brief wartime domination by Japan they never managed to regain their control. Christian missionaries failed to convert more than 20 per cent of the population, and Islam, brought by the Arab horse-merchants, proved equally unattractive, and the vast majority of the Sumbanese still live by animist beliefs, ritually keeping the balance between the Merapu gods of the sky above, and Nyale, the Sea Goddess, of the world below.

The arid but more accessible eastern half of Sumba is recognized for producing some of the finest ceremonial ikat textiles of the Far East, whereas the verdant west of the island is known only to a few, chiefly for its unique 'Pasola' rite, which has managed to survive in two villages almost intact up to the present day. The Pasola is an annual war sport in which two teams of several hundred mounted warriors charge each other at a full gallop, hurling javelins from close range with intent to kill. The spectators, by being as legitimate a target as the warriors themselves, are really participants – for the Pasola, as we were to discover, is a veiled form of human sacrifice. . . .

Lorne and I had spent years trying to see, let alone film, the Pasola, and Lorne had already made one abortive trip to Sumba in the company of the remarkable Zac Saklofsky, who was one of the few outsiders to

182 A nineteenth-century textile embroidered with cowrie shells and antique beads from the kingdom of Pau

183 A sandalwood horse with its proud owner

have spent any time there. Travelling west from the arid Sumbanese capital of Waingapo, they had been profoundly impressed that the desolate tundra characteristic of the east so abruptly surrendered to emerald valleys and sweeping hills still topped with dense stands of sandalwood and cinnamon forest. They had talked excitedly of this hidden world, and of the granite megaliths weighing up to twenty tons used to seal the graves of dead nobles who were buried with their valuables including – up to only one hundred years ago – their freshly sacrificed horses and slaves. But, for all Lorne and Zac's enthusiasm, they had not been able to establish exactly when the Pasola takes place.

'It's up to the Ratus, the priests,' Lorne had reported sheepishly. 'They watch the moon and stars for a few months and then predict the one day a year when the beaches will swarm with wriggling seaworms. The arrival of the worms signals the start of the Pasola – and it is different every year. . . . But', he added, when he saw my sceptical expression, 'the chieftain of Wanokaka told us it *has* to happen in the first two moons of the year.'

In fact it wasn't until three years later that Lorne and Zac claimed to have pinpointed the exact day and made the appropriate arrangements, and I found myself taking a gruelling twelve-hour bus ride across Sumba towards an improbable-sounding rendezvous.

I hoped they knew what they were talking about, and that I was in the right island at the right time. There were three thousand square miles of territory up ahead of me, and fellow-passengers on the bus told me that no one drove this route at night, for mounted highwaymen armed with shotguns still preyed on it from their fastnesses in the forested hilltops just now coming into view. . . .

I'd been churning in the bus for about six hours, when it finally ground to a halt halfway across a dried riverbed, and we all had to get out to push it. I was straining away with my fellow-passengers when a jeep veered down from the opposite direction, thundered past in a cloud of dust, braked and reversed.

'You're late!' shouted Lorne from one window.

'And you're going the wrong way,' added Zac, from the other.

Disengaging my duffel bag from beneath the sun-stricken chickens and goats lashed to the bus roof, and forsaking my colleagues in the chain gang, I climbed gratefully aboard the jeep, which continued back in the direction from which I had come.

'So much for the two Pasolas only taking place during the first two moons of the year,' Zac announced. 'The first moon's barely begun and Lamboya held their Pasola three nights ago – the government forced them to do it early. Something to do with controlling the event.'

'We filmed it, by the skin of our teeth,' Lorne said excitedly. 'It was unbelievable – I've never seen anything like it! We saw one guy killed instantly. He was knocked off his horse by a blunt spear hitting him on the temple.'

I really hadn't thought it was still going on, and I was outraged at having missed it, but they told me a second Pasola, following the timing of the Ratu priests, rather than the government, was yet to take place in

Wanokaka, and the taboo month leading up to it started in five days.

'Then, why the hell are we heading back east?' I demanded.

There was a tense hush, then Lorne ventured, with heavy irony: 'Well might you ask. Zac has had a "psychic experience".'

'A what?' I expostulated. 'You are a rational man, are you not?'

Zac continued looking rather fixedly and uncomfortably ahead of him. He was a pragmatist, inclined to dismiss any sort of psychic phenomena, so his occasional lapses were to be taken seriously. Lorne explained what had happened.

Having filmed the Pasola two days previously, they were relaxing on the street-front veranda of the digs at Waikabubak when they had heard the news about Zac's greatest friend and benefactor on the island, the redoubtable eighty-five-year-old Raja of the fiefdom of Pau, in East Sumba, a fierce guardian of the island's traditions. A couple of textile merchants were just telling Zac that the old man had recently returned from medical treatment in Java with yet another sixteen-year-old wife, to the chagrin of his existing stable of spouses, when Zac, who had been idly scratching his neck, leapt up with blood streaming down his shirt and went indoors. Looking in the mirror, he told us, he had been horrified by the amount of blood still pouring from that tiny scratch, then much more disturbed by what he took to be the face of his old friend Raja Pau behind him. Zac had had two bad nights after that, and had woken up insisting on immediately heading east again to visit the old man in the brief interval between the two Pasolas.

It seemed like an exhaustingly ill-timed red herring to me, but we began the journey back to Waingapo, pausing at one of the infrequent petrol pumps and fruit stands. Unbelievably, the proprietor handed Zac a note, having obviously been asked to keep an eye out for a tall white man with a big moustache.

Zac read the note aloud, turning white with fright.

'Mr Zac, come quickly. Raja Pau died two days ago. You know just what time.'

Pausing in Waingapo just long enough to buy an ikat suitable for a royal funeral, we eventually clattered exhausted into Pau, only just managing to dodge the severed head of a horse on the track.

'Pau's favourite stallion,' said Zac. 'Its ancestry was as old as his. They used to kill off his whole stable, when the king died.'

A few yards from the main, high-roofed palace was a low building from which issued a chorus of gut-rending wails. The doorstep was the skull of a water buffalo, with horns spreading as wide as I had ever seen. Inside I discerned a triangular-shaped bundle, about four feet high, draped with a royal ikat. This was solemnly introduced to us as the late Raja Pau. His body was squatting upright – in Sumbanese burial pose – with his elbows on his knees and his palms on his cheeks – beneath not one, but dozens of superb ikats, representing the finest examples of antique royal Sumbanese weaving anywhere outside international museums. But these were to be used for their intended purpose; they would be buried with the Raja beneath a four-ton megalith.

As our eyes adjusted to the darkness, we could make out the throng

184

184 The entrance to Raja Pau's death-house

215

of family and royal retainers. Some squatted and wailed, softly and deeply in their throats. Others sat chewing rouged wads of betel nut, gossiping comfortably as if at the market. The dead Raja himself was flanked by two youths with little red and green flags brushing away the flies which were attracted to the rank and costly bundle, and to the offerings of food and cups of tea at its feet. He would be 'fed', like the Toraja kings of Celebes, every day, sometimes for many years, until his funeral could be properly prepared. Zac was greeted warmly by a number of his friends, who confirmed that Pau had indeed died at exactly that sunset time when Zac's throat had bled so profusely. Apparently the surgeons who had operated on Raja Pau in Java had failed to sew his throat up properly – and it had suddenly opened up again after his return home. In fact the reason why these normally secretive and suspicious East Sumbanese accepted us so readily was due largely to Zac's story having preceded us here. To them it indicated that a genuine connection existed between Zac and their late king, the great lover of their traditional arts.

The Raja's brother then formally introduced us to yet more ikated bundles with offerings at their feet, which we had missed amongst the shadowy crowd. This party was attended by three generations of unburied Paus squatting in the living room. There was his mother, father, brother, wife and sister-in-law. Some had been waiting for more than twenty years. Every time Raja Pau had painstakingly managed to assemble the required herd of sacrificial-quality buffaloes, the neighbouring Kingdom of Rindi had rustled them, forcing the postponement of the funeral yet again.

The Rindi explanation, as we heard it from them later, was that in the 1920s, when Pau's father had been a brash young chieftain, he had orchestrated the theft of the Rindi clan's most magical and powerful golden heirlooms. Until these were returned, the Rindis had sworn that no dead Pau would enjoy the pleasures, indeed necessities, of a proper burial. Since the treasures were long since scattered about the private collections and museums of the world, we were witnessing the perpetuation of an Edgar Allan Poe-like curse which seemed to have no end in sight. Our present host, heir to the much diminished family assets, but a still larger kitty of unburied remains, was too preoccupied with the present to anticipate the future.

'The last of our real treasures', he said, 'must be buried, not sold, with my family.'

'You mean those fine ikats draping them now?' Zac asked.

'No,' replied the new Raja, 'these ones.' In a corner of the darkened room he opened a large rattan basket, patina'd with age, containing hundreds of what Zac later described as the finest single collection of ikats anywhere in the world.

With permission we pulled them out, and filmed them, yard by shimmering yard. Layer upon layer of multi-coloured creatures danced on an indigo background. The pattern is dyed into the stretched-out warp threads before the textile is woven. A few threads at a time are tightly tied with grasses which will leave a pattern when the ikat is

185 Megaliths are still raised to honour the dead

186 Intricate ikat textiles such as these would accompany the dead raja into his grave

187 Three generations of Paus patiently awaiting burial

186

187

dipped in the dye. This is repeated many times. A four- or five-colour ikat, all of natural dyes, can take two years to produce, mainly due to the need to wait for the proper season for each of the required plants.

Certain patterns and symbols are the unique prerogative of specific kingdoms and clans, and experts can instantly detect where an ikat comes from. They differ from the family crests or tartans of Scotland, for instance, in that no two ikats are ever the same. Many of the symbols are also magical 'power-shapes', whose secrets are understood only by the elders of the clan, and jealously guarded from neighbouring households. It is through these powerful motifs that each clan maintains what it sees as its unique political and mystical contribution to the whole. The best ikats are not only powerful magical 'runes' but, like Buddhist or Hindu Tankas and mandalas, are also maps of a hidden cosmology.

It was a remarkable piece of good fortune to have seen these finest examples of the famed East Sumbanese art and much more than we had bargained for, but we were more concerned with what was about to happen in the west of the island. After a little difficulty in persuading Zac to tear himself away – for none of these ikats had ever been seen by outsiders – we withdrew from the scent of death, and the shadowy intrigues of the dwindling house of Pau, and headed towards our original destination.

Topping the final ridge before Wanokaka we entered one of the greenest valleys I have ever seen. About five miles deep and three wide, it swept down from lush hills to yawning wild beaches, contained between high cliffs. Here we were greeted warmly by the chieftain, Haba Kodi, whom Lorne and Zac had met three years earlier.

A slim and energetic man in his mid-forties, Haba Kodi was Christian for convenience, but an animist at heart, and a cosmopolitan type who had roamed as far as Java. He informed us with obvious pleasure that the previous year's Pasola had been a great success.

'We had only one death, but that was really quite enough, and anyway the omens were good.'

'You mean it doesn't matter if somebody dies?' I asked in surprise.

'Oh, it's not terrible if nobody dies, just better if they do. What is important is that enough blood is spilled.'

'Then, it's true that the Pasola *is* human sacrifice!' Lorne said with increasing interest.

'Not exactly. Not like the sacrifices we used to make for the Andung Tree.' Haba Kodi pointed to the bleached tree with truncated branches, propped upright in the village graveyard of megaliths.

'There was still a human skull on that when I was a child,' he said, 'but those sacrifices were *asking* the Merapu gods for something. The Pasola is different: in it we are offering *ourselves* to the gods, to be used in their task of keeping a balance between the Upper and the Lower Worlds.'

He pointed out that the entire valley was organized to reflect this duality, with the inland villages of Upper Wanokaka representing the Upper World, and the coastal villages of Lower Wanokaka represent-

188

189

188–189 All Sumbanese villages are built around the megalithic graves of their ancestors

ing Nyale, Goddess of the Lower World of the sea. The Pasola, in which these two sections of the valley fight each other, is not so much a reflection of the cosmic conflict, he explained, as an actual part of it.

He had arranged to have us stay in Puli, one of the most spectacular Lower World villages, close to the Pasola action, and overlooking a wild and sweeping beach, bookended with great green-topped cliffs. We were to spend two months there altogether as guests of the chieftain, Malira, and his wife, both hardworking rice farmers, part-time fisherfolk and horse-breeders, with whom we got on famously. The house we shared with them was tiny, and we slept cramped into little bunks around the central cooking fire, but it was as near the centre of things as we could have hoped for.

Our first exploration of the village revealed that every hilltop behind us appeared to be crowned with dark clusters of rocket-ships awaiting liftoff from alien launchpads. These were the high, pointed roofs of traditional Sumbanese houses, ringed by fortifying stone walls, and a clear reminder of the very recent days of neighbourly warfare and human sacrifice.

A spacious roofed-in porch ran all the way round the square foundations of the house. The gently sloping ceiling and intricately carved wooden pillars were almost completely covered with the jawbones of sacrificial pigs. The slightly raised central living area was reached by stepping over the skulls of four water buffalo – their horns spanning more than five feet across.

There are several floors of windowless attics above the main living area, beneath the high, steeple-like roofs. In the lower ones are stored the family's rice and working tools, while the highest are reserved for their most cherished treasures: the ceremonial ikats, totemic effigies, and gold jewellery beaten from the sovereigns once used by colonialist nations to pay for their sandalwood horses.

Almost every square foot of space between the houses was occupied by carved gravestones weighing many tons. Even my host had no idea how his forefathers had managed to drag them up to the hills.

'Since before my grandfather's day,' Malira told me, 'there's been no more room for them up here. We've been burying people under stones down in the flatlands since then. Even that takes a great effort to haul the stones ten kilometres from the sacred quarry.'

'Trucks must make that easier now?' I ventured.

'Oh, no! That wouldn't do at all. Once the blocks have been hewn from the quarries with the right ceremonies, hundreds of our friends must help us drag them on rollers. It takes many days, and we must give our friends much palm alcohol or they lose all their strength!' He went on to explain that the few people who had tried technological short-cuts had become the objects of popular scorn.

It wasn't long before we met the Ratus, mysterious, shrivelled old men, jangling with amulets. They crouched beneath the Andung trees, uttering incantations, and slitting the gizzards of live chickens to observe the omens in the fall of their entrails. They had been carefully observing the night sky for several weeks before our arrival, and now

190 The Ratu priests carefully observing the movement of the heavens to determine the correct day for the Pasola battle

191 Ornaments of gold beaten from sovereigns traded for horses and sandalwood

announced that the official month of taboo leading to the Pasola itself had begun. We were mortified to learn that this put the dramatic beach beneath the village out of bounds, for it would now become the most sacred piece of coastline on the island, and Nyale, the South Sea Goddess, would tolerate no swimming, fishing, levity or rowdiness until the Pasola began.

We slipped comfortably into the rhythms of Puli, crawling out of our hammocks each morning to the rhythmical pounding of rice, and to the operatic strains of our host's wife calling the pigs to breakfast, and lovingly feeding them, one by one, with individual ladlefuls of food. The village dogs were the politest we had met anywhere in Indonesia, but the probable explanation for such charming manners revealed itself at dinner that first night, with the arrival of a bubbling dish of chillied hound. The Sumbanese cuddle, pamper and eat their dogs with the same alacrity as they do their pigs and goats and chickens. We were in fact to eat more dog meat than anything else – it tasted somewhere between rabbit and goat, but richer in protein than either, and tended to make one sweat while eating it.

While we waited out the taboo month, we took sacrificial gifts of chickens, and our own questions, to the wizened Ratus who dwelt at the furthest reaches of the valley. We did not find them forthcoming, but they ate all our chickens with relish. We even tried riding the famous sandalwood horses, which were as game as ourselves, although our feet tended to drag along the ground, and on one occasion, while trying to persuade his mount to turn left, Zac was actually bitten on the foot by the horse.

Instead of a gradual build-up to a frenzy of anticipation, our community became more and more sleepy and withdrawn as the taboo month progressed. On the night preceding the Pasola, however, a strange fear seemed to grip everyone. We remained wakefully silent and crouching indoors, to avoid the spirit entities which prowled outside. Our household was electric with anticipation, with the family, like all their neighbours, reading chicken entrails and trying to remember if they had offended the spirit world over the previous year. Only the Ratus ventured out, those of the Upper World villages wandering downwards to be joined by those of the lowland villages to assemble

together on the beach. At the first hint of dawn, we all descended to join them and stood very still as the chief priest chanted to the fading stars.

'Nyale! Nyale!' the crowd began shouting, as the first rosy glow of dawn began creeping across the sea. But as I looked closer I realized the redness was more than the dawn – the seaworms were swarming, wriggling multitudes staining the beach with every wave. The high priest was the first to wander sedately into the surf to sample this 'gift of the Sea Goddess's body', and to announce its portents to the waiting throng. Our host whispered to us that from the colour and condition of the 'Nyale' – the seaworm and the Goddess share the same name – the Ratus could tell us what to expect of the coming rice harvest.

'If the worms are healthy and plentiful, it will be good year,' he said. 'If they fall apart at the touch, then enough rain can be expected to rot the rice on its stem. And if they are pitted and damaged, then a plague of rats or insects is probable, and we can take precautions in our planting methods.'

This year the worms suggested the latter diagnosis, but no one seemed too perturbed at the time, since the day of the Pasola was upon us. As soon as the high priest had given his verdict, the crowd rushed into the surf themselves to scoop up the seaworms in their cupped sarongs or woven baskets for a holy breakfast, which they quickly cooked over small driftwood fires and ate.

With a growing sense of excitement we joined the throng now climbing up to the Pasola ground, dramatically perched above and to the west of Puli. Several hundred magnificently bedecked horsemen were already cantering around in tight circles, working themselves and their mounts into a preliminary frenzy. This sweeping battlefield over-looking the Indian Ocean was edged with scattered burial megaliths, but these were now mainly hidden by a milling swarm of enthusiastic spectators who had gathered from miles around.

As we waited, a great hush descended and even the horses stood still. All we could hear were a few bird calls and the surf beating below. Suddenly, the two high priests of the Upper and Lower Worlds broke their ranks and galloped their horses at full speed towards each other into the centre of the field, waving their spears and invoking the energies they represented to come and join the battle. Then, with unexpected

192–196 On a signal from the high priests, two hundred armed warriors join battle

197 (over page) A pause in the battle after the first blood is drawn

violence they hurled their javelins from a distance of about fifteen feet – intentionally missing each other by a hair's breadth.

This was the signal for the battle to begin, and as they withdrew from centre stage they were engulfed as the first thunderous onslaught of spearsmen charged each other at the gallop, their vivid orange, red and green turbans and ribbons streaming in the breeze.

We had tried these horses ourselves, and seen them being ridden home through the fields, or next to the road, but now I realized something of what was meant by the spirit of the sandalwood breed. Small, but as heroically proportioned as the Arabian horses to which they are believed to be related, they moved, as unshod as their riders, with sure-footed exuberance. They were ridden bareback, and stirrupless, their riders gripping far forward with their knees, while manoeuvring expertly at full speed in unbelievably tight curves. Their bits and reins were mainly of hemp and cloth, rather than of leather – for they were very gentle-mouthed, and responded better to pressure from their riders' knees than from their wrists.

We could only film, change magazines and go on filming, as violent waves of warriors ebbed and flowed around the field, occasionally charging straight into the ranks of the spectators, tossing their spears with abandon. But after a while a pattern began emerging. For the most part, they rode in two great circles reflecting, it was explained to us, the orbits of celestial bodies. Only where the oppositely rotating circles converged, like the teeth of intermeshing cogs, did the warriors loose their spears at each other.

I saw a number of riders struck heavily off their mounts by spears, rolling into balls and being cantered over by scores of other horses. They then leapt to their feet and limped hurriedly off the field. Another man was knocked unconscious, and carried off almost triumphantly, only to come to again – rather to everyone's disappointment – and shout angrily for his horse, mount it and charge off into the fray once more. This was a true medieval pageant, and for the first time in my life, amongst the noise and blood and horse-sweat, I sensed something of those past centuries of warfare in which our own ancestors had fought on horseback to establish the national frontiers of Europe.

Thankfully there were periodic pauses, like those natural lulls in conversation, when everyone withdrew to catch their breath for a few moments, before beginning again. It was during one of these that the atmosphere was altered by the arrival of a dozen military jeeps and trucks, with armed soldiers bouncing around in them. Without announcing themselves to the chieftains or the priests, they took up belligerent postures around the field, and watched.

Lorne was satisfied now with the wide shots we had taken, and was eager for more detail. Perhaps feeling that the presence of the authorities would mitigate the custom of attacking onlookers as well as riders, he suggested we set up his tripod in the centre of the field, with Zac on second camera beside him, and myself reluctantly wielding the tape recorder and still cameras. We were barely installed, when a wall of howling spearsmen charged towards us. While Zac and I blanched and fumbled with the wrong buttons, Lorne contentedly glued his eye to the viewfinder and began shooting. Once the riders had passed, he was surprised to see three spears, closely grouped, protruding from between his camera's tripod. They had been hurled with such force that, despite their blunted ends, they protruded from the earth like well-grouped darts in a dartboard.

It was clear by now that these people had no trouble with accuracy, even at a gallop, so it surprised us that relatively few of them were actually hit. This was mainly due to their equal skill at avoiding the spears. They swerved and ducked, and swung almost from the bellies of their horses like the Red Indians of the cowboy films, and a number of them excelled at actually catching the incoming spears, or expertly deflecting them with their forearms.

Later we interviewed a number of the veteran riders, who insisted that when the government had decreed the use of blunted spears a few years previously the Pasola had actually become more rather than less dangerous. They explained that since the spirits were as satisfied by spilled blood as by a death, and as blunt spears provided little of the former, they had to concentrate on the latter, and therefore aimed directly at such spots as the temple or throat, where the blow alone could kill.

The Pasola continued throughout the morning, and well into the afternoon. Some blood was drawn, a few limbs were broken, but there were no serious injuries. The participants were all still enjoying themselves, when some of the soldiers began beating a horse and rider whom they considered to be out of control. The Ratus rode up furiously to intervene, and were abruptly pushed back by the uniformed officials. An ugly scene seemed on the verge of erupting, and although it resolved itself, and the Pasola continued, from then on the mood changed and the festiveness had gone.

Before the game had officially ended, we noticed the chief Ratus trotting surreptitiously away from the Pasola ground. Shortly afterwards, and long before the darkness which usually ends the Pasola, the crowd and the warriors alike began drifting back towards their fortified villages of the Upper and Lower Worlds. The balance between the two, and their deities, even if not between themselves and the brave new world, had been restored for another year.

The armoured jeeps and soldiers with their battered rifles pulled out past the column of homeward-bound cavaliers, overtaking their own chivalric history. Some of them jeered at a trio of late-departing and scowling Ratus – the priests who could tell, from the moon and stars, as they always had, just when those seaworms would swarm.

We had come to Sumba for a glimpse of our earliest beginnings, of megaliths and the origins of war, where a warrior still looked his opponent in the eyes, but we had found something more. It seemed there was no animosity here but, rather, a recognition that we are all participants in the interplay of light and darkness, order and chaos, reflected in the life-giving seasons of the planet itself, if we but knew how to interpret them like the Ratus.

198

9 The Dream Wanderers of Borneo

The summer of 1977 found us blissfully and impecuniously at home in the Balinese highlands. To the sound of the cicadas and the laughter of the village children taking their early-morning bath in our stream, we crawled amongst our charts and files spread out on the tiled ground floor, planning what was to be the silliest of all our Indonesian adventures. An insanely enlightened group of American investors had offered to finance our next film project, whatever it might be (within recoupable reason), and in Jakarta, only three weeks beforehand, we had bumped into Sutan Wiesmar, the Sumatran 'Whizz' of diplomatic paper-wangling whom we had come to know well in *Lindblad Explorer*. It was perfect timing. The Whizz was going to Borneo as a guest of the governor, he told us, to make a survey for Army Intelligence, and we were welcome to come along with him.

Borneo! Ever since childhood just the sound of its name had filled me with excitement. Headhunters, poison blowpipes, the 'Wild Man'. . . . It was about the last place I ever actually expected to explore.

The third-largest island in the world (after Greenland and New Guinea), Borneo covers an area more than twice that of the British Isles. The top quarter of the island is occupied by the two Malaysian states of Sarawak and Sabah, and the independent oil sultanate of Brunei, whereas the sprawling southern three-quarters is now Indonesian Kalimantan, a name derived from the Malay words meaning 'river of diamonds'. Kalimantan accounts for 20 per cent of Indonesia, but less than 3 per cent of her population – about 5 million people, some 4 million of whom dwell on the coast, in the handful of burgeoning oil and timber cities. The remaining million or so, the indigenous Dyaks of Borneo, live somewhere in the interior, beneath a barely explored forest which spreads wider than France.

Of some two hundred distinct Dyak tribes, virtually all of them, until very recently, were river-dwelling headhunters, with the mysterious exception of the nomadic Punan Dyaks, of whom remarkably little is known or written. They had always fascinated me.

Some time in the distant past they had withdrawn from the riverbanks, where the headhunters marauded, and struck out on foot to become the free-roving masters of the interior, the 'dolphins' of the forest, knowing every plant and creature by name and sound. The shyest, most jungle-wise of all the tribes, they wandered with the migratory seasons of their game, hunting monkeys and flying squirrels with poison blowdarts, spearing pig and bear, making instant shelters at night, and moving on at dawn; men, women and children, scrambling fast and silently through primary forest so dense that no other tribe could follow them. As time went on, the fierce riverine Dyaks began to value the Punans less for the prestigious value of their lopped-off heads than for their skills at obtaining inaccessible plant and animal products

199

200

198 The proboscis monkey of Borneo which, because of its long pink nose and silly face, the Indonesians call 'Belanda' – meaning 'whiteman'

199 Trophies from a head-hunt displayed in the longhouse

200 1940s photograph of head-hunting party subsequently gaoled by the Dutch

from the deep forest. Amongst the aristocratic headhunters it became rather poor sport to pick off a Punan – and almost bad luck. They were also thought of as a fey and ghostly people, barely human, rather like the pixies of Ireland. Some tribes called them the 'green people', and early Western explorers remarked that their very pale yellow skins, never exposed to the sun, did indeed reflect the forest green.

The official Indonesian position was that nomadic Punans no longer existed in Kalimantan – they had all settled down like sensible folk, and their children were now wearing shoes to school and saluting the flag. The Whizz, however, was convinced that there were still wild Punans living in the interior – and that we might be able to find them.

Kalimantan represents a kind of Everest for the independent explorer. The military severely restrict travel passes and film permits, and just getting there is a logistical nightmare, with poor odds on returning, if at all, with anything on film of sufficient value to justify the effort. When questioned about permits the Whizz was surprisingly nonchalant.

'No problem with permits. I'll get them in three weeks. I'm Army.'

'I thought you were Student Union!' I said sternly.

'Student Union, Tour Leader *and* Army,' the Whizz replied, brandishing and quickly concealing again a number of battered but alarming-looking badges and identity-cards.

Examining our charts on the floor in Bali, we began to realize what an awesome undertaking a search for the Punans might be. This would certainly be our first large-scale expedition, and we would have to be responsible for a lot more than ourselves. The most striking thing was how little difference exists between the earliest and the most modern maps of Borneo. Only the shape of the coastline has changed, but the interior still remains astonishingly blank.

I now produced an encouraging paper I had found, by an anthropologist named D. B. Ellis, who in 1972 had spent some time in Malaysian Sarawak amongst a group of now sedentary Punans (or Penans as they are called north of the border) attempting to learn from their elders something of their migrations within living memory. They had told him that several decades earlier they had broken away from a group of their kinsmen which they believed still wandered in Kalimantan somewhere on a line between the coastal town of Samarinda on the east coast and Long Nawan nine hundred miles away in the highland interior. Right in the middle of this imaginary line, according to our latest edition of the International Aviator's Chart, lay a large empty patch representing an area 350 miles long by 200 miles wide, its virgin whiteness marred only by a few hesitant dotted lines hinting at the presumed courses of jungle-hidden rivers and the boldly printed 'RELIEF DATA IRRECONCILABLE', which is the modern equivalent of 'HERE BE DRAGONS' or 'HERE YOUR GUESS BE AS GOOD AS MINE, CHUM'.

We hoped we could learn more from people in Samarinda itself.

It was to be three exasperating months, mainly spent haggling for permits between Sydney and Jakarta, before – much poorer than we had begun – we finally ground to a halt on the heat-shimmering airfield of Samarinda. The beauty of her name belies the town's dark history of

201

201 Sutan Wiesmar, our mysterious Sumatran companion

202 A collection of Dyak weapons

piratical sultans and internecine blood-letting, though much of its flavour emerges in Joseph Conrad's steamy masterpiece *Almayer's Folly* (1895) for which Samarinda was the model. Crumbling Dutch colonial mansions and exotic Chinese temples crowned the low hills, which gave way to rambling bougainvillaea and wild vegetation descending to the stilted homes at the river's edge. Nobody here had the slightest clue as to what might go on in the deep interior.

Although the Chinese unquestionably traded with Borneo for rhinoceros horns and hornbill ivory before Christ, the first outsiders in more recent times were Malay and Chinese pirates who were attracted to the coastal rivermouths by the funeral canoes of the inland Dyaks which came floating downriver with headless corpses, accompanied by their treasures of beads, gold and even diamonds. Yet efforts to ascend these rivers to the source of the wealth were for centuries thwarted by the fierce tribes which ruled them. Today, there are still no roads into the interior, and the only means of access remains the great rivers, now controlled by a handful of frontier barons. They now float downstream not the valuable corpses of their dead, but jungle trees by the million to container ships waiting in the rivermouths. The great headhunting tribes – the Iban, the Kayan, the Kenya – were the sophisticates of their race. They forged their own bronze and gold jewellery, and filigreed steel 'mandaus' – the decapitating-swords of Borneo. They also developed unique forms of musical and artistic expression, and these most creative exponents of their culture were also the first to succumb to the great bore of change which is rolling up the very rivers they once ruled.

We checked into a naked-lightbulb boarding-house on the waterfront, changed our clothes, and set off up the hill with Wiesmar to present ourselves and our permits proudly to his friend, the governor of East Kalimantan. Unfortunately, communications had somewhere gone awry, and the present incumbent was a brusque stranger, in a spotless safari-suit, smelling heavily of Cologne. He glanced at our papers, which contained the signatures of at least fourteen separate government ministers and department heads, and tossed them back to us.

'Don't these ministers *know* there are no more nomads left in Kalimantan?' he asked with some vehemence. 'What century are they living in? You're wasting your time. Look!' He pointed out of his broad window overlooking the bay. 'See all those floating trees being loaded? The Dyaks are all doing better cutting those down now than wandering around. They're all working for Sumber Mas now, the biggest timber company round here!'

'Then, we'll film the highest timber camp on the river,' Wiesmar announced archly. 'And we'll show the world what a good job our nation's doing. How do we get up there?'

'I haven't a clue,' the governor told us. 'I've never been, thank you. But I can tell you it's easier to get the missionary pilots to fly you in than to persuade those secretive Chinamen to take you. But you'd better be a very powerful Christian, or very sick. . . .'

With these discouraging words we returned to our lodgings for the night, and resumed the customary procedure of terrorizing the bedbug

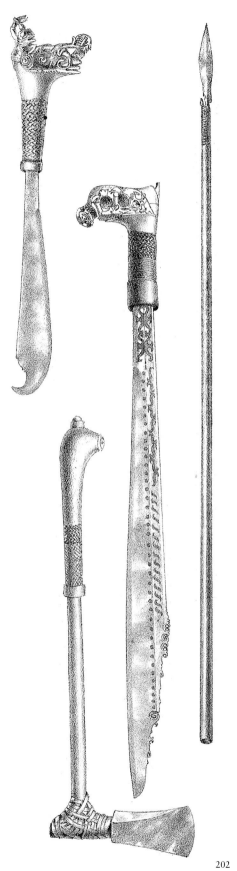

202

community by tiptoeing into the darkened rooms, violently ripping the thin kapok mattresses off their plank frames, switching on the light and quickly flattening as many of the scuttling multitudes as possible before they vanished between the cracks. The few inevitable survivors would exact a bitter revenge on us during the night in order, it would seem, to spawn parthenogenetically their entire tribe again by the morning.

The mission pilot was away, but the Whizz's brazen manner, battered identity-badges and silver tongue now worked wonders with the local timber lords, and we were shortly aboard one of their powerboats and roaring hundreds of miles westwards along the Mahakam river and then northwards up its tributaries to where various logging camps were scattered along the southern edge of the big white patch on our chart, which Wiesmar had christened 'Punan Putih' – 'the Punan White'. But at each of these moonbases of heavy machinery and deafening trauma, at the very shores of the unknown, we found ourselves as isolated from our nomadic Punans as if we'd been back on the coast. Even here, few people knew anything about them, and the local populations of riverine Dyaks, newly hypnotized by the rewards of aiding and abetting the slaughter of their environment, were neither interested in nor capable of taking us inland on foot. We got a number of responses about the Punans: 'All gone'; 'Cannibals'; 'Sure they're back there, where nobody goes'; 'You mean the Orang-Utans?'

Where we could, we commandeered the powerboats and explored deep up the other tributaries bordering on the Punan White searching for guides or ways inwards. Our pilots shattered our propeller shafts on submerged obstacles, our welcomes with the logging lords waned, and yet again we found ourselves forced to return to where we had started, taking the 600-mile two-week downstream chug on the regular river-bus system to Samarinda, packed cheek by jowl with livestock and

203 Our last powerboat ride for a very long time

204 The curling horns of the forest gods distinguish a storehouse of the Kenya tribe

203

humans, all patiently rotting beneath permeable tarpaulins in thundering rain. I decided to comfort myself by catching up on my already disintegrating Borneo research material. As a tonic, it was a mistake.

The only way to get *in* to Borneo is during the rainy season, when the inland tributaries are swollen enough to be navigable. Between downpours, this is also Insect Time. There are appalling accounts by the early explorers of the hostility of Borneo's insects. Phenomena like the Ant Marches, when glistening rivers of warrior ants, eight miles long, hundreds of yards wide and a foot deep, arise from apparently nowhere, consume everything in their path, then mysteriously dissolve again, are credited as being one of the main reasons for Borneo's long isolation.

Back in Samarinda, four months after we had called our investors from Sydney to tell them we were heading back to Jakarta and thence Borneo the following day, we rustled up one last desperate chance.

Sumber Mas, the dominant monopoly, was Wiesmar-warbled into taking us 300 miles west along the infernal Mahakam again, then 150 miles north up the Belayan river, to the remote seedling logging camp at Tabang from where it was the shortest direct line – just 200 miles – across the Punan White to Long Nawan. If we could cover the distance, even if we didn't see a single nomad on the way, at least we could return with a film about a lost tribe which remained lost!

204

It would be a dangerous gamble, so before leaving Samarinda we decided to visit Ted, the mission pilot for Christ. Tall, stooped and awkward, Ted was remarkable for combining a distinctly hazardous profession with a singularly narrow world-view. Despite his and his teenage wife's three years of residence in their box-like billet, not a thing in their living-room gave any clue that we were outside Kentucky. Their walls were bare, and the bookshelf contained only a bible and flying magazines. We distrusted each other on sight. His charter was to ferry Church bigwigs and occasionally sick Dyaks around the island, though he was occasionally prepared to moonlight for an exorbitant fee.

'Never heard of the Pooh-nans,' he told us. 'They're all natives to me. I do an occasional run up to Long Nawan. Never been into the village, though – just drop 'em off at the airfield, fly back in time for supper. I know what they're like. Here,' he said, 'look at this.' He showed us a cutting from a Singapore newspaper which was taped to the fridge, and the only visible sign of decoration in the whole house.

It reported an industrial quarrel in the major coastal town of Balikpapan, when the picketing Dyak employees of a Javanese-owned sawmill had not merely assaulted their white-collar management, but separated a number of them from their heads.

'There's your Pooh-nans for you,' he commented. 'Give 'em a head start, and they start taking yer head.' He was amused by this little crack, and nearly laughed. We brayed quite loudly, partly because we needed his help, and partly at the news that, contrary to official assertions, head-hunting in Kalimantan was not entirely a thing of the past.

'We've got to walk through the big white patch, Ted,' I told him. 'Are you sure there isn't anywhere you could put down for us in there, if things don't work out?'

When we produced our International Aviator's Chart he laughed.

'It's all wrong, you know,' he said. 'Here, look at mine.' He unfurled his own well-crumpled and doodled-upon copy, and pointed at several pencilled crosses in the big white. 'There's only about two usable landing-spots in here and they're usually out of the question in the rainy season. They open them up, and they grow over or sink all the time. Maybe they're building another one round here, somewhere.' He pencilled a circle in the heart of the white patch.

We were puzzled. 'You mean they just sprout in the jungle like mushrooms?' Lorne asked.

'Don't you know?' he said. 'It's a good system. We send the native evangelical scouts in to reach the remote pagans on foot, like you foolish characters. They pray with them, tell 'em what they're missing in life, and leave them exact instructions on how to flatten an airpatch. Length, flat as the river, and all that. I check them every few months to see if they're safe enough to land on with preachers.'

He said he could not promise anything, but would make some fly-bys if he hadn't heard from us in Samarinda or Long Nawan in two months' time. On that cold comfort, we prepared to leave, but he called our attention back to his chart.

'About there!' he said, squinting forward again, triangulating with his plastic instruments, and he drew yet another neat crucifix in the white void, with a longitude and latitude which I quickly cribbed. 'There's a waterfall,' he said with some excitement. 'Coming off the Apo Kayan plateau. Looked like heaven to me. Drops sheer to the Mahakam jungle – minimum fifteen hundred feet high. That ranks near Angel Falls in Venezuela, amongst the highest in the world. But it ain't marked on any map, and nor is its river. Keep a look out for it if you're in the neighbourhood. I'll keep an eye out for you, too. Thursdays is the only day you can expect me, but I'm not risking any hairy landings.'

Three and a half days of breakneck river-travel brought us to Tabang, a handful of Kenya longhouses adjacent to the hastily built timber barracks. The following day a group of seven alert-looking Punans swept into town in their dugouts. They were the first we had ever seen, and we delightedly accosted them before they had barely set foot on the bank. Leah, their leader, was to become a closer friend than we could have imagined. They laughed a lot, spoke a slow and thoughtful Indonesian, and looked us directly in the eye. They were the semi-acculturated cousins of the wild nomads – weathering the tide of progress better than any other of the island's tribes. These free-ranging amphibians rode the bow-wave of change; as equally at home in the deep forest as with their wives and gardens at Tabang, they were sophisticated travellers and linguists. When they tired of the frontier villages, they could return to the more rewarding skills of hunting bears, pythons, and the valuable bezoar stones from the crops of monkeys, and collecting aromatic and medicinal plants.

Yet even they were not sure whether their pure nomadic cousins still existed. If anyone knew, Leah told us, it would be Bereyo, a renowned old Punan rhinoceros-hunter who apparently lived a six-day scramble through the forest away in the longhouse of Long Belinau, on a river system which, enticingly, was no longer marked on our map. On the understanding that the old rhino-hunter might well have gone 'walkabout' by the time we arrived, Leah then set about inspiring his colleagues to lead us in at least as far as Long Belinau, for a small fee. They would take us no further, as they would have to return to their families, but at least we would be going in the right direction. . . .

205

Wiesmar was now wearing his paramilitary costume, topped incongruously with an Aussie bushman's hat, and sported a revolver in his belt. It was a dismaying symbol of authority, and a number of our porters came close to resigning with indignation on the spot. We gave him yet another opportunity to return home and leave us to our private madness, but we could see the glint of nineteenth-century empire-building in his eye, and nothing would dissuade him from continuing with us. He managed to talk Sumber Mas into providing their outboard-powered dugout to take us the four hours upstream through the rapids to where the Belayan Falls made it impossible to continue by boat. It required two journeys to take what were by now eighteen of us, so half went ahead in the afternoon, with the straggling porters and the rest of the equipment joining us the following morning. During those few sunlit hours waiting for the rest of the team to arrive, I experienced one of those rare moments which seemed more than to compensate for the entire effort thus far. We were filming clouds of butterflies, attracted to the uric acid left by drinking animals at the water's edge. Our technique for screen-filling close-ups was simple, and periodically effective, even if it did have our Dyak companions in hysterics. I would lope around with my home-made butterfly-net in one hand, and in the other our medical kit's aerosol freeze-can, intended for anaesthetizing sprained muscles. A brief blast would instantly freeze an insect or a small reptile long enough to focus on and film it before the sheen of ice left it and it obligingly hopped or flew off screen. We were actually talking about the Raja Brooke Birdwing, one of the most coveted butterflies in all Borneo. Being a denizen of the high canopy, it is so rarely seen in the wild that it is bred in captivity for high-paying collectors. It was first caught and catalogued by Alfred Russel Wallace, who named it after his host and friend in Sarawak, the British Raja Brooke. Wallace's memorable description in *The Malay Archipelago* of first catching its closest cousin, *Ornithoptera croesus*, rang clear:

206

The beauty and brilliancy of this insect are indescribable, and none but a naturalist can understand the intense excitement I experienced when I at length captured it . . . my heart began to beat violently, the blood rushed to my head, and I felt much more like fainting than I have done when in apprehension of immediate death. I had a headache the rest of the day, so great was the excitement produced by what will appear to most people as a very inadequate cause.

205 Leah, who would lead us to the Rhino Hunter

206 An anthropologist's nightmare! Our own porters decided they would dress up as wild Punans for our benefit. Asun wears the kettle-spout nose

I had seen them in photographs, and a few dusty corpses in display cabinets, but now amidst this flittering carpet of Lepidoptera I thought I saw the real thing. Barely ten feet away, with a vivid red collar, and seven-inch blade-shaped wings of deepest black slashed with bars of iridescent green, was a monstrous Raja Brooke Birdwing. I was as frozen as if struck by my own freeze-can. Then two more alighted, and a fourth swirled by. I stalked a step closer, and they soared upwards – real fliers, rather than flappers. With my heart in my throat I hunted them, to our porters' increasing delight, for ninety minutes.

Then to my disbelief, and to a rousing cheer, I netted a perfect adult. Lorne hovered close with the camera, I froze it (perhaps, I thought, too enthusiastically for its own good) and unveiled it, at which it instantly ascended to heaven. Within a few seconds it swooped downwards again and I swiped it out of the air. We froze it more vigorously, shot some film, and then released it. As the ice-sheen left its wings, it quivered for a few moments, then flew up to the tree-tops again – an hallucination which has somehow remained captured on film.

Our expanded party now included the surprise of Leah's nine-year-old nephew, M'bau, who was to eat, walk and talk the rest of us off our feet. Fourteen porters might seem rather excessive, but half of them were needed to carry the rice required to feed us all on the planned two-week journey. The rest carried out 'movie chattels' and quantities of salt, which in the iodine-poor interior is the best currency.

The Dyaks went barefoot – for balance and for sensitivity to the terrain, they said. We set off in single file up the jungled escarpment at an Olympic pace. Our companions carried an average load of eighty pounds each – more than twice the international airline allowance. Everything, including whole ice-chests of film stock, was strapped to their backs in rattan baskets, leaving their arms free for balancing, climbing and cutting a swath with their mandaus – the distinctive machetes of Borneo, which we were warned to carry at all times. We three novices, in our canvas United States Army jungle boots, and carrying only our mandaus, had a devil of a time keeping up with them. We panted so hard that we couldn't even talk to each other. M'bau, like a leprechaun, clambered jauntily upwards singing to himself, examining things closely, doing cartwheels and splashing in the mud where terrain permitted, suddenly shouting at us from the tops of boulders or the forks of trees, and showing not the slightest signs of fatigue.

After a gruelling first day we reached the top of the ridge, where we had our first experience of what it would be like to sleep in the jungle proper. Our companions had it down to a fine art. Entirely from scratch, and within twenty minutes, they built an elegant bungalow large enough for us all. It required three particular trees: pliable saplings for the frame, firmer supports for the slightly raised floor platform, and a forty-foot tree for the flooring itself. This particular species was felled solely for its bark, great tubes of which were unfurled to provide a seamless floor-covering whose top side made a spongy mattress and whose underside oozed a noxious insect-repelling sap.

'Very lucky you bring this big sheet of plastic,' Leah said, referring to the item which Wiesmar had liberated from the timber company to protect our equipment, and which we now saw had been unpacked to

207

208

207 Both a grave-marker and a warning to outsiders, this indicates we have entered Kenya tribal territory

208 Leah's intrepid nephew, M'bau

209 The Raja Brooke BirdWing butterfly, a good omen for our quest

210 The Punan guides don't pitch camp, they build a house from scratch every evening, and abandon it again next morning

210

cover our Jungle Hilton. 'Without that, it takes twice as long to make a house. The trees with the big leaves for the roof are harder to find.'

We reserved a section for our most perishable gear, ensured that Wiesmar was satisfied with his 'master nest', observed the equitable democracy with which our party established their sardine-like sleeping positions, and retired to our own arrangements, into which we had put considerable thought in advance. The seamstresses of our village of Pengosekan had produced two enormous banana-shaped mosquito-nets, which could be attached to the ropes of our magnificent Yucatecan 'matrimonial' jute hammocks. Topped with tarpaulins, these baroque tensegrity structures were ingeniously suspended on a number of in-dependent wires. Assembling them required locating the appropriate pair of trees, cutting a number of correctly proportioned 'spreaders', and a certain clear-headedness. The first two requirements abounded, but assembling these aerial mobiles before darkness or exhaustion set in became a sort of malarial nightmare.

But here, this first night on the jungle ridge, our companions breathing contentedly in the instant longhouse next to us, I remember sinking exultantly into the arms of the night music, suspended in my muslin cocoon. Things flashed and flickered around me in the dark. I felt like the pioneering oceanographer Professor Piccard, cosy in his deep-submersible bathyscaphe, 12,000 feet down in the sea. And I slept.

At first light, my feet felt numb, and my hammock was stained with blood. Three black leeches, like enormous ticks, were burrow-ing between my toes. A fourth, also swollen like a chewing-gum ball, nestled behind my earlobe, and several more were optimistically tightrope-walking down my hammock rope towards me. . . .

They had sensed us from the ground, climbed the supporting trees, descended the hammock ropes, wormed their way through the folds of the 'banana's' tightened drawstrings, and made it to the lunch-counter. The tortuous brilliance with which these little suckers achieved their goal was a disquieting indication that, evolutionarily speaking, they were a very far cry from the blind worms I had imagined them to be. We were to encounter multitudes over the months that followed, some areas being so infested that we would have to struggle on in semi-darkness before pitching camp. In some places, if we stopped for a moment, they would detect our rising warmth and drop down like rain.

We abandoned our instant longhouse and moved on. On one side of the ridge, immediately below us – and seemingly only a stone's throw away – lay the ruffled ribbon of the Belayan river, which it had taken all the previous day to struggle up from. On the other, rolling for ever into the haze, were the untouched jungled hills of the Big White. We left the ridge, and any links back to the safety of the outside world, and submerged beneath the unremitting canopy of the deep forest.

For six days we struggled in single file, through vegetation so thick that we could never see more than two or three companions before and behind us. Leah spearheaded the column, hundreds of yards ahead of us, while the three novices slithered and panted near the tail where the ground had been pretty well cleared by the time it was our turn.

At night, round the dwindling cooking-fire we would question and listen to their forest stories for those all-too-brief moments before we surrendered to exhaustion. They talked of Bereyo the Rhino-Hunter, a legend for many rivers around, and of how much gold he had once been given for his rhino horns by the Chinese merchants. Wiesmar hung back from these sessions, aloof, exhausted, in a sort of trance, but at the mention of Bereyo's gold he jerked visibly into greater consciousness.

On the sixth morning we reached the Belinau river, and found the rather astonished Bereyo in magnificent residence. At first he was wary, but he had not seen his wandering cousins for more than twenty years and was intrigued by the idea of finding out how they were doing. After we had spent a few days as his guests, Bereyo decided he would lead our search, a journey which he said might take twenty-five days.

'Difficult to hunt and find in rainy season,' he told us in halting Indonesian. 'First we hunt deer, and harvest our rice to feed us all for long journey.' This was a relief, since we now had supplies left for only another week.

Two of our new party were the impressive Hidjau and Raja, master trackers and blowdart hunters, and without them we would probably not have survived. Leah and the boys also changed their mind about leaving us here and going home when they heard Bereyo would be leading us, and his community providing free food.

Young M'bau remained with his mother in Belinau, and with six canoes and a party of now twenty-two people we embarked on an even more demanding journey, beginning with three days' poling our way upstream against a boiling current.

'Modiking', as the technique is called, is an impressive speciality of Borneo's riverine Dyaks, in which, working to a single and perfectly poised rhythm, five to ten standing men punt their way upriver. It is wet and frighteningly precarious. The bows must be kept directly pointing into the current, and the most dangerous moments are at the riverbends when one must 'tack' from one side to the other. As one porter observed with skilled understatement: 'If we turn over and get this lot wet, it'll take a whole week to dry out, won't it, Tuan?' We were ordered on no account to move a hair, and we crouched with our passports and money in our pockets, our cameras and tape-recorders on our trembling knees – even when they had to get out to haul the canoes ahead over boulders. It was in the wicked inland rivers of Borneo's rainy season that so many other expeditions had come to grief. But our team propelled us with the dexterity of surfers to where at last the river was too shallow for us to proceed, and we tethered our canoes for whoever might need them, striking out on foot again behind Bereyo the Rhino-Hunter.

Bereyo was proud and humorous, and was treated like royalty by everyone except Wiesmar (who was Sumatran royalty, and treated him almost as an equal), but he was usually so far in the lead that we hardly ever saw him during the day. By the time we caught up with him at the rest-stops he had already been there for half an hour and was ready to move on again, while it was our turn to rest and remove leeches until the person immediately ahead of us followed his leader onwards. Thus our

211

212

211 Bereyo, the Rhinoceros Hunter, gathering his dry rice before our long walk inwards

212 Bereyo in evening dress, with his best blowpipe

239

213 Bereyo, with our best hunter, Hidjau, mixing poisons for the blow-pipe darts

213 Bereyo, with our best hunter, Hidjau, mixing poisons for the blow-pipe darts

214 The occasional whisky-coloured rivers, which we all had to stop and swim in for their alleged medicinal properties

whole party moved through the forest like a giant leech, contracting at points of rest, and extending itself onwards again, for what would be twenty-five days before we saw another human being.

Our guides and providers, teachers and playmates, house-builders and cooks – for they were all of these and more – were also as responsive to our inquisitiveness as they were alert to our general welfare.

'Never touch that,' they would say, indicating an innocuous-looking green shrub. 'Cannot see its teeth – but bites like red ants.'

Or: 'Quickly, this way! Never get closer than ten men to those.' It was a bulbous brown swelling on a bulbous barked tree – a nation of sleeping bees condensed to a camouflaged nucleus a yard across. 'Very bad-tempered when they wake up. Whole travel-parties have been killed by bees.' The man in front grinned back at me.

The terrain was far more treacherous and the pace faster than anything we had yet experienced, and as the days progressed we discovered how varied were the ecological islands hidden beneath the forest, and how different from the monotonous 'green hell' so often used by foreign travellers to describe the jungle. We crossed deep gorges and roaring whisky-coloured streams balancing along the slippery skins of immense fallen trees. Sometimes these were so rotten that we would halt for a while to fell our own arboreal bridges. We crossed quagmires, expertly disguised as firm land, hundreds of yards across, tiptoeing along gangways of freshly felled saplings which gradually sank. The least-experienced went first, for the last would be up to his knees.

There were eerily dark freshwater pools, where we harvested bamboo shoots, asparagus-like water plants, the first edible vegetation we could reach, which, even when boiled, tasted like bitter raw cabbage.

I saw these again, I thought, by a smaller, clear stream, but was dragged away by a Dyak who pointed out numerous tiny transparent globules clinging to the reeds like glistening droplets of resin. He held his hand over them and they extended towards it like watercress sprouts. These were the disagreeable thread-leeches, which prefer to suck your blood from within and can infest the mouths, nostrils, lungs and oesophagi of unwary drinkers – to say nothing of the urogenital linings of careless splashers.

On one rare occasion I was actually within a few yards of Bereyo when I noticed a colourful confident little twelve-inch snake, coiled in the loam watching us.

'What is it?' I asked him.

'A snake!' he replied with an air of authority.

'Yes, but is it a dangerous one?'

He came back a few paces, hunkered down and squinted closely, then to my amazement began jumping up and down on it with his bare feet, rendering it quite flat.

'Yes, very dangerous. It can bite people dead.' And he moved on.

At night round the camp-fire, while Hidjau and Raja meticulously fashioned their blowdarts and mixed their venoms, and Wiesmar lolled in the shadows, Bereyo would enthrall the company with his stories. He told of being a child in Sarawak across the border, and having to flee

213

with his parents from river-borne war-parties of head-seeking Ibans. He described a hidden highland lake, where he and a few companions had watched under a full moon while five or six enormous pythons, so aged that their markings had been replaced by a silvery grey, 'danced together' round and round in the water. 'Old snake religion,' he said, 'maybe dancing for Aping, the forest god.'

He was asked about rhinos.

'Sometimes three moons we travelled, just five of us, tracking one rhino. He knows we follow him. He has strong "dream wanderer". Very difficult.'

I whispered to Lorne that rhinos were supposed to be very sensitive to vibrations, but that 'dream wandering' was not in the literature.

'He hears our soft feet on the ground,' Bereyo continued, 'from many rivers behind him. I look in his dirt, and talk to him. Tell him where to go, so we corner him. "You need more bamboo shoots," I tell him. "You love them. Head east, O Rhino, to the bamboo forest at the end of the Deng gorge." Or: "River roots, Rhino, so sweet, so tender – go back a bit, for a week or so, towards the trap where the great rivers meet." We can only kill him when he turns towards us in anger.'

'How do you kill him, Bereyo?'

'I used to kill him with a spear, in eye or ear or mouth. But Bereyo is a "modern man" now,' he said, thumping his chest. 'I take a gun.' Closer questioning revealed this to be a sawn-off double-barrelled shotgun, which he had left hidden in his longhouse at Belinau.

'He's talking about *Rhinocerus sumatrensis*,' I remarked to Lorne, 'of which the World Wildlife Fund says there are only about a hundred and seventy left anywhere, and only twenty-five of those in Borneo!'

'How many have you killed, Bereyo?' Lorne asked him.

'Last year, one!'

'No, altogether . . . how many?' the others chorused.

The old man leant back and wrinkled his face for a long while, then he splayed the fingers of both hands five times.

'Round about . . . *fifty*,' he announced at last with satisfaction.

'Fifty!' I spluttered. '*Our* people, who fly aeroplanes and things, say there are only twenty-five of them left!'

'Maybe those white men walk through here so fast, counting them, we can't even see them,' Bereyo countered. Everyone howled at this reference to our abilities to keep up with the pace.

'Maybe they land their planes in the Kinabalu mountains and count them,' someone suggested.

'Maybe they learn their language and ask one of them how many more there are,' said another.

Our supplies were disappearing fast, and we slowed our pace so our hunters could range around poison-blowdarting gibbons and leaf-monkeys. We had refused them at first, with their singed baby-like hands and limbs, but now we looked forward to our share with as much relish as everyone else. From our two expert hunters, Hidjau and Raja, we learnt how their darts are smeared with as many as five different kinds of poison, each required for a different prey. The difficulty with monkeys is getting the dose just right. If it is too strong, then the monkey dies clinging to the tree-tops; but just the right amount and it tumbles down and gives you your dart back. Care must be taken only to cook it directly over the fire, for if it is boiled or fried, then the poison which poisoned it poisons the poisoner.

As I hungrily picked the slivers of flesh from between the charred fingers of these primates, Lorne took some relish in pointing out that they were listed as an 'endangered species', and that the gibbons we now ate fetched a good five thousand dollars a mating pair on the black market. At this, our hungriest hour, we were eating by far the most expensive dinners of our lives. Gibbons and the occasional large monitor lizard were now our only protein, yet nobody but ourselves seemed unduly worried. A Dyak blowpipe, which is usually from seven to nine feet long, is far more than a poisonous pea-shooter. Whereas the Kenya tribes had excelled in making them, the Punans – despite their shortness of stature – were the undisputed masters of their use. Rather than the hollowed reeds or bamboo laths used by certain South American Indians, the Dyak blowpipe also serves as a spear, so consists of a single piece of hard wood, meticulously rifled down the centre, to spin the dart on a straight course. The blowpipe is not straight, but subtly curved to compensate for the downward sag resulting from holding it by its extreme end. In the hands of a master, it can be accurate to within a range of some seventy-five yards and is a terrifyingly effective weapon in jungle warfare. Its very silence conceals the source of the dart which delivers an agonizing death by nerve-poison – and of course the killers never run out of ammunition.

It remained a complete mystery as to how Bereyo was finding his way through this pathless tangled universe. I was aware that virtually nothing was known about Punan religion, and many authorities, somewhat puzzlingly, assert that they do not even have a coherent form of animism of their own. Yet they are referred to as being amongst the peoples who claim to 'psycho-navigate' their way around, with the help of visions and lucid dreams. Other 'psycho-navigators', as they have been called, include the Australian Aborigines, the Dinka of the Sahara, even the Bugis seafaring tribes; but whereas they, like pigeons, it has been argued, may rely on some innate sensitivity to celestial signposts the Punans are divorced from the sky by the forest canopy, and hardly ever see it. When I again challenged Bereyo how he knew where he was going, he replied: 'We Punans know we have two souls. There's the physical, emotional soul, this' – and he smacked his forehead with the palm of his hand – 'and the "dream wanderer". In sleep and special trance, the dream wanderer travels, sees with different eyes, sees pathway of wild animals or lost people.'

Bereyo seemed to recognize the giant waterfalls mentioned by Ted, the mission pilot, and one morning he led us up a high ridge to an astounding sight.

The forest curved away beneath us to the vertically soaring cliffs, about eight miles distant, which rose to the Apo Kayan plateau above us. Pouring off its edge we saw not one but *two* mighty feathers of water

— as high (and the pilot should know) as any in the world. Both they and their rivers remain to be named — perhaps Teddy Falls, One and Two. Although Lorne, wanting to keep it in the family, thought Two Fools Falls might be appropriate.

'Four days and nights to get there and back,' Bereyo said. 'But I don't feel the Punans there.'

'Then, forget it,' growled Wiesmar. 'Let's keep going.'

'I've never been there myself, either,' Bereyo continued. 'My grandparents have. They said there's a cave there. All crystals inside, like diamonds.'

'Just four days and nights?' queried Wiesmar with more interest.

We knew where we were all right, barely halfway through the Big White — and the way things were going we'd never make it through, let alone find our nomads.

'Relax. We find them,' Bereyo told us. 'Everything perfect. No rain, no insects, nice day.'

'Sure!' I gasped to Lorne.

Days later we were deep in the forest again when we came upon a Punan message-stick — which required highly trained vision to distinguish from its surroundings. A four-foot stick was notched with six curling spirals of bark, and hung with two circular and one semicircular scale of bark, topped with a leaf woven back on itself. Leah explained this Punan code to us.

'Six people passed this way,' he said. 'They've been travelling for over two months — these bits of bark tell us. And this bent leaf', he said,

pointing out a refinement of the message, 'means they're hungry, like us. Not much game. Punan professionals. Only about a week ahead of us.'

Our spirits soared, but within a few hours we were halted by a river dangerously swollen by a highland storm somewhere ahead, and which presented no suitable tree for felling across it as a bridge. We barely had time to find the ingredients for a camp before the storm broke over us, too, crushing us to that sodden clearing at the river's edge for eight days. We were down to the last of our salt and rice, but it could no longer be cooked. We could neither advance, nor retreat, nor stay where we were for very long.

The rains sometimes dropped as solid lumps, making it hard to breathe. On the first night our hammocks' roofs and banana nets collapsed, and we crawled like rats into the community shelter where morale was high, despite the dark and asphyxiating atmosphere.

Bereyo remarked that the nomads didn't like this weather, either, and they'd much sooner squat in an abandoned longhouse until it was over. In fact they were squatting there now, just half a day down this angry river. He had seen them clearly, he announced. The longhouses, built and abandoned by Kenya tribesmen, he had seen as a child, with his own nomadic parents. He had seen them again twenty years ago, he said, empty and falling back into the forest like dead trees. But the Punans were there now!

It would be days before the river abated enough to cross it, but as soon as the rain stopped Bereyo sent a six-man scouting party along the banks to verify whether the longhouses were more than a dream, while

215 Our sodden, fragile camp in the heart of darkness

216 Poling our way up another uncharted river

we endured the anxious days of waiting. A science-fiction sun, looking more like the moon, emerged and peered down on our clearing as if through a giant polarizing lens surrounded by a halo. With it came the insects again, and there was no escapting them now.

Only about half of them were there for our blood, for the rest had different tastes. Some came for our eye mucus or urine stains. There were minute bluebottles which liked earwax and crawled around in the mines, making it hard for us to hear each other above their amplified buzzing. A few, a flying black beetle in particular, were content to divebomb in from nowhere, sting for the hell of it, and drone adroitly off. Many arrived just for the party – to eat each other. By far the most nerve-racking were swarms of tiny brown bees with an exceedingly virulent sting. They were solely after the salt in our sweat, and settled softly all over us, like fur coats of venom, causing us to move, if at all, with the ridiculously exaggerated self-awareness of puppets. Since the greatest danger is getting them caught, and peeved, in the folds of one's clothes we followed the sensible Dyak procedure of going naked except for shorts (which items were preserved not for modesty, but for security against unlawful entomological entry). 'You can feel their mood, and where they are, with no clothes,' Hidjau the hunter told us. 'Remember, as with the leeches, just surrender what they want to them. If they feel happy, you will, too.'

There had been a frightening occasion several weeks earlier, on the trail, when Lorne had been stung so viciously on the back of the neck that he thought it was a tree snake. He was completely blinded for almost an hour. The man behind him had identified the culprit as this same species of bee – and now there were thousands, and we studiously avoided getting them trapped behind our knees or under our arms.

Then came the magical morning when both the river and the insects had subsided, and our missing scouts came jubilantly poling upstream to us towing a train of almost toy-sized canoes.

'They're there!' they shouted. 'Some have lived there for years, but the *others* are there, too. They're frightened. They think we may be from the government, sent to track them down and put them in prison.'

'I'll put them in prison if they *aren't* there!' Wiesmar growled.

Perched in these precarious canoes we now thundered down into a hidden fairyland. After a few hours the river slowed and broadened beneath a cathedral-like archway of interlocking trees. Then we heard it: an eerily hollow drumbeat seemingly coming from the river itself.

'That's it, Tuan,' our companions shouted. 'The famous Punan water-music.'

Sweeping round the bend we surprised a circle of seven all-but-naked nomadic Punan girls, up to their waists in the river, beating out a superbly syncopated rhythm with their cupped hands on the water. They scrambled up the bank faster than monitor lizards, and were gone.

Then the dilapidated longhouse came into view on our left, silent as a grave, without a soul to be seen. 'They're here,' Bereyo said. 'They wouldn't have left the girls behind. But let me go first.' He stepped ashore. We had waited for perhaps ten minutes, when the longhouse

217

began to erupt with the keening wail of a traditional Punan welcome, and strange and wonderful faces began to reveal themselves. The older men and women came cautiously down to the bank to greet us. They wore vivid loincloths, were latticed with tattoos, and great clusters of earrings dangled unashamedly from their long earlobes.

At first they were aloof as we squatted together in the strangely empty longhouse, but as the evening wore on the population silently expanded. Sinewy, exquisite, bare-breasted women crept in like does to peer at us from the edge of the circle, their wide-eyed babies cradled on their backs peering over their shoulders.

Our own Punans, who throughout our journey had become increasingly more interested in finding these lost relatives, were now enthralled. Their different dialects found common ground, love-affairs blossomed instantly amongst the young, while the more senior citizens sat down to lengthy and rewarding comparisons of each other's genealogical tree. A tremendous bond of love seemed to unfold around us, as all of our porters were adopted by individual families to be taken in and spoiled as their own.

There were about thirty-five families here, each with their individual compartments opening on to the long communal veranda. To avoid being eaten alive, we had to be individually introduced to all the hunting dogs. About ten of the families had been living here for five years, yet still relied more on hunting and gathering than on their rudimentary experiments with growing dry rice. The rest spent most of the year still wandering freely through the forest, sheltering during the heaviest rains at any number of abandoned longhouses, such as these, scattered through the jungle.

Surprises came thick and fast. The first was to learn that Suleh, here, on the Long Eut river, nowhere near any of the pencil marks we had cribbed from Ted's chart, was just the first of three other such communities, all within a day's canoe-ride of each other. The second surprise was the news that Suleh had been reached several times the previous year by a team of zealous young Indonesian missionary scouts,

218

217 We found the Punans sheltering from the rains in long-abandoned longhouses

218 A hunting party returns home

219 (over page) The young orchestra responsible for the famed 'water-music' of the nomadic Punans

led by 'treacherous Punan guides from the north'. Suleh, with no help from any of the other three villages, had obeyed precise instructions and built a landing-surface, just atop the hillock on the other side of the river. It was an astonishing coincidence. The old chief spoke little Indonesian, but his son was an enthusiastic interpreter.

'We're very modern,' he explained. 'We finished it just two moons ago. Got our first plane just before last big rain, maybe ten days ago. We all rushed over the river and climbed up the hill. It never landed, just fly around and went away again. Didn't even drop a banana!'

We were dumbfounded. Could it be Ted? Could this really be one of those landing-spots he was talking about, right on our doorstep, and hadn't even been landed on yet?

We had to fish out a watch from deep storage to see what day of the week it was. Thursday was just two days away, and the appalling thought of having to be suddenly airlifted out before having a chance to film the people we had come so far for conflicted with the awful suspicion that we might not get flown out at all.

Nor could we walk out, unless we returned with our porters the way we had come. They would have to leave within a few days, to return to their families. If we stayed, the plane might not come, and we would have no sure means of escape.

Next morning an engine sent us roaring across the river and panting up to the airfield, to find it was indeed Ted, nonchalantly waiting for us to catch up to him.

'Hi, guys,' he said humourlessly. 'Fun walk?'

With never a word to the amazed Dyaks who had sweated so long to build this field, and who had never seen a plane so close before, Ted took off fifteen minutes later. With him went a very thankful and much slimmed Wiesmar, agreeing to meet us in Samarinda, and taking much of our valuable footage. Ted's last words to us were: 'God willing, I'll pick you up next Thursday – or whichever subsequent Thursday I can.'

It was with an uneasy sense of abandonment and danger that I watched that little plane clear the trees, but it was forgotten on returning across the river to Suleh, where a whole new level of festivity was taking place. With Wiesmar, the shadow of authority, finally gone, these divided limbs of a dwindling people had come together and struck a fiery spark. Throughout the night, to the haunting sound of single-stringed instruments, the twin fans of black and white Hornbill feathers were passed from dancer to dancer, so each would reveal his soul by dancing solo before all the rest. Toothless old ladies howled with laughter as Bereyo flirted and waggled his ears at them. Our young guides were looking their best, love-affairs blossomed more extensively, couples withdrew into the darkness, some made love in the river like otters, to reappear again hours later, sleek-haired and lustrous-eyed, at the Dance of the Hornbill.

Bereyo, Leah, all our guides and companions would be leaving, replenished with love and food to help sustain them on their long way back to the edge of civilization. They longed to stay, learn more of themselves, but their families and fruit gardens called them. They would

220 An awkward welcome from three Punan priests

221 Hilo hears his voice on a tape-recorder for the first time

222 Our new family in Long Huruk

223

225

226

223 The baby-carriers, encrusted with ancient beads, coins, bear-claws and dogs' teeth, are magical shields against both psychic and physical dangers

224 Our friend Gajet, with his bamboo poison-dart quiver at his belt

225 It is the long ears which are really the objects of beauty – the bronze earrings are only worn occasionally, to stretch the lobes

226 A whole life's worth of tattoos

accompany us for one more day – down to the next longhouse of Long Pipa, the Punan community of rattan-weavers and tattoo artists.

Everywhere people were making the superb shoulder-baskets and sleeping-mats which, for all the Punans' obscurity, has won them recognition as amongst the finest weavers of rattan in the world. Intricately patterned, and extremely practical, their mats and baskets gradually acquire a lustrous chestnut-like patina from human skin oils, making them resistant to weather, wear and rot. The Punans also appear to have been amongst the first people prepared to harvest rattan – an incredibly tough and slender parasitic vine, hundreds of feet long, which clings to the forest with multiple thorned tentacles and is considered even by modern loggers as the most difficult of all plants to extract. Rattan, for wickerwork, for furniture, hampers, and even headmasters' canes, became fashionable in Victorian Europe as a symbol of Imperial reach, and is still much prized. But the Punans use only the surgically shaved skin of the rattan vine, with which, in effect, they spin complex three-dimensional fabrics, rather than basketry.

A nomad's most valuable material possessions must be easy to carry. Chief amongst these are their beads, of astonishing age and variety, some of which were equivalent in value to an entire bride's dowry; Chinese, Portuguese, Arabian and Indian beads attested to centuries of contact with the ancient world. There is even a bead now believed by experts to be identical to those extracted from Mesopotamian graves 2,300 years old, except that they are in better condition for having been lovingly worn round the necks of numerous generations of Dyaks. They also wear centuries-old coins which were once traded by the spice-warring nations. These, together with bears' claws, crocodiles' teeth and magical amulets, encrust their highly prized baby-carriers which serve to shield their young against both physical and psychic dangers. But the chieftain of Long Suleh pointed out to us that, valuable as these few material objects are, it is really a Punan's inner memories which are his most precious possession, the shape of his destiny. For the major experiences of a Punan's life, whether an inner dream or an outer adventure, are commemorated with a ritual tattoo. Most of the men wore tattoos on their chests, throats and arms, and the women on their wrists and legs. Many of our guides, who had shared this hazardous and unexpectedly rewarding search for their own roots with us, were now inspired to submit to being tattooed for the first time, which was a moving experience for everyone.

The following morning, boldly displaying the fresh symbols of their new-found cultural pride, our companions set out on the long journey for home again, amidst a tumultuous keening send-off and thumping water-music from the girls at Suleh.

We were left alone to explore the four villages on this unmarked river, the oasis for a dwindling caravanserai of Borneo's last nomads. Every Thursday we would struggle back to the airfield and anxiously wait from dawn till dusk, but it was to be many weeks before Ted managed to airlift us out. It was our long journey through the forest that prepared us for so easily sinking into the subtle rhythms of the

227

228

227 Hidjau was the first of our porters to be tattooed

228 Weaving the rattan shoulder-baskets and mats for which the Punans are so famous

229 Punan musical instrument

community. With Bereyo and Leah we had learnt something of the Punans' outer way of life; we were now open to what lay behind the symbol which looked back at us from their tattoos, baskets, beadwork and jewellery – which they called the face of Aping, the Tree of Life.

We entered a pool of dream time, in which one event melted into another as we passed from household to household, to be spoilt, cross-examined and passed on again. When our novelty wore off, our medicines ran out, and our total inability to contribute food or any other useful social activity became fully apparent, we continued to be tolerated with affectionate sensitivity and inquisitive humour. I became very close to a middle-aged couple called Gajet and Mera, who were still shaken by their encounters with the overland Indonesian missionary scouts earlier that year, who had even carried paint-pots and brushes through the forest to leave murals of hellfire on their longhouse walls. On our journey inwards, the mysterious Punan water-music, which few had heard and none could describe, had become for ourselves and for our bearers an alluring symbol of the lost forest maidens. Now, each dawn and dusk, the almost frog-like booming rhythm produced by the girls' skilfully cupped hands beating the surface of the river sent a hypnotizing heartbeat through the jungle and ourselves. After dark, several other musical instruments were passed around to add their haunting sounds to those of the forest. There was the nose flute, and two strange stringed instruments, the *satung* and the *sapeh*. The former is merely a cunning resonating cylinder of bamboo, with thin slivers of its own skin stretched over it to provide a murmuring, lilting hum. The sapeh, or Dyak 'mandolin', is carved like a miniature canoe, with three vine strings. The top string is used for the melody, while the lower two act as drones, as with the Indian sitar. This instrument produces a rousing light-footed sound which, for its similarity to hillbilly music of the southern United States, we called 'Borneo blue-grass'. It was the sound of these instruments, perhaps more than anything else, which gradually awakened us to the realization of having actually reached the scent of paradise, a scent which had guided us through so many Indonesian adventures, and quite suddenly one morning, like our guides before us, we both wished for our own tattoos.

We approached the two couples who had earlier suggested we be tattooed along with our guides, and were glad to find that their offer still held firm – though they reminded us that this was a serious matter. We could either choose from the glossary of Punan symbols, or else give free rein to the shamanic art of the tattoo master, whose hand would be inwardly guided to draw the design. Long past any sense of self-determination in the matter, we both surrendered the responsibility of choice to the tattooists, rather as one might to a hairdresser.

They always work as a couple – a man (for whom it is taboo to draw blood, except in anger) to trace the symbol, and a woman laboriously to open up the wound and hammer in the dye. Our tattooists took less than half an hour to paint the design on our chests, but their partners took closer to six hours to make it permanent. I thought it was finished after the first three, when I was asked to stand up

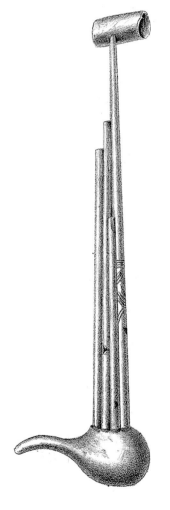

229

and wash the blood off my chest, but there was only a patterned pink wound, an eighth of an inch deep, into which she went on meticulously to beat the carbonized wood dye. This was achieved with a strip of bamboo tipped in Lorne's case with two semi-straightened fish-hooks, and in mine with two rusty nails, which were tapped by a secondary hammer with the unwavering precision and regularity of a sewing machine. During the more painful moments, our skilled tormentors would cluck commiseratingly in our ears, without altering their tempo. The ache, when we'd recovered from the psychological impact, came not from the wound itself, but from the glands beneath the armpits.

In our dazed state, and freshly instructed in how to surrender to, rather than fight, the insect bites of the forest, it was a surprisingly painless experience. It was with some astonishment that we afterwards stared at each other's angry carbon-stuffed wounds. Being the rather forgetful 'doctor' of the outfit, I now realized that our once quite sophisticated medicine-chest had long since been emptied of even its last plaster and anti-malarial tablet. An extensive rummage through all my mildewed pockets, however, revealed a few errant capsules of antibiotic powder, which we superstitiously dusted over our chests as a magical potion against infection. I had never been the slightest bit interested in having a tattoo – or anything else which couldn't be changed – yet the very permanency of the act now seemed to exert its own irresistible attraction, stronger even than the flattery of accepting the high honour of a Punan tattoo, which is so seldom granted even to other Dyak tribes. Yet it has neither faded nor worn out its welcome, and several years

230

later, when I was to rush from my burning home in Los Angeles, thinking that my tattoo and the body it marked were all that remained of my eastern adventures, it was still a comforting reminder of the dream wanderers.

Our new protectors shared with us everything they hunted or gathered: lizards and snakes, flying squirrels and monkeys, sago and bitter ferns. They even fed us the occasional egg, usually reserved for young children and requiring considerable labour to discover in the nests of their semi-wild jungle fowl. Yet we were weakening now, and we both knew that, even if any of these people could be persuaded to lead us the remaining 150 miles on foot out to Long Nawan, we no longer had the strength to follow them.

Another Thursday came and went with no Ted, and we decided to risk making the five-day return journey to Long Huruk, the furthest of the four villages and the occasional abode of Nanyet the high priest. We went in a single canoe, with six powerful young men, including the interpreter son of Long Suleh's chieftain.

We felt strangely vulnerable now, with such a small party, but the beauty and ease of the downstream journey softened our apprehensions about making it back up again without rainstorms or mishaps to delay our appointment with an airlift to safety.

It was at Long Huruk that we encountered the vortex of the dream time of which we had so far only touched the periphery, for this was the semi-nomadic community of mystics and dream wanderers. As we tottered up the bank towards the crumbling longhouse, Nanyet came purposefully down and embraced us both – an unheard-of greeting between Indonesian strangers. He was as impressive a figure as one might hope to see at any international gathering of wise men. Perhaps sixty years old, tall and fine-faced, it was not so much his dramatic countenance of tattoos, bronze earrings and priceless beads which placed him apart as the quality of his gaze and his voice. In addition to being the philosopher and shaman of the community, he was also the possessor of the healing touch, which he laid briefly on the heads of each of our grateful boatmen after embracing us. When he later laid his palm on my scalp, too, I felt a warm current trickling through my head and down my spine.

'Tell us about Aping,' I asked, after we had been sitting comfortably in the shade for a while.

'You bear the symbols of his face, I see, the leaves of the Tree of Life,' he replied, clear as a bell, through our awed young interpreter from Suleh. 'In trance and in sleep, or even awake, our dream wanderers can ascend the Trunk, the Kayu Abilau, to talk with Aping.'

'What else can the dream wanderer do?'

'You have walked through the forest with Bereyo,' he said, clearly well informed of our movements. 'How did he know we were here? We might have been across the border in Sarawak, or sheltering in other hidden longhouses many moons from here. With Aping's help,' he went on, 'our dream wanderers can direct our way not only through the forest, but also at the major crossroads of our inner lives. Most of us

231

232

230 The syncopated rhythms of the Punan water-music, played with cupped hands on the river's surface

231 Submitting to an indelible record of our Borneo adventure

232 Hidjau, performing the Dance of the Hornbill, wears the beadwork 'Face of Aping', the Forest God, at his forehead

spend our lives wandering throughout amongst the roots of the world – but our dream wanderers, once awakened, can move amongst the upper branches of the Tree of Life, encompassing all things.' It is this dreaming, flying body, he told us, which knows our beginning and our end – and which binds all times and tribes and creatures together as one.

That evening, he said, he and the community would be sending up their dream wanderers to move amongst Aping's branches, and he invited us to attend.

To retain our already dangerously slender safety margin over making our regular Thursday appointment with the elusive Ted, we would have to leave almost immediately and travel through the night. But when darkness had fallen, and the moon was playing games with the river, we were still there. About fifty men, women and children sat cross-legged around Nanyet, who crouched by the glimmer of a single oil-lamp on the longhouse floor. After some throaty personal murmurings, he began to 'speak in tongues', a sort of canting glossolalia, which was soon taken up in different forms by the surrounding throng. It was a language with no meaning, they told us, except for those with fully awakened dream wanderers. It was called the tongue of 'before being born and of after dying'.

We were well aware of how little was known of the Punan religion, and here, on the eve of our hoped-for departure, we found ourselves with the unique opportunity of capturing a moment of it on film.

Our hitherto stalwart cameras, lights, tape-recorders and generator now all embarked on a succession of cardiac arrests, and while Gajet's and the assembly's unperturbed dream wanderers floated amongst the branches of Kayu Abilau, Lorne and I carried on like Laurel and Hardy, stumbling amongst our machinery, blinding them with our lights, and tripping over our cables.

Afterwards Nanyet informed us that the whole ceremony had been for our benefit, not for posterity but to awaken our dream wanderers. We would know whether the rite had been effective, he predicted, if within a few days one or both of us had an unmistakable dream.

We were all a little shaken when we set out after midnight on the long punt up to Suleh. We climbed the hill at dawn, dizzy, weaker than ever, and waited with our companions until night fell. But no Ted.

We would have to wait another week, or perhaps longer.

Our hosts at Suleh were sensitive, and left us to retire early to our hammocks, strung on the longhouse veranda. They talked quietly, and for a while a one-stringed 'Borneo blue grass' refrain reached out to us, and we slept – heedless, now, to anything but the patience to make it through another week, and the prayer that Ted would come.

'Lawrence! Wake up!' Lorne's voice came urgently from the dark.

'What the hell is it?' I jerked awake in alarm.

A couple of cocks crowed, and a dog briefly barked.

'I've just had a *dream*. A damn good one.'

'It had better be,' I said.

'It's so vivid. I was in a massive tree which stretched from coast to coast of Borneo. One Tree. There were creatures in it, all around me, some of which should have been afraid of me, and others which I should have been terrified of. There were enormous praying mantises, and tiny orang-utans, yet none of us was in the least bit frightened. It was . . . as if I saw myself in all of them, and they saw themselves in me.'

I heard the enthusiasm in his voice from a long way off, as I drifted back to sleep. I had expected something more dramatic from a dream which couldn't wait to be told over a healthy breakfast of scrambled monitor lizard.

I next awoke to the sound of an engine. It was *Friday*, not Thursday, for God's sake! But we were packed, and up the ridge in a flash.

Ted was kicking his wheel with his back to us when we came up to him, trailed by our panting helpers with our gear. He turned sharply.

'Can't get all that on board, boys. Soft runway. What's it to be, you or the film?'

'Both!' we said quietly, with one voice.

We reached a quick compromise by giving our bewildered friends, who were still totally unaddressed and even apparently unnoticed by Ted, everything but our essential footage and equipment – generator, hammocks, clothes and precious reference-books. After very brief goodbyes, Ted was grumpily lifting us over the tree-tops into another world, and we watched that hitherto hidden oasis of Punans dwindle behind us into the one great tree.

'What kept you, Ted?' Lorne asked at length.

'Mission convention,' he replied, pulling a large sandwich out of a paper bag and munching into it. 'Kept me real busy. Marvin, the third pilot in this island, dropped his bird up by the Kayan river a few weeks ago. Just broke bones and the aeroplane. So there was just two of us to ferry the priests around. Did you see my waterfall?' he asked between mouthfuls. 'Let's go take a look at it, shall we?'

I was much more interested in ripping the rest of the sandwich from his grip, but Lorne reckoned he had another thirty feet of film left in the camera, and wanted to hang out of the window with it.

'There it is!' Ted announced at length, and welding our diaphragms into the roofs of our mouths he plummeted down the edge of the Apo Kayan shelf, right next to the mighty cataract. But it was not it at all. It was indeed only one, rather than the *two* we had seen, and it poured from a differently shaped ledge; nor, we thought, was it as high. So Bereyo had shown us something else – not Teddy Falls, as these were, but Two Fools Falls after all. The cruel irony we were experiencing of having covered what we estimated to be more than 800 miles by canoe and on foot to reach a spot with a new airfield was now softened. The walk had been worth it after all.

I looked beneath my shirt to see if my tattoo was still there. Nanyet's last words to us had been: 'Remember, from now on, wherever you go amongst the tribes of man, you will bear the mark of Aping, as a reminder that all life forms are part of a single tree.'

As we settled back into the long straight flight over the flat forest to find Wiesmar amongst the gambling-dens of Samarinda, I felt distinctly ill and very happy.

10 The Shadow Play of Life

A short walk from our Balinese house there is a temple, in a sacred forest, towered over by a giant Banyan tree, which the Balinese say links heaven and earth. Dedicated to Durga, the goddess of death, it is a dark gateway, carved with hideous demons, festooned with human skulls. It is known as the 'monkey temple' because, according to the village, the spirits, in the bodies of monkeys, rule there, and even the locals can find themselves tricked or even terrorized by the bandalog.

The monkey folk must be kept in their place. Not, we were told, by any outer show of force, but by inwardly never letting them forget that you always remember who you are, and what you'll put up with. After a number of years, I no longer dropped my peanuts; but neither, in the presence of the monkey folk, did I ever want to nod off. But things seemed very different, after Borneo, when I returned one soft evening to pay my respects to the monkey forest and its sacred Banyan tree.

I sat very still, cross-legged, at the foot of the tree. The tattoo was still as fresh on my chest as the words of Nanyet, the Punan sage, were in my mind. The bandalog arrived, but sat down in a semi-circle some distance away, quietly watching me. The dominant male, with enormous yellow fangs and a wilful, unpredictable nature, was feared by some of the Balinese, but he usually remained in the background, disdainfully aloof. This time, he stalked up to me alone, looking closely into my face as he came. Then he gently laid his warm, coarse paw in my palm, and left it there. I closed my eyes, and his paw remained. When I opened them again some time later, he was still studying me very closely, his wrinkled, rather brutish old face seemingly on the brink of cracking into laughter. Something seemed to have changed.

On the day we returned to Bali from Borneo, Gusti Nyoman Lempad, the great Balinese artist, died a conscious death aged 116 in the nearby village of Peliatan. John Darling, our Australian anthropologist friend and an immediate neighbour of Lempad's, brought the news. I was shocked at first, but the Balinese attitude was that it was high time he moved on, and that after 116 years of conscious living a man ought to know how to die.

I had interviewed Lempad a few years earlier, for a BBC film called 'Balinese Vision', in which he had discussed some of the secrets of his longevity. He was very small and extraordinary – rather like an extra-terrestrial – and I feared that just touching the long-nailed claw he offered me in greeting would cause him to crumble and vanish.

Lempad spoke Balinese, and his son translated for us. When I asked him if he was frightened to die, he replied that he just couldn't see the way or the time yet, but would know them when they came.

'How do you manage to be so old and healthy?' I went on.

'Compared to my grandparents, I'm still just a baby.' He grinned.

233 This girl's dance welcomes the gods to their temple

234 Sangiang Widi, the Supreme Being, stands above all other gods in Bali

235

'But when I was young an old sage told me that if I never learned how to read and write, and my soul remained unburdened with worldly learning, then I would flower into my destiny and live out my time.'

Despite his nominal illiteracy, Lempad became the oracular source of every variation of Balinese Hindu/Buddhist mythology and teaching, and even in Europe in the 1920s was recognized for his remarkable religious and erotic art. There was hardly a medium to which he did not turn his hand – from making musical instruments, to designing and carving scores of spectacular temples. His peculiar characteristic was never quite to complete any of his works. 'Perfection is for the gods to achieve,' he would say. 'Foolish of me to try to emulate them.'

Not only had Lempad chosen the holy day Kadjeng Kliwon on which to die, it was also when the sun rose at its closest point to Gunung Agung, the Volcano of the Gods. He had had himself bathed in holy water from the temple spring of his patron, Saraswati, goddess of Wisdom and the Arts, and then formally dressed in white. He called his large family about him, and when they were patiently assembled he sat up, said a few words, smiled, and died.

Given that the island was littered with his almost-finished masterpieces, his final words were rather wry: 'I leave it to you, my descendants,' he had said, 'the task of completing what I haven't had time to finish in my short life.'

In his hand was the wooden mask he had been carefully working on for three years, and had laid aside that morning. It was unpainted, peaceful. 'The face of a young soul', he had called it.

When John Darling, as is customary for immediate neighbours, had asked the family what he might contribute to the funeral, he'd been told to get our assistance in making a film of Lempad's life and death.

'A film may be the only funeral gift to last,' John told us. 'Most of Bali's top artists were his students at one time and they're all contributing to the funeral pyre. Imagine, all the best painters of the West donating one of their canvases for a burning!'

Over the next weeks the family were to reveal to us the intimate details leading to a cremation, from the tender washing of the body, to the progressive releasing from that body, before it is burned, of the layers of spiritual essence. Although a corpse is legally required to be either buried or cremated within two weeks, Lempad had insisted on six weeks elapsing between his death and cremation. He smelt, as they said – and I smelt it, too – like frangipani and myrrh, right up to the forty-second day. Making the resulting film, 'Lempad of Bali', opened our eyes to the fact that the arts of dying still flourished in the islands.

It was the scent of living mysticism which had first drawn us to Indonesia. We had escaped the ashram walls and had rambled instead through many an outer, *Boy's Own* adventure, yet each time we returned to Bali to digest and heal. It was this flavour of mysterious wisdom, forgotten in our own lands, which eventually led to an eleven-month filming marathon, with Zac and our Balinese soundman, Bobby Radiasa, in search of the sages, mystics and healers of the islands.

We found ember-eaters and hypnotists, fakirs and charlatans. There was trance of every kind – even, in the Gorong Islands, a sinister form of mass possession, in which an entire village was victimized by a giant money-eating serpent, cannily articulated by prancing shamans. We also encountered some very impressive sages and skilful manipulators of unseen energies.

Perhaps the most remarkable was the enigmatic man we named 'Dr Dynamo Jack', an ethnic Chinese of many generations in Java, whom I first met at his spacious home on the outskirts of a burgeoning East Javanese city. He claimed only to be a healer, using acupuncture needles in the traditional points, but he sent a powerful 'electrical' current through them, from within his own body. He claimed to have derived these powers from a Taoist master, a forest hermit, since dead, with whom he had studied for seven years.

'I use acupuncture needles some of the time,' he told me, 'but usually just my hands, from a slight distance. Look, I'll show you.'

He stood up, undid his belt, lowered the top of his trousers and underpants, placed the flat of my hand on his bare stomach a few inches below his navel, and ordered me to try to keep it there.

I found myself having to lean against him with all my strength, and still my hand was being pushed away from his stomach by what felt like a dry but irresistibly strong jet of water. Then he exhaled, and my hand shot back to his stomach again, nearly sending him off his feet.

'That's one of the two chakras I use to generate the energy,' he said, tightening up his belt again and stretching out his arm. 'This is another!'

I touched his outstretched hand. He inhaled and released such a powerful jolt through my arm that I howled and snatched it away.

He then asked an assistant, a tall, serious-looking man called Mohan, to bring us a wooden stool and a new packet of bamboo chopsticks, and invited me to push one through the inch-thick wooden stool. I tried several times, nearly broke the chopstick, and failed to make the slightest dent in the stool.

'No, it's like this.' And taking my chopstick between the tip of his thumb and two fingers, he pushed it with one swift movement vertically down through the plank and halfway out the other side.

I touched the points of entry, both above and below, for some clue as to what he had done. I could push the chopstick no deeper, but was able to withdraw it easily; the hole, rectangular, like the chopstick, was perfectly smooth-walled and compressed back into itself.

'It's very simple,' Dynamo Jack said. 'Just a matter of practice. Like an electric eel, we all have this Yin–Yang polarity,' and he pointed downwards from his navel with one finger, and upward from between his legs with the other. 'I use these two chakras. My positive and my negative. One comes up from the earth, the other comes down from the sky. It's just a matter of learning to harness and project them outside the body. I've been practising this for seventeen years now, meditating every day. One has to be very careful of one's emotions, though – like anger, for instance, which can be very dangerous. It can kill as well as heal. My student, Mohan here has been practising for four years. By the

236

235 Gusti Nyoman Lempad in the last of his 116 years of life

236 The money-eating serpent of Gorong

237

238

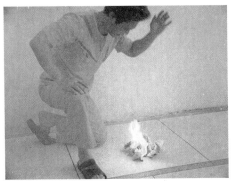

239

237–239 After eight years, 'Dynamo Jack' finally allowed us to film him setting our newspaper on fire – without a match

240 Scaring the Demons of Bali

time he can do these things he won't be too interested in them any more. It's what's awakened inside you that gets interesting, much more interesting than impressing the world, or even yourself.'

Over the ensuing months we saw him on many occasions, following him around the country, questioning him, watching him heal his patients, and occasionally demonstrating his astounding powers.

I even managed to take my mother, a rigorous judge, to meet him in a suite on the ninth floor of a plush hotel in Jakarta.

'Very difficult to work with these energies when so far from the ground,' he told us. 'Hard to earth.' He then crushed our newspaper into a ball, held it in his left hand, pointed at it with his right, and ignited it into a blossom of flame. There was a sudden strong smell of ozone in the room, and I remember the scramble to get all the burning, floating pieces into the metal wastebasket before they singed the carpet.

But he would never consent to our filming him.

'I'm not interested in tricks,' he said. 'I am a healer. If Western people see this on film, they will assume I am a market conjuror'.

I knew he was right, but I was frustrated not to return with some evidence on film of what we had seen and felt him do, and under such varied conditions. On a final trip back to Indonesia, in the midst of writing this book, I decided to try once more. It was a hurried journey through the islands, to gather some last footage for our series. We had the luxury of a film crew for a change, and found ourselves in Jakarta, with a full seven hours before our plane took off for Northern Celebes, and I used it to track down Dynamo Jack again, 400 miles away.

'How are you doing? What do you want?' he asked, immediately recognizing my voice over the crackling phone line.

'I'm with a film crew. Lorne's got a sick eye. Can we fly down to see you for half an hour? It's all the time we've got.'

'The eye isn't very sick, is it?'

'No, not *very* sick,' I replied. The phone line crackled for a while, then he said: 'Bring all your eyes down. You can't film me, though.'

When we got there, not only did he treat, and cure, Lorne's infected eye, but he suddenly agreed to appear on camera. He explained that he was depleted from the healing he had done that day, but went on to ignite our newspapers, push chopsticks through stools, and 'electrocute' our bodies and those of our sceptical film crew. When Lorne first had his temples touched he began jerking around so violently that I asked him not to ham it up so much, or no one would believe anything on camera. I shut up, though, when Dynamo Jack touched my hand, and jolted me into remembering what it had been like the first time.

When I asked him why he had suddenly consented to being filmed, he replied that, now his students were starting to get the hang of it, it seemed time to show more of this to the world.

'Even if most people do think it's simply a trick,' he said, 'some will recognize that we all have these powers, sleeping within us.'

To believe in our 'superhuman' ability, is one thing, to see it is quite another, but actually to capture it on film, however fleetingly, seemed like a final benediction on all our travels.

It had been four years since we had returned to Indonesia. After our struggle to produce the series, and my shaking off the ashes of the Los Angeles fire, and then this breathtakingly fast trip through the islands, we finally managed to spend two blissful days at home in Bali.

As usual, Batuan and the village of Pengosekan embraced us like returning prodigals. The house had grown, like a tree, into a fragrant haven, enveloped by palms, hibiscus and night-blooming jasmine. Carved in the sandstone blocks at the foot of our roof columns were new beasts and deities, already enmossed with the illusion of age. The resident ghecko population in the roof thatch was large and talkative, and the walls glowed with the new forms of painting with which the villagers were experimenting. A number of the villagers were now artists of some repute, selling paintings to foreign collectors for several thousand dollars apiece. There were several jeeps in the community; they were richer, more cosmopolitan, but as creative and ingenious as ever, and still spending most of their income on the festival rites. But they were not that impressed by my stories of Dynamo Jack: his remarkable feats made no ripples in their already supernatural view of the world.

240

On the final afternoon of our stay we joined Batuan and his family on their annual pilgrimage to the mother temple, high on the slopes of the Holy Mountain. It was raining that evening, warm and scented, and the peak of the mountain was hidden by cloud. The towers and carved escarpments of the mother temple, built over layers of thousands of years of earlier shrines, sprawled ahead through the mists like an abandoned science-fiction city.

We paused at a stone chair set above us which stayed empty waiting for Sangiang Widi, the invisible Balinese God of All Things – beyond all the deities. Batuan said he might sit there now, if we were very still. We were still, and the mountain rumbled; but it often does.

The Bird of Paradise, it seemed, had beckoned us on and led us in, to stand here in this place high in the land of volcanoes. It was here in Bali, after returning from the Toraja Star Children, that I first recognized what they meant by us all being born half of heaven and half of earth. And after the mounted warsports of Sumba it was in Balinese ritual that I saw with new eyes the battle for balance between light and darkness. And after Borneo, returning to the sacred Banyan tree and its simian custodians, I had felt that all great trees, what's left of them, do indeed link heaven and earth in a single forest of life.

Standing there on the sacred mountain, I felt very much like the man who wasn't sure whether he was asleep, dreaming that he was awake, or awake not knowing that he was part of a larger dream. After all these years we really were about to fly back to eighteen months of film editing and word-processing and a chance to unburden ourselves of some of this adventure. It was to be a chance, too, to point towards the Ring of Fire hidden at the bottom of our garden, which remains, it seems, both a cauldron of our earliest beginnings and a womb quickening mysteriously with our unknown future.

Bibliography

NOTES

1 Lawrence Blair, *Rhythms of Vision: The Changing Patterns of Belief* (New York: Schocken Books, 1976).

2 Alfred Russel Wallace, *The Malay Archipelago: The Land of the Orang Utan and the Greater Bird of Paradise* (London: Macmillan, 1869).

3 Tom Simpkin and Richard Fiske, *Krakatau, 1883: The Volcanic Eruption and Its Effects* (Washington, DC: Smithsonian Institution Press, 1983).

4 Three books on the Wallace–Darwin relationship, as fascinating as they are undeservedly obscure, are: Wilma George, *Biologist Philosopher* (London: Abelard-Schuman, 1964); H. Lewis McKinney, *Wallace and Natural Selection* (New Haven, Conn./London: Yale University Press, 1972); and the trenchant Arnold C. Brackman, *A Delicate Arrangement: The Strange Case of Charles Darwin and Alfred Russel Wallace* (New York: Times Books, 1980).

5 Alfred Russel Wallace, *The Wonderful Century* (London: Macmillan, 1898).

6 Carl Sagan, *The Dragons of Eden: Speculations on the Evolution of Human Intelligence* (New York: Random House, 1977).

7 An authoritative source on this theory is Austin Coates, *Islands of the South* (London: Heinemann, 1974).

8 Rosemary Grimble, *Migrations, Myth and Magic from the Gilbert Islands: Early Writings of Sir Arthur Grimble, Arranged and Illustrated* (London: Routledge & Kegan Paul, 1972), p. 37.

9 Joseph Conrad, *Almayer's Folly* (Harmondsworth: Penguin, 1984), p. 9.

10 Wallace, *Malay Archipelago*, p. 311.

11 We were later to track down two books written by Collins of his intriguing experiences: G. E. P. Collins, *East Monsoon* and *Makassar Sailing* (London: Jonathan Cape, 1937).

12 Lyall Watson, *Supernature* (London: Hodder & Stoughton, 1973).

13 Wallace, *Malay Archipelago*, p. 341.

14 The collection is now housed in the Michael Rockefeller Room at the Metropolitan Museum of Art in New York.

15 David Attenborough, *Zoo Quest for a Dragon* (London: Lutterworth Press, 1957).

16 Walter Auffenberg, *The Behavioral Ecology of the Komodo Monitor* (University Press of Florida, 1981).

SUPPLEMENTARY READING

Chapter 2:

T. Bigalke, *A History of Tana Toraja* (USA: Wisconsin University Press, 1981).

David Devine, *Certain Islands* (London: Macdonald, 1972).

Robin Hanbury-Tenison, *A Pattern of Peoples* (New York: Charles Scribner's and Sons, 1975).

R. A. Kartini, *Letters of a Javanese Princess* (Kuala Lumpur: Oxford University Press, 1976).

Walter Kaudern and Henry Wassén, *Art in Central Celebes* (The Hague: Martinus Nijhoff, 1944).

J. F. Sheltema, *Monumental Java* (London: Macmillan, 1912).

Chapter 4:

Shirley Deane, *Ambon, Island of Spice* (London: John Murray, 1979).

Clifford W. Hawkins, *Prahus of Indonesia* (London: Macmillan 'Nautical Books', 1982).

Chapter 5:

Willard A. Hanna, *Indonesian Banda* (Philadelphia: ISHI, 1978).

E. Thomas Gilliard, *Birds of Paradise and Bower Birds* (New York: The Natural History Press, 1969).

Chapter 6:

D. Eyde, *Cultural Correlates of Warfare* (Yale University, Doctoral dissertation, 1967).

A. A. Gergrands (ed.), *The Asmat: Journals of Michael Clark Rockefeller* (New York: Museum of Primitive Art, 1967).

Milton Machlin, *The Search for Michael Rockefeller* (New York: Putnam, 1972).

Chapter 8:

Monie J. Adams, *System and Meaning in East Sumba Textile Design* (Yale: University Press, 1969).

Fritz A. Wagner, *Indonesia: The Art of an Island Group* (New York: MacGraw-Hill, 1959).

Chapter 9:

Carl Bock, *The Headhunters of Borneo – A Narrative of Travel Up the Mahakam and down the Barito* (London: Sampson Low, Marston, Searle and Rivington, 1881).

Tom Harrison, *The World Within: A Borneo Story* (London: Cresset Press, 1959).

John Mackinnon, *Borneo*, (Amsterdam: Time-Life Books 'The World's Wild Places' Series, 1975).

Redmond O'Hanlon, *Into the Heart of Borneo – An Account of a Journey Made in 1983 to the Mountains of Batutiban with James Fenton* (Harmondsworth: Penguin, 1985).

M. T. H. Perelear, *Ran Away from the Dutch – Or: Borneo from South to North* (New York: Dodd, Mead & Co., 1887).

Guy Piazzini, *The Children of Lilith* (London: Hodder & Stoughton, 1960).

B. E. Smythies, *The Birds of Borneo* (London: Oliver & Boyd, 1960).

Chapter 10:

Miguel Covarrubias, *The Island of Bali* (New York, Knopf, 1956).

Colin McPhee, *A House in Bali* (Toronto: Asia Press, 1944).

Lyall Watson, *Gifts of Unknown Things* (London: Hodder & Stoughton, 1976).

Acknowledgements

Of the numerous people who have, over the past fifteen years, helped make *Ring of Fire* possible, and who are not already mentioned in the book or credited in the films, we would particularly like to thank the following:

Monie Adams; The Keraing, Andi Banawa and his wife, Ibu Desa; Julian and Julis Boileau; Jan Butchofsky; Soedarmadji Damais; The Tans Hans family; Raden Temenggung Jarjonagoro; Virginia Holshuh; Indonesian Directorate-General of Tourism; Michael and Robert Kennedy; Perry Kessler; Claire Leimbach; Donaldine Lourensz; James and Aune Nelson; Sydney Perret; Dorothy Pittman; Putrayala; Robert Seiffert; James Seligman; Gusti Made Simung; Alyson Steffen; Hal Stone; Harifin Sugeanto; Charles Twing; Jack Weru.

Index

Figures in **bold** type refer to pages containing illustrations

Flores, **36–7**, 109, 191, 202, 207
Flores Sea, 57, 112
flying Frog, **39**, 42
flying snake, 42
flying Fox, *see* bats
Fort Rotterdam, **140**
Fumeripits, 161
funeral rites: Bali, 262; Batak, 50;
    Dyak, 231; Sumba, 215–18; Toraja,
    11, 57, 63, 67–89, 216

Gaisseau, Pierre-Dominique, 163, 170
Gajet, **252**, 255, 258
Ganeesh, 43
Garuda bird, 43
Gerard, Hillary, 9, 149, 159
Gigantopithecus, 41
Gilbert Islands, 46
Gnostics, 23
Gold-Lipped Oyster, **151**, 152–4
grave-robbers, 58–9, 92
Greater Bird of Paradise, *see* Birds of
    Paradise
Gunung Agung, 23, 47, 261
Gusti Nyoman Lempad, 260–1

Haba Kodi, 218–19
Halim, 92–5
Harvard-Peabody Expedition, 166
Hawaii, 35
Head-hunters of Borneo, The (Boch),
    13
head-hunting, **36–7**, 70, 71, 161, 162,
    163, 169, 170, 229–30, 231, 233,
    242
Hernandez, Robby, 205
Hidjau, 239, **240**, 242, 246, **254**, **257**
Hilo, **250**
Himalayas, 67
Hinduism, 43, 44, 54, 72, 119, 218,
    261
Holland, 34, 59, 130, 131, 135, 138,
    163, 171, 179, 189, 213, 231
Hong Kong, 194

Iban tribe, 231
Ibu, 98–102, 115, 126
ikat textiles, 213, 215, 216–18
India, 34, 42, 43, 51, 119, 254
Indian Ocean, 30, 33, 191, 213
Indonesia: Darul Islam, 63, 104;
    geography, 12–14; geology, 48;
    independence, 47, 63; population, 48
Irian Jaya, 162
Islam, 44, 47, 72, 127, **149**
Italy, 136

Jakarta, 44; zoo, 203
Japan, 71, 99
Java, 29, 41, 47
Java Man, 41
Java Sea, 57
Jayapura, 166

Jogjakarta, Sultan of, 47

Kadjang Kliwong, 261
Kalimantan, 229, 230, 231, 233
Kasuso, 95
Kayan River, 259
Kayan tribe, 231
Kayu Abilau, 257–9
Ke Islands, **147**, 148
Kenya tribe, 231, **233**, 234, **236**, 243,
    245
'keraing', 98
Ketjak, **20**
Kinabalu mountains, 242
King Kong (film), 202
Kipling, Rudyard, 29
Komodo Dragon, **16**, 24, **42**, **190**,
    191–211, 213
Krakatoa, 24, 29–33
Krander, 109
Kukoi, 175, 176, 178, 182, 184, 186,
    187
Kurum, **163**, 176, 178, 179, 184–6,
    187

Laba, 102, 105
Ladjang, 106–7, 109, 110, 111, 127,
    131, 143, 146–7, 152, 158
Lamboya, 214
Lampong River, 29
Lancaster University, 11, 135
Lang Eiland, 29
laweri, 139–40
Layard, Austen, 38
Leah, 234–50, 255
Leimbach, Bill, 163, 167, 171, 176,
    179, 183
'Lempad of Bali', 262
Leod, John, 138
Lesser Sundas Islands, 42, 199
Likangloe, 103, 105, 110
Lindblad Explorer, 134, 183–4, 191,
    194–6, 199, 203, **206–7**, 229
Linnaeus, Carolus, 155
Linnean Society, 39
Loho Liang, 203, 204–6, 207, 208
lombok, 41, **91**
Long Belinau, 235
Long Eut river, 247
Long Huruk, **251**, 257
Long Nawan, 230, 233, 234, 257
Long Pipa, 254
Long Suleh, 247, 250, 254, 257, 258
Lontar, 131, 135
Loro Kidul, 47
Los Angeles, 18–19, 22, 24–6, 54, 163,
    257
Lost World, The (Doyle), 199

Ma'badong, 80–1, 83, 84, 89
Macawali, **90**
Made Widjaya, 55
Madra, 51

Magellan, Ferdinand, 34
Mahakam river, 232, 233, 234
Mahommed, **147**
Makale, 89
Makassar, 11, 57, 59, **90**, **91**, **92**, **93**,
    116, 136
Malacca Straits, 44
Malay Archipelago, The (Wallace), 12,
    13, **39**, 235
Malira, 219
mandalas, 19, **20**, 218
Mansur, 110, 112, 131, 134, 143, 152,
    158
'Maya', 10, 23
Mayans, 10
M'bau, 236–9
megaliths, 214, 215, **216**, **218**, 223,
    227
Melanesians, 44, 151
Melville, Herman, 91
Mera, 255
Merapi volcanoes, 47
Merapu gods, 213, 218
Mexico, 10, 11, 156
Meyer, Dr Werner, 62–4, 67, 69, 71,
    75, 78, 79, 84, 95, 114, 142
Miami University, 204
Michel, John, 9
Micronesians, 44
Moera Takoes, 43
Mohan, 262–3
Moluccan Blue-Ringed Octopus, 105
Moluccas, 35, 48, **56**, 136
Moluccas Sea, 57
monkeys, 103–4, **228**, 260
music, 248–9, 254, 255, **256**

Nanyet, 257–8, 259, 260
Napolean, 130, 136
New Guinea, 9, 35, 57, 91, 119, 127,
    150, **151**, 152, 161. *See also* Irian
    Jaya *and* Papua New Guinea
New York, 189, 191, 195;
    Metropolitan Museum of Art, 162;
    Museum of Primitive Art, 162
nutmeg, **129**
Nuang Ase, 107
Nyale, 213, 219, 222, 223
Nyoman Batuan, **20**, 22, 23, 264

O'Brien, Willis, 199–202
O'Keefe, Mary, 62
Omanasep, 170, 182
orang utan, **39**, **40**, 43, 48
Origin of Species (Darwin), 35
ornaments, **168**, **221**
Otjanep, 162–6, 170–83, 184–9
Ouwens, Van, 191

Pacific Ocean, 33, 44, 119
Padar, 191
Pa'gellu, 81
Pakubuono XI, Sultan, 47–8